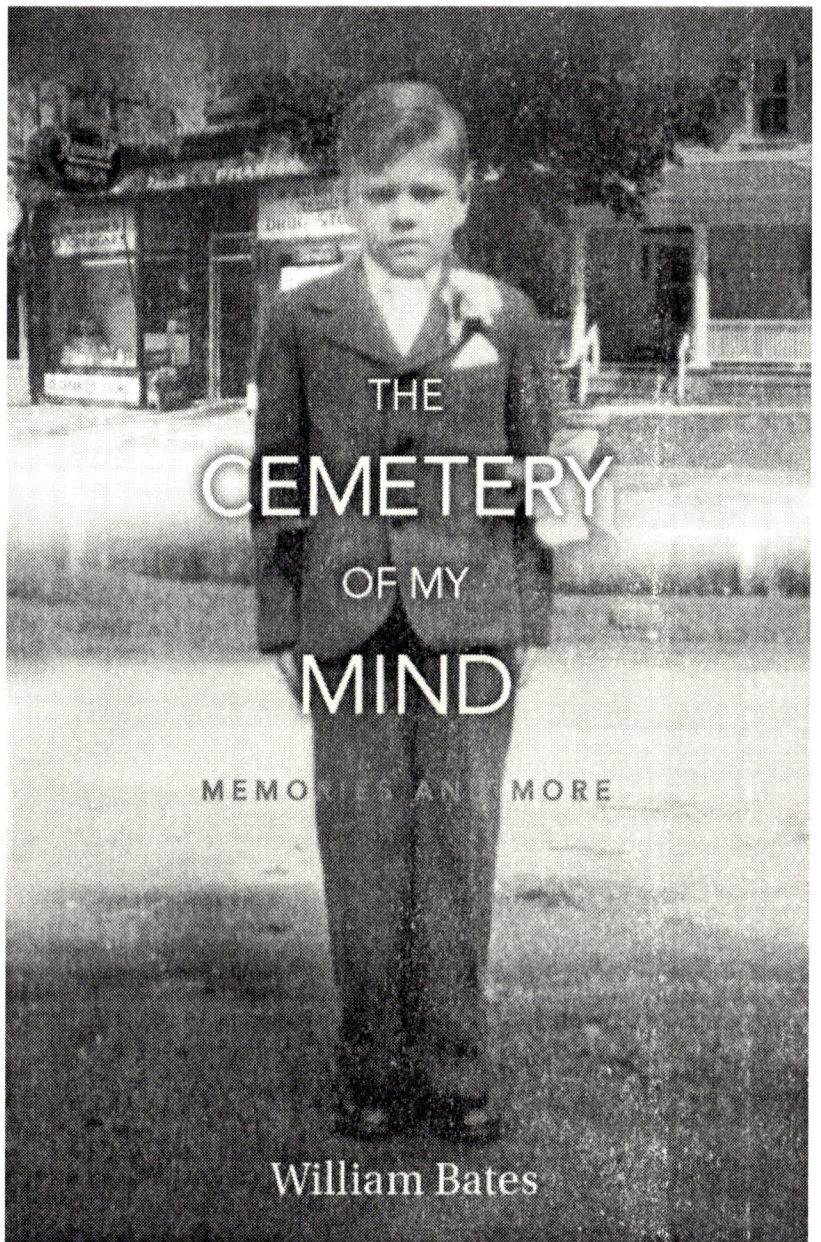

THE CEMETERY OF MY MIND

MEMORIES AND MORE

William Bates

Copyright © 2014, William Bates.

All rights reserved.

Cover design Copyright © 2014, Wendy Butler.

Various photographs are copyright © Jim Smith, all used with permission. The model of the *S.S.Cayuga* was constructed by Jim Smith.

Photographs of Doug Unsheared and Sheared courtesy of the *Kitchener-Waterloo Record*.

Other photographs are copyright by the author.

Disclaimer: All content is based on memories of the author, of other individuals, on information published in newspaper articles and other media. Some names, places, events, and their descriptions have been altered out of respect for individuals living or deceased. The content expressed in this book is solely the responsibility of the author. The designer and publisher hereby disclaim any responsibility for the book's contents.

Book design by Mike Miller, pubyourbook@gmail.com.

Table of Contents

DEDICATION	2
OVERVIEW	3
INTRODUCTION	4
PART ONE - MY NIAGARA HISTORY -	5
THE WAY IT WAS	6
Wham!	6
Determination	7
Sparing the Rod	9
NIAGARA-ON-THE-LAKE	13
NIAGARA VERY EARLY CHILDHOOD	16
Maw's House	16
Maw and Pop	20
Mother	22
My Dad	29
The Store	35
The Honeymoon Is Over	38
Strung Along	39
Her Majesty, The S.S.Cayuga	40
Maiden Voyage	42
Number Two!	43
DETROIT	46
Chuga-Chuga-Chuga	46
Welcome to Detroit	49
Down the Drain	51
Trick Knot	52
Between Us Men	53
WAR STORIES	57
Meanwhile, Back At The Store	57
Christmas Surprise	59

'Fraidy Cat	61
War Time Uncles	62
Inside the Box, Outside the Box	62
A Pot and a Grate	65
Excitement Next Door	66
Maw's Chili Sauce	67
The Ming Vase	68
Why, Oh Why, Can't I Fly?	69
Broadcast News and Bedtime Bunnies	71
Learning Curve	71
DOWN ON THE FARM	**73**
How Are You Going to Keep 'Em Down in Niagara, Once They've Seen the Farm?	73
Poop, Poop, and More Poops!	75
Professor Dickey	78
Uncle Wendle's Farm	82
SHORT NIAGARA STORIES	**84**
C-A-T	84
Fire!!	85
Artists At Work	89
V-E Day	90
What, Me Worry?	91
All For One, One For All	93
X-Ray Vision	94
Accidents Will Happen	95
How Holy Am I?	96
"Cousin" Pat	98
Picture This	99
Ride 'Em Cowboy	100
King George's Bum Spot	102
Jack Green's Livery and Philosophy	103

Haunted Legacy	105
The Songs of Regent Street	111
Missing: One Appendix and Two Kittens	113
Raise a Glass To Prohibition	115
Small-Town Canada	116
The War Is Over, But Not the Rationing	118
Gun Running	120
Tag, I'm "It"!	123
Gainfully Employed	125
In The Money	129
Breaking News: Summer, 1947	131
Diving	133
Peep	138
(Almost) Forbidden Fruit	140
Fire at Fort Mississauga	141
Donnybrook	142
I Am Here	147
Technology to the Rescue	148
Drugstore Confidential	151
The Store Was My Living Classroom	152
Not the Girl for Me!	154
When Reasoning Stinks	156
English, What a Strange Language	159
You Are Not My Boss	161
New Life?	163
Blood Brothers	165
Potential Fathers	166
We Owned the Water	168
Ice and Escapades	169
Car Skiing	173

Enamored	175
A Red Hot Lesson	177
Father Weaver Serves Me Peppers	178
Ready, Aim, Fire	180
Finders, Keepers	182
More Balls and More	185
Much More than Balls	187
Ye Olde Spring	190
Breath of Life, I Have You Back	193
Baby Death	196
Resurrection	200
A Love Lesson	206
Brother's Blood	207
Niagara, the Movie	209
FIRST LOVE	212
Too Young to Love, Too Engrossed to Care	212
Safety First	213
"Marty" and "Joyce"	215
"Bust"-ed	216
Custard	218
Know-It-All	219
Pizza	223
Thunder in August	224
Lenny, Nailed	225
KITCHENER	227
St. Jerome's Off to Boarding School	227
School Daze	230
Always Hungry	232
Love Letters	234
Thanksgiving	237
Say Goodbye to Love	241

EXPELLED	243
Thank You, Pauline	243
Scandalous	244
Inspiration	245
Discussing Sex and Religion	246
Fun and Games	249
A "Sheared" Doug	251
AWOL	255
MY FIRST REAL LOVE	257
Joan Tank	257
School Food	261
Father Feeney's Vendetta	263
EXPLORING THE GRAVEYARD	267
My Secret The Secret is the Cornerstone	267
Evil Enters Like a Needle and Spreads Like an Oak Tree	269
The Secret is Always Wrapped in Fear	273
Double Barrel	275
BACK TO THE OLD TOWN	280
Premonition or Faith?	280
World Scout Jamboree	283
The Cayuga's Last Days	288
Homecoming	289
PART TWO - LIFE AFTER NIAGARA -	293
LOVE DETERMINATION, LIFE EXPERIENCES	294
The Greater the Challenge, the Greater the Reward	294
I Never Walked Alone	302
Back to the Ring	306
Follow Me	309
Business "Plan"	310
Who Has The Keys?	316
Michael, The Archangel	319

Goodbye	328
Encountering Marriage	335
Search	339
Our Last *Search*	345
DON QUIXOTE RIDES AGAIN	349
A New War	349
The Journey Towards Confrontation	350
Another Candle Lit	359
Tom Economus	360
Deliver Us From Evil	365
My Own Warrior	368
Ray Brown	370
Richard Sipe and Tom Doyle	372
Nancy Mayer Helps Me Bear My Cross	373
To Sleep Or Not To Sleep . . .	377
The Fight Continues	379
2013 - 2014 UPDATE	383
REVELATION	390
The Keys	390
What Is This Journey All About?	392
EPILOGUE	399
And Finally . . .	399
ACKNOWLEDGEMENTS	404
SURVIVORS NETWORK OF THOSE ABUSED	406

THE
CEMETERY
OF MY
MIND
MEMORIES AND MORE

William Bates

DEDICATION

For my Children and Grandchildren.
That they understand the Good and Evil in my life.

OVERVIEW

A young boy's sheer determination frees him from his Stockholm Syndrome-scenario. He becomes a survivor who transforms into a thriver. With the assistance of his wife, they are committed to helping others.

His story is a no-holds-barred description that begins in his town, Niagara-on-the-Lake, "Where Canada began." It is his personal journey you will not find in history books.

The author courageously reveals how abuse occurs, why it occurs and with the help of others, what can be done about it.

He shares his abandonment, his humor, his woundedness, his strengths, his weaknesses, his love, his commitment, his successes and failures.

The reader will appreciate his sharing's of what it was like for this couple to challenge the most powerful, to fight the unbeatable, to try to right the unrightable wrongs, to overcome all odds and to come out whole. Ultimately, the author discovers the "keys" to loving the unlovable and forgiving the unforgiveable.

The author's personal history is a fabric of Niagara itself. His experiences cover many decades, yet they are very relevant to current, international issues.

INTRODUCTION

This little light of mine . . . and as we let our own light shine, we unconsciously give other people permission to do the same. –Nelson Mandela

If I have a quest and do not share my journey, it is but a lonely journey indeed.

At first I did not even know I had a journey—it was only later that I learned that I had to let "this little light shine." It is my firm conviction that we have indeed given others permission to search out their quest.

This book is much more than my history. It is about the journey of my soul and all the souls that gave me the courage to write a book with no experience doing so, a story that only I had to tell and with many friends guiding me.

All sharings encompass risk, courage, and fear. Sharings of the good are a joy.

I cried, I laughed, I thought, I reasoned, we did.

PART ONE
- MY NIAGARA HISTORY -

I learned not to dread problems because it is in the whole process of solving problems that life has meaning.

adapted from M. Scott Peck, *Road Less Travelled*, p. 16.

THE WAY IT WAS

Wham!

It was the middle of the night. The shock of the bright light woke me. Then, wham! Wham! I was being beaten with a hairbrush. As I struggled to get out of bed: Wham! Across the mouth then, crack! The bottom half of my front tooth, bloodied, toppled from my mouth onto the bed.

My mother, in one of her drunken rages, was assaulting me.

I jumped up, tussled with her, and dragged her back to her own bed. Her wailing remorse awoke my dad, who had been asleep on the couch downstairs.

Dad assessed the situation and produced ice and cloves. This reduced the swelling and stopped the toothache. We all went back to an uneasy sleep. My dad called the dentist first thing in the morning. The dentist installed a temporary cap, but eventually the tooth developed an infection and had to come out. I was left first with a flipper plate, and then a permanent bridge.

Although I was just eleven years old at the time, I had endured quite a few of these bizarre episodes already. But this was the first time my mother had tried to beat me to a pulp. Add to this insult, another type of abuse from a so-called mentor was beginning.

Usually, I was able to restrain her until she tired herself out. Once, though, when I was trying to hold her back as she took a wide swing at me, I blocked her hard and heard a snap. My mother's arm had broken from the force of the blow she aimed at me. From then on, according to her, it was me who broke her arm.

Determination

By the time I was fourteen, Mother's episodes weighed heavily on my mind and my disposition. One early evening, which concluded a very warm summer's day, my little brother Lenny and I were waiting for Dad to come home from work. We were going "over the river" (a term used by both sides for crossing the border) to Lewiston for a late supper—and I got into a shouting fight with Mother. I sure did.

It was useless to try to reason with her. My tamped rage vaulted up, and I bolted out the front door and ran the block down to the river. There, I sprinted up and down the top of the bank in a fit of frustration until I was exhausted; then I slid part way down the bank and must have dozed off.

The next thing I recall was Dad's voice calling me to the car. I didn't respond. I wouldn't. A real stubborn "feeling sorry for me" streak welled up, and while Dad called repeatedly, pleading for me to answer, I just stiffened myself and let him call.

After my father gave up and left, I sat at the edge of the bank, numb, staring out at Fort Niagara. It was starting to get dark. As the embers of the day slowly dimmed, the lighthouse searchlight brightened to a glare. It held me in a hypnotic trance. I focused on the rhythmic sweeps of light flashing across the Niagara River. They seemed to be searching out the very essence of my being. I went into another world.

Have you ever been lone in body and soul? Not just a normal lonely, but truly lone. I was. I felt like a lone tree growing in a vast desert of loneliness. It was a scary, fear-filled, quaking lone. Imagine the darkest-night-thrown-down-an-even-darker-well lone. That evening, I felt my whole universe drop into a black hole, dragging me with it. I was totally abandoned, without any sight or light.

My mother had repeatedly cursed, damned, and abandoned me. What did I have left? She had stripped the love from my mind. What would it be replaced with? Hate? Remorse? Despair?

Where was Michael, my trusted Guardian Angel? He had been the anchor of my life, but he seemed to have abandoned me, too. I swore at Michael. He must be just a made-up fairy tale like Santa Claus and the Tooth Fairy. I swore at God. He must be a fairy tale, too.

Then, a transformation overtook me. Did this change reflect the determination of my father's hero, Winston Churchill, who swore to never give in? Maybe. But I like to think it was a response to the culmination of all that I had experienced in my young life, all that was threatening and negative.

My spirit just rebelled, retching from the guts of my soul, and, suddenly, my depressed rage was changed into an erupting volcanic power of determination. I vowed that never again would anyone hurt me. Not my mother. Not that other Stockholm Syndrome adult who kept me gripped in an even deeper, more frightening secret. In that moment, I was imbued with a subtle but magnetically powerful strength and peace. Somehow, I just knew that I would now have the ability to overcome any adversity.

This seemed an answer to my angry prayers, so, at first, I thought my experience was similar to that which I had learned occurs to the saints when they are given the gift of redemption. But unbeknownst to this fourteen-year old, as I perched on the bank overlooking Fort Niagara, my own redemption would have to wait for many years.

Still, between sweeps of the lighthouse's powerful beam, something inside me had changed. I had been given a gift, not of redemption, but of determination, the determination that I would need to survive. And I definitely needed this gift to survive the prejudices, judgments, and nightmares that were to litter my life.

I know that when a mother's love is withdrawn, a scar remains in one's heart forever.

When a disguised evil invades the soul, the penetrating scar pain shakes one's entire being to the very root of faith.

Sparing the Rod

Life is surely in the eye of the beholder, but one's perceptions of it are influenced by those surrounding one.

Thus, as an adult, I can now look back and perceive those Niagara years quite differently than the way I experienced them at the time. As a young child, my understanding of what was "normal" was defined by the adults—family members and others—around me. As I grew older, it was my friends who had the greater influence on me. And when I became a father, myself, I had to revise my perceptions yet again.

But during my Niagara, at-home years, all I knew was that I was "bad"; that if there was discord, it was my fault. My mother, if she did not create this perception entirely, certainly reinforced it by repeatedly saying that she had been a very different person—a happier one, I assumed from her tone—before I was born.

As difficult as this "it-was-my-fault/I-am-bad" attitude made my early life, I was not alone in feeling this way. Other children, too, were "disciplined" to make the "little buggers" obey like robotic soldiers.

Although in my house it was my mother who did the punishing, in most homes, it was the fathers who meted out the "justice." For example, Friend A had the devil exorcised from him with a horsewhip. Friend B would become penitent after repeated lashes of the belt or bashes with the fist. Friend C would recant after several strokes of the rubber strop.

The mandate "Spare the rod and spoil the child" was commonly cited. "The rod," usually a thick yardstick, was applied by fathers when deemed necessary. Mothers, on the other hand, tended toward the use of a wooden spoon or hairbrush banged against a rear end after repeated warnings had been given.

Despite my mother's physical expressions of anger, I can remember my father slapping me only once—and that was clearly in response to me and my big mouth overstepping the line.

As a child, I was unable to understand the rights and wrongs of the complicated system of "crime and punishment" that I was growing up amidst. Like all children of abuse, particularly those of alcoholic parents, I was confused. So I shoved as much of it as I could—my faults, my denials, my justifications, and my unworthy feelings—into the cemetery of my mind until they festered there and eventually erupted.

When a child is subject to physical, sexual, and/or mental abuse, those experiences form the foundation for the person's continuing dysfunction: simply put, children to whom evil is done respond with anger in return.

It was not until I was older, a parent myself, that I was able to unravel the web of abusive experiences with which my childhood had been inculcated. But before the unraveling could begin, I had to admit that I had problems, problems which I could no longer control.

I believe that we are born for a reason, for what the Church says is our calling. Whatever my reason for being, Niagara-on-the-Lake was my nemesis. I had to escape in order to find myself and live out my destiny. As much adventure as misadventure, my journey from those "at-home Niagara years" has followed a steep learning curve.

From Dale Carnegie classes I understood that the most important thing a person possesses is his name. And from someone else I learned we never forget the place where we are born. Together, birthplace and name become a reference point for us, a foundational concept about who we are.

***

I was born in Niagara-on-the-Lake. I almost died there. I became a survivor there. And even now I can hear the voices of my experiences calling, in contrast to the town's yearly two and a half million visitors viewing it as simply *quaint* or *charming*.

Some treasured memories of my time there have faded and now are hard to recall. Other precious memories have been destroyed – as the sadness of loss lingers still. Some still-tough memories scorch as I touch on them. But all keep calling from my past.

The Cemetery of My Mind is my story – my life as I remember it.

NIAGARA-ON-THE-LAKE

YE OLDE TOWN "WHERE CANADA BEGAN"

Winston Churchill considered the Niagara area, from Fort Erie to Niagara-on-the-Lake, "the prettiest scenic spot in the world." The millions of visitors who make Niagara their destination each year agree with Churchill and understand just how unique this town is.

Located at the mouth of the Niagara River, which borders the United States, and only ten miles from Niagara Falls, Niagara-on-the-Lake, also bounded by Lake Ontario, is a peninsula. Boasting many Canadian firsts—including first Parliament, first library, and first museum—as well as the Underground Railroad, Niagara-on-the-Lake is listed among the most historic towns in Canada.

First known as Newark, Niagara-on-the-Lake was founded on Masonic principles and was home to such prominent Masons as Governor John Graves Simcoe, who convened the first Parliament of Upper Canada, and John Butler of Butler's Rangers. Indeed, the rigid roots of the Empire were transplanted into the soil of this newly conquered territory, establishing British heritage as the cornerstone of Upper Canada.

The town's signature is the Cenotaph, a clock tower that stands sentinel at the center of Queen Street and represents those townsmen who died fighting socialist dictators in Europe.

Considered a monument dedicated to freedom, for me, the tower is actually a giant, redbrick tombstone. My Uncle Jack Dietsch's name is engraved on that tower and, to me, that is his gravestone. I think of Uncle "Big Jack" every time I pass the clock, and every time I hear it bong, memories flash across my mind, memories that put the Cenotaph at the very center of "The Cemetery of My Mind."

Neighboring the tower, period stores line the main street. One, the Niagara Apothecary, which stands at the corner of King and Queen Streets, is the oldest drug store in Ontario.

The stores are not the only vestiges of times gone by, though. Crazy King George's England contributed two forts to the town, one in 1799 and one in 1814. The first, Fort George, is a wooden structure now rebuilt to its original majesty. The second, Fort Mississauga, is a unique brick and plaster structure built from the rubble resulting from the fire of Newark caused by "the Americans" on December 10th, 1813. The only five-star Canadian fort, Mississauga spreads across more than three acres on Point Mississauga, close to the edge of Lake Ontario, and is ringed by a fifteen-foot moat. Some say the fort's roof was designed to allow for the firing of an internal, rotating cannon.

Although Fort Mississauga is now closed, it is surrounded by the oldest golf course in North America. Fort Mississauga faces both the Niagara River and Lake Ontario, while Fort George is turned towards the river, and both are but a cannon shot from the elegant, mid-eighteenth century stone castle, which is the United States' Fort Niagara.

Outside the historic town lies lush farmland where grapes, cherries, peaches, nectarines, and a medley of other fruits and vegetables grow. In fact, the area has so many award winning wineries it is often referred to as the "Napa of the North."

Truly, then, Niagara-on-the-Lake would seem a sort of historical paradise, a place so unique the fantasies of Walt Disney could not match it. But beneath the beauty lies a tension so dark, even the horrors of Steven King could not meet them.

And there you have it: my town, my life, is built from equal parts of these.

NIAGARA VERY EARLY CHILDHOOD

Maw's House

VICTORIA STREET, 1938-1946

When an egg allows a sperm to enter, together they immediately form a zygote. The energy created at this nanosecond is akin to the initial reaction of an atomic bomb. Indeed, it is an atomic-level reaction. In my mind, I consider this instant the birth of the soul. This phenomenal reaction keeps the cells dividing and sub-dividing until death—that moment when all that original spirit energy is released into a different form.

Since I was born on June 24th, 1938, my own atomic-reaction moment must have been sometime in the early fall of 1937, bringing me along just before World War II.

Fortunately for me, my maternal grandmother, whom we called "Maw", was a bit of a nuclear reactor herself: a four-foot-something, one-hundred pound "love reactor." She generated a radiating kindness to everyone who came into contact with her. For me in particular, she was my special, one-person caring dynamo. And I needed her.

While I longed for my own mother's smile (and remember each time she did smile at me), my brothers and I only sporadically received either a smile or a twinkle from our mother's eyes or warmth from her voice. Sure, I remember a few times when her laughing smile dispelled my tears, but sadly, I remember a lot of bad stuff more.

I've been told that Mom and Dad had been out partying just before I was born, so it seems probable that I came into this world with a hangover. I certainly used to cry a lot. This could have been from alcohol withdrawal or from the fact that she didn't bond with me. My mother had her own drummer—and it clearly wasn't me.

That's why Maw was so important to me. Maw ended up with nineteen grandchildren, and gave each and every one of us a special piece of her spiritual energy, but when I was with her, it was like I was her only grandchild.

Maw and me

In one of my first memories, Maw is filling a large galvanized washtub with warm water for two little tykes, my cousin Donna and me. We were to sit in our own private spa. The hot summer sun is flickering with a soft breeze through the hollyhocks, producing a dance of white, red, and pink blossoms along the pale green stems that stretch up the side of the white garage. A hummingbird darts in and out of the flowers; the pail is pouring; Maw is singing, "This is the way we wash our chickadees: Splash, splash," and giggles as she splashes us.

Our Garage - Our Spa

Water sparkles before our enchanted eyes. In the magic of the moment, Maw's smile and laughter are magnified, creating a circle of love around this slice of innocent heaven.

Our galvanized "spa" was placed in the backyard of a magnificent, ten-room, white, wood-frame house, circa-1880, located on Victoria Street. It was just a dozen kicks of the can from Queens Royal Beach. Maw had bought the house for herself and her extended family.

It was a church-blessed house. Fear and hope were both instilled in us by the religious pictures and crucifixes that adorned the walls. When Maw would put us to bed, she would instruct us in the proper way to say our prayers. First, she would tease us by sometimes speaking them in lilting Gaelic, which sounded like spiritual music to my young ears. Then she would repeat them in English, telling us to always include a special prayer to our own particular saint or guardian angel.

Donna's saint was St. Teresa, who helped little girls. My guardian angel was St. Michael the Archangel, protector of children and defender of God. I never tired of hearing Maw tell me how Michael beat up on the Devil's angels, and I felt very special having this hero available to guard me.

In addition to our night-time prayers, Maw also gave us special prayer cards to connect us with our guardians. My card featured a young boy with a large, kind-looking angel standing behind him. I was enthralled with this picture and kept it next to my bed. It was clear to me that the boy in the picture was me, and that Archangel Michael would always have my back.

In addition to these more typically Catholic spiritual helpers, Maw also hosted a full complement of Irish entities of superstition. This meant that "gonies", "banshees", and guardian angels all cohabited with the families and friends who lived there.

And then there was the flag. A star flag hung in our window. This confused me, because, unlike all the other symbols in the house, it seemed to bring Maw sadness. Visiting soldiers would stand at attention and salute the flag, and Donna and I would mimic them, but we didn't really understand why.

When I finally asked Maw, "What is that flag?" she answered, with choking tears, that it was my Uncle Big Jack's memorial flag.

That Victoria Street house, with Maw as matriarch, was an open house, holding many people close. But it harbored strife, tension, fear, anger, sadness, too—and me. For this was my home, from shortly after my birth until I was eight years old, in those in-between years, those mostly war years, from 1938 until 1946.

Maw and Pop

Maw tried to fill all of us grandkids with the love we were missing from our own parents, but she was only one for so many. And, from what I can see looking back, it seems obvious that she had her own demons to deal with. In writing this story, I tried to learn as much as I could both about Maw and about my mother's father, but met with only limited success.

This is what I discovered:

Maw's husband, my grandfather Emile Dietsch, was born in a tiny village called Grishenheim, outside Colmar,

Alsace, France. From a very large family, he was one of at least a dozen children, all of whom were born in a one-bedroom cottage. As was the practice in that village at the time, the babies slept on the main floor as infants. When there was no more room, the biggest of the little ones were sent to sleep in the attic. When the attic became too crowded, the Dietschs, like others, would ship their oldest boy to America.

That's how it was for Emile, who, towards the end of the 1800s, at the age of ten, immigrated to the United States to live with his older brother in the American Midwest.

For her part, Maw, born Margaret Kelly, fled the Irish Famine with her parents. Her family established itself in Toronto, Canada, where Great-grandpa Kelly worked for the City of Toronto. (I have a picture of my great-grandparents Kelly in which I am told Great-grandpa Kelly is blind.)

I have heard varying stories of how Maw and Emile, whom we always called "Pop", met. And while I cannot even guess which of these might be correct, I do know that Maw was his second wife, and that his first wife died, and that Maw took on not just Pop, but his young daughter, Mamie, too. I also know that Pop gave Maw a clock, dated 1900, as a wedding present. (I know, because I own that clock now.)

From there, Maw and Pop's life leaps off into a half-dozen different versions—amid which lies the truth. It is certain that Pop was a chef. Maw once showed me an invitation for a gala event for Prime Minister Sir Wilfred

Laurier to be held at the Royal York Hotel Toronto. According to the invitation, Grand Chef Emile Paul Dietsch coordinated the banquet.

But one of my uncles maintained that Pop was the inventor of Honey Dew Orange, a drink that was extremely popular at the Toronto National Exhibition—and was also a great mixer for bathtub gin during the 1920s prohibition; a different uncle said that Pop earned millions and owned a block on Bay Street, in the financial district of Toronto—until his partner stole all the money and fled to South American, leaving Pop bankrupt.

Not so, my brother Doug says. His version is that Pop became partners with a lawyer and bought the Ford Hotel. Then, when Pop died, probably of alcoholism, the lawyer got the best of the deal. But Maw fought her way to at least a portion of Pop's holdings and used that money to bankroll her real-estate career of buying houses, fixing them up, and flipping them. Cousin Jim Goode agrees about the Ford Hotel, but says it burnt down, and Pop did not have insurance.

Ultimately, we do know that Pop died in Beamsville, of pneumonia caught because he did not have a winter coat. But before he died, my grandparents had six more children, making seven in all.

Mother

The first rule of our family concerned secrets: We hid them. Even though others may have already known our secrets, we were not to speak of them. Not even to each other. Instead we were to ignore anything that was not as it was supposed to be—in our own family and in everybody else's family, too. I can't remember being taught this. It seems that I always just knew it. For instance, I knew to talk about my mother as a very special person at my dad's store. This continued even after she stopped going in to work.

There must have been a time when my mother was happy and gay, because her family nickname was "Irish", after the song "When Irish Eyes Are Smiling". "When Irish eyes are smiling/Sure, it's like a morning spring," my uncles used to sing to her, so she must have smiled a lot when she was growing up with them.

Even in her grown-up years, Mother put on a gregarious face for the world at large. And early in my own life, Mom did have what seemed to be genuine extended periods of sobriety and kindness, during which, she offered me what passed for the love that I hungered for. One precious memory I have from back then has sustained me through a lot of uglier moments: It was a beautiful, sunny, June day. I was just a toddler, and Mom and I were skipping the three blocks to Dad's store. As we held hands, skipping and giggling, she sang, "Skip to My Lou, My Darling". I have treasured this little crumb of my childhood for many years, and wish there were more such moments to hold onto.

One secret that could not be kept, though, was Mother's lack of care for her children's cleanliness. When Maw was around, we kids were clean and presentable. But when she wasn't, we looked like street urchins.

When I was nine, I received an early birthday present. My baby brother Lenny arrived. This is when Dad got some help at the store so he could help out more at home. Now he could cut his hours to fifty plus per week.

Dad did the laundry, we emptied the dirty diapers, sloshed them in the toilet and put the wet remains in a pail for Dad to launder. Dad tried to steal time from the store and came home to make dinner. We made our own breakfast and lunch and dinner, when Dad couldn't get there. I ate out as much as possible, just to get out of the house when Dad was working.

I slept in the same room with my Lenny in his crib. He was about two or more. It was early morning when I felt a whack on my head. I looked up to see that my angry brother had thrown his empty bottle at me. It was time to get up, change him and fill that bottle.

Strangely enough I felt like a responsible grown up. I had taken over what Doug had done for me. Len was my responsibility. This was magnified when Jack moved to Toronto and Doug went off to cut tobacco.

I usually knew where my Dad was, but only too often my Mother's mind was somewhere else. I suspect she was dealing with her demon.

I wish for my children and grandchildren to understand that writing about my Mother was not an easy task. After all I had only one mother. First I had to go through a kaleidoscope of feelings. I felt like I was rejected, dejected, in fact I felt abandoned. I had to deal with my feelings of anger bordering on rage, regret, and remorse, even blaming her for everything bad that happened to me.

When I was proof reading my eighth draft everything came together.

Being very sentimental, I will often get tears in my eyes when watching sad movies. When I got that ah-ah moment, I was hit with teary mist that enhanced my vision.

It was through both a TV ad and then a movie when I got the revelation that put my mother in her proper perspective.

It was sometime in June 2014, that I saw a Florida ad on T.V. from placeofhope.com. It took me a few seconds to figure out that this ad was about me. It hit deep into my heart!

It is about two very wholesome looking brothers. The younger is about six. The older is around eleven or twelve. The camera focuses on a stark light bulb, then the youngster's face as his brother helps him wake up. The camera pans the mattress on the floor, two toothbrushes on a not so clean washcloth, a toy dinosaur, the messy shelves and the pot of water on the stove. I am into it when the younger beams with pride as the older one washes him, then finishes dressing him. The sweater goes on with loving care as it pops over his head. He angelically smiles with admiration as the older brother fixes his hair. The last shot that really does it is of the two of them, back packs full of books, the older brother leading the way, the younger one playfully by his side as they start off to school. This is all to the back ground music of Five Hundred Miles.

The caption reads "Neglect" followed by the next scene "Not all child abuse is obvious."

It is left up to the viewer to ask, "Why is the older one taking on this parental role? Where is the Mother? The Father?"

I first related to it that the older boy in the ad was Doug and the younger one me. In thinking about it further, I realized that as time passed, the roles changed. I took Doug's role and Len took mine. I know that siblings may fight among themselves, but most have a protective nature for the ones more vulnerable.

It was July 2014 when my wife Joan and I were watching a 2003 movie "The Missing" on Netflix.

This is when the second part of the revelation fell into place.

The following lines said it all:

"Inside you are two dogs. One is evil, the other is good. The mean dog fights the good dog all the time." "Which one wins?" "I don't know. Whichever one I feed the most."

As children we used to relate to the two angels sitting on our shoulders. The one on the right was the good angel, the one on the left was the devil angel. The devil angel was always tempting us to do wrong. The good angel was encouraging us to be good. However, I like the evil dog versus the secure loving good dog. Unlike angels, dogs have to be fed.

I know from friends, relatives and business associates that alcoholics feed the devil dog. The only way they can stop is with the help of a supreme being and their community, each helping each other, lending their ability to quiet the devil dog, keeping it at bay, i.e. the AA Organization.

Hair of the dog:

Alcoholics often take a drink to relieve the morning after pain. This is called the hair of the dog. There is some scientific backing that when suffering withdrawal, another drink lessens the pain.

I was shocked when after a heavy party at our house, I saw Mom and an aunt glug down a huge shot of whiskey followed with water. The wild dog had to be fed. It was at ten o'clock on a Sunday morning. They were getting ready to go to mass.

I try to think of what was going through my mind when being around sloppy drunks. I suspect like most kids, I shut it out the way I did with all the things I could not or did not want to understand. I buried it. I laughed at it. I denied it. I just depressingly daydreamed my way around it. I ran away from it to become more carefree. However, there was always a lingering, misunderstood, uneasy, scary void-am I part of the problem? I could easily skip school by hiding under the covers, pretending to be sick. This menagerie paid a big toll on my schooling. Even though I had a so-called mentor supposedly tutoring me, I failed grade eight. That was the summer I received my gift of determination.

In some ways, my father and we four boys reacted in a protective mode by joining forces in a dysfunctional family circle. What happened in that circle was protected by all of us. The outsider got the story we gave them.

Every once in a while Doug and I dumped Mom's booze down the sink. True to form, Len helped me to do it a few years later.

It was not long after one of these episodes that I was determined never to cry over her again. In fact I had had enough of her. I soon divorced her as my mother. I still cared and was a friend, but never again would I feel responsible for her or would she influence my life.

The sad part is that like a lot of kids of alcoholics, I grew through it but did reluctantly take some of the blame for it. However growing through it was not easy and it did leave its deep imprinted mark in my heart. When I had grown into my late teens, I understood that alcoholism, like smoking, over- eating, bulimia and drugs, can be addictive. The user is out of control. Any love that I had for my mother was replaced with pity.

It was only then that all the nightmares and hopelessness about my mother were able to be set free. The loss stays forever. I lament and question why my mother, who had so much potential, continuously chose to feed the wrong dog.

I do not think it has merit to elaborate on my mother's sickness, except to say that when I was older, on one occasion, she and I were alone. She was very remorseful saying she did not want to be that way. I convinced her to phone AA's. I looked up the number but told her she had to make the call. She did and talked to an AA person for the longest time and even made an appointment. I felt full of hope. However she never kept the appointment. Most of the family denied she was an alcoholic. She was just a heavy drinker. My mother grabbed at this frail life preserver. When I was going for counselling myself, I learned that when someone decides to make a drastic change, the others in that dysfunctional circle are at a loss as how to handle it. People like the familiar. They like what they have grown accustomed to. At my stage in life now, I understand how easy it is to make someone else a scapegoat for our problems. It was easy to blame my mother for my problems, because she did not protect me. Be that right or wrong, I had to reason that I would not ask a cripple to run a race against me. But she was my mother. I know she was seriously handicapped but Mothers are supposed to protect their children aren't they? I cannot blame those in the family who instinctively wanted to keep the status quo.

All this being said, because of my 'woundedness', the so called caring mentor who cunningly vacuumed me into his clutches, is sadly a horrendously different story. Both my dogs had a lot of fierce fighting to do before I could survive that one.

Regardless of my convoluted history, I just know that placeofhope.com ad is about me.

My Dad

Everyone in town knew my dad for his place behind the counter of his very own Bates Rexall Pharmacy. The owner of a store that contained answers to every human need—including hand-compounded medicines, birth control devices, and a few yards of gossip strung in between—my father was a man who liked to see the other person's perspective and who did not like confrontation.

He was very quiet, yes. But if you sought him out, he would respond. And he knew everything. You could talk to Dad most times, but I learned very young when not to interrupt him: Of course, the customer always came first. But also, when my father was manufacturing a new medicine, it took his complete concentration, and any idle questions on my part were put on the back burner.

Most of the time, though, my dad could talk to me, compound his prescriptions, listen to the chatter going on in the background of the store, and still think his own thoughts, all at the same time. And as quiet as he was, in later years, his trademark became a cream-colored, Gene-Autry style jacket, complete with fringes!

Dad

As a Catholic convert, Dad was considered a bit of a turncoat in Masonic Niagara. Freemasonry had been viewed with some suspicion by the Catholic Church. If a Catholic should become a Mason it meant automatic excommunication from the Church. In the mid-twentieth century, Niagara was still a predominately Protestant town with its Masonic roots dug deeply into the soil.

While a slight counter-bias against Catholics was in evidence at the time, fortunately some businessmen had the sense to put business first, and there were instances of both Catholic and Protestant business people supporting each other as the town struggled to survive.

I've been told that when my father first arrived in Niagara, in the Depression year of 1934, he and (Presbyterian) Scotty Stewart struck up a friendship. But in the 1950s, when Scotty decided to sell what was known as the "Stewart Block", a section of the street which housed my dad's drug store, he refused to sell it to my by-then Catholic father, whom Scotty considered "a turn-coat Presbyterian." Instead, Scotty sold it to Jim Gullion a Niagara Falls clothier—who, understanding the situation, subsequently a few years later sold the building to my dad.

My mother, attuned to these undercurrents, used her personal charm and her business wiles to offset the potentially negative consequences. From the war on, she was famous for her negotiations. For example, she befriended what seemed to be the entire army camp, men who didn't care whether they purchased necessities from Catholics or from Presbyterians.

Also, since most of the (exquisite!) summer mansions were owned by successful businessmen from Buffalo and Ontario, in the summer, Mom arranged for the Buffalo Sunday News, the three Toronto papers, and the St. Catharines Standard to be delivered to the store. Dad took the baton from there, and sold these papers as a loss leader to those same wealthy businessmen, creating loyal, supportive customers of them.

Too, Dad and Mom welcomed new immigrants, earning their business by helping them out whenever possible. For instance, the hard-working Dutch and Mennonite farmers knew Mom and Dad would give them store credit when necessary, allowing the farmers to pay when their crops came in. Mom also made sure the parents knew how to register their children for school.

Then, in 1946, my parents vacationed at Williamsburg, Virginia, and Dad was struck by Williamsburg's success as a tourist Mecca. He immediately saw that historically significant Niagara-on-the-Lake had the potential to be a north-of-the-border Williamsburg.

Although Niagara had slipped into a slump that made the town little more than a poor backwater to St. Catharines and Niagara Falls, my dad felt that Niagara-on-the-Lake could be revitalized. But, as he said, "Niagara had to go backwards in order to go forward," and return to its colonial-era quaintness just as Williamsburg had done.

When they returned from their vacation, my father was on fire with his new idea and attended meeting after meeting, trying to promote his vision. Mom, instead of supporting his efforts, was frustrated with his spending so much time trying to get the town's businessmen involved in his concept. She felt they were too rooted in a conservative attitude to respond to anything new. And it's true that some of the meetings got heated. But Dad had a quiet, non-combative approach and was able to move things along despite initial resistance.

In March of 1947, the then-dormant Niagara Businessmen's Association got a push. While some of my dad's business peers still offered stiff opposition, the majority agreed to have my dad (J.W. Bates), M. Morgan, W. Kirby, and others approach the St. Catharines Chamber of Commerce with a view toward forming their own Chamber. This group brought back much information, including the fact that one of the ideals of the Chamber is to block the rise of communism.

Well, this was fine with all involved, and with St. Catharines Chamber mentoring the group of forward-thinking Niagara businessmen, the Niagara-on-the-Lake Chamber of Commerce was formed. One of Dad's friends, Don Shaw of Potter & Shaw Pharmacy of St. Catharines, arranged for Dad to hold the meetings. And then, to put a cherry on the top, James Connelly supported Dad's greater vision by announcing that he was going to renovate his own store front to reflect the architectural style of Colonial Canada.

Now officially associated with Chambers of Commerce across Canada, Niagara-on-the-Lake finally had the recognition and support it needed from both the Provincial and the Federal Governments.

I am proud to say that my dad, John Bates, was the first Niagara-on-the-Lake Chamber of Commerce president, attaining that office on May 12th, 1949, and remaining president for several years.

So it was, in issues of politics and business, my dad was a person who would stand his ground. But when it came to my mother, it seemed she could get the better of him every time. I loved Dad, but he had a different personality than I did, especially when faced with Mother's problems. I often questioned how he could be so soft, tolerant, and enabling with her. But I misunderstood him. It took me decades to appreciate and learn from both his personal strength and his quiet aptitude for leading others. First I had to find who I was.

Dad, Mom, Doug, Len, and me

The Store

There were other drug stores besides Bates Rexall in town. The main competition was McQuillan's, with locations in Niagara Falls and St. Catharines, as well as in Niagara-on-the-Lake. Others came and went. Fields lasted. It officially became the oldest drug store in Ontario, and with everything in its place on antique shelves and in old, Western-style glass cases, its décor properly represented the tired, drab, museum-like store that it was. Owners Earl and Eugene Fields stocked only a limited amount of drugs, and then they relied on some of my dad's stock to keep them supplied so their customers wouldn't have to come to our store.

Dad in "The Store"

I couldn't understand helping out our competition in this way, but Dad's view was that we had to help each other out, so we could all survive against the big cities.

Donna and me in front of "The Store"
on Ash Wednesday

Dad's store, known to most in Niagara simply as "The Store", was an entirely different matter from the dusty, scantily stocked Fields. The Store had four seasons full of life. Its two large, glass-front windows showcased the vibrancy of what was happening inside.

In winter, The Store offered the townspeople help with colds, flu, and "the blahs." Vitamins, Neo-Chemical food, Buckley's cough syrup. One of the most in demand was 222s -one-quarter grain codeine and aspirin, which were over-the-counter products in Ontario, but required a prescription in New York. Sun lamps gave customers hope that they would make it through to spring. Spring and fall brought the famous Rexall one-cent sale. For Easter there were chocolates, pastille fruit drops, and the big favorite,

McIntosh Toffee. The Mother's Day display featured Estee Lauder cosmetics and special perfumes.

The Storefront Window

With summer's arrival, The Store offered bathing caps, sun tan lotions, sunburn treatments, and the famous aviator sunglasses, as Niagara welcomed the return of the tourists. Fall was back-to-school. Through the windows passersby could view books, note pads, scribblers, rulers, pencils, nib pens, and erasers. Although ballpoint pens were banned by teachers because they thought their use would corrupt the students' writing, and banks would not accept a ball-point signature on a check, The Store still displayed them. The forbidden ballpoints made a pricey, enticing addition to the standard fountain pen.

Christmas, of course, was the biggest retail season, with a third of The Store's goods being rotated in and out of the windows. There were French and German perfumes, brush sets, costume jewelry, specialty English soaps, and specialty face powders for the women, and watches, cameras, imported snuff, Irish pipe tobacco, Burrell wood pipes, shaving brushes, razors, knives, lighters and pocket and wrist watches for the men.

During World War II, the right-hand window showcase was dedicated to the local lads fighting overseas. There, my father displayed photographs of all "our boys", set against a backdrop of two Union Jacks angled in such a way as to form a proud "V" for victory.

For a young kid, The Store was a cave of wonders—a place full of noise and people and shelves and stacks and rows and aisles filled with all of the things the townspeople needed. As early as I can remember, The Store offered glimpses, now just snapshot memories, of the world into which I had come.

The Honeymoon Is Over

Exactly six months before I was born, a real-life nightmare occurred that left scars, not on me, but on the landscape for the entire Niagara region to see. It was January 23rd, 1938, when a sudden wind-storm on Lake Erie sent a huge deluge of ice down-river and over the Falls.

Within hours, the river below the Falls was jammed with such an extraordinary amount of ice that the pressure against the abutments and hinge supports of the upper steel arch bridge, which we knew as the Honeymoon Bridge, caused irreparable structural damage.

Honeymoon Bridge collapsed

Witnessed by the thousands who had come to watch its collapse, four days later, at 4:20 p.m., on January 27th, the entire span of the Honeymoon Bridge broke free and fell into the river below. And while this event should not have had any effect on my soon-to-be life, like so much that happened in Niagara, it sure enough did.

Strung Along

My Uncle Big Jack had dragged a remnant of the Honeymoon Bridge, a wooden post, out of the river shortly before I was born. Hauling the post home, he planted it in Maw's back yard and strung a clothesline from the pole to the house. This was one of the last gifts Maw received from Big Jack, who would later be memorialized on the clock tower on Queen Street.

By the time I was a toddler, I was walking and talking quite normally—even to the point of being a (cute) pest. Then, suddenly, after months of babbling and toddling along, I quit. No more walking, no more talking for me!

The accepted explanation was that my brothers had been doing everything for me, and that I was so lazy and spoiled, I let them.

The doctor was called in to consult on the case. As his prescribed exercise, he told my family to hook me up to Uncle Jack's clothesline in a harness arranged so that it would let my feet touch the ground but would not allow me to sit back down. My brothers were to crank the clothesline slowly back and forth, forcing me to walk. In order to get them to stop, I had to speak up and instruct them to stop.

My brothers had fun with this new game, laughing as they pushed me faster and faster. On the first day, I passed the test, but then regressed, so we went back to the same routine the next day. This lasted until I finally capitulated and was willing to walk and talk on my own.

But even as I write this, a question lingers in my mind: Why would a capable toddler suddenly stop the most important tasks of early childhood, walking and talking? Was I really lazy? Or was there some other cause? And how did the force to which I was subjected affect that little one who was me?

Her Majesty, The S.S.Cayuga

When I was three years old, and walking and talking quite happily again, my brothers Jack and Doug would take me out to the middle of Victoria Street, where we could look directly at the mouth of the Niagara River and wait until we saw the S.S.Cayuga approach the river from Lake Ontario. Then my brothers and I would jump up and down, shouting, "BLOW! BLOW! BLOW!" until the Cayuga heard us, and blew its horn with three spaced out mighty blasts.

S.S.Cayuga—model built by Jim Smith

I was so proud. My smart brothers knew how to make that big boat toot on cue.

One day, my cousin Donna and I were playing outside and heard the three Cayuga blasts. We ran out to the middle of the street looking for my brothers, but they were nowhere in sight. What happened? How did the boat know to blow its horn without them?

We went in to ask Maw. She explained that the Cayuga always tooted at that spot to warn boats in the area that she was coming through and also to let people on the dock know she was coming into berth.

Oh. In an instant, the magic my big brothers had created for me disappeared. Still, this knowledge did not stop me from joining Jack and Doug in their hollering ritual for a few more years to come.

Maiden Voyage

That same summer, I was a lucky three-year old when Maw decided to take me with her to Toronto. We were to sail across Lake Ontario aboard the Cayuga, instead of just watching her pass by on the river. I was so excited!

Maw and I were standing on the dock as the big boat came in. The Cayuga threw her propellers in reverse just before reaching the dock, which made everything vibrate. Suddenly, I had the sensation that the dock was moving, and the ship was standing still. In my excitement I got a bit scared, but Maw gripped my hand a little tighter and assured me that everything was all right. Still, I was glad to see they tied the boat up tight before we boarded.

Maw and I climbed up to the second deck, clutching onto railings that seemed to beg someone to slide back down them. I resisted that urge, though, and, instead, once on the deck, Maw and I sat on the boat's seats and ate the picnic lunch she had packed.

I was enjoying lunch and having Maw all to myself, until we ran into a storm that made the ship roll back and forth, back and forth, and back and forth. After a few minutes, it was goodbye picnic, goodbye lunch, and the sailors had to put the mop brigade in full action.

By the time we landed at Toronto, the water—and my stomach—was calm once more, and I had the fun of getting to watch the boat tie up alongside the dock. The steward gave me a Cayuga pin as a souvenir for being so brave.

If only I had that pin now.

When we sailed back home a few days later, the weather was fine. This time, I was allowed up in the wheelhouse with the captain. I was right there when he pulled the cord that sounded our arrival. I couldn't wait to tell Jack and Doug exactly how the big TOOT, TOOT, TOOT was made.

Number Two!

One morning, Maw was in the back kitchen, dressed in her yellow-flowered housecoat, adjusting the wood stove with more kindling. Doug and I took our usual seats in the dining room at the large round oak table. We heard the scraping of metal as the stove plate was removed and smelled a slight whiff of smoke as Maw slotted another piece of wood into place.

She was making us oatmeal porridge, which required long, slow cooking to create the delicious, creamy mass. After a few minutes, Maw brought our bowls to the table, and we topped our porridge with brown sugar and covered it with creamy milk, transforming a simple breakfast into a wonderful dessert.

From my seat across the table, as Doug slurped his porridge, he was silhouetted by the light coming in from two large dining room windows. These were my morning windows to the outside world. Through them, I watched the varying weather. I always knew when it was spring for sure because, like all the other windows in the house, these were cleaned inside and out to get rid of all the soot from the coal furnace.

On this morning, even in silhouette, I could see that Doug had a silly smirk on his face. Doug was a great seven-year-old brother; he was my protector and my teacher, but he was also every bit a wise-ass boy.

It was definitely the wise-ass in him that made him reach his hand across the table and say, "pull my finger." Of course, I did it.

Doug looked straight into my eyes and let two big stinky farts, and we both broke out laughing. Then, all of a sudden, Doug hopped up off his chair and undid his knickers. He bent over and put his hand into the back of his pants and proceeded to pull a handful of brown you-know-what. As I stared, mesmerized, he smelled it. Then he stuck his dirty pointer finger right into his mouth.

"Want some?" he asked, offering me a finger-full.

"Maw," I screamed as I ran into the back kitchen, "Doug is eating Number Two!"

I followed behind Maw as she shuffled her slippers to the table.

"Douglas," she said, "what are you doing?"

"Nothing, Maw. I was just licking peanut butter off my fingers," was his smart-ass reply.

Maw figured out what happened and laughed.

Doug laughed, too, pointing at me. "Got ya!" he crowed.

What? I felt so stupid. Doug, my teacher and protector, had betrayed me. Did he think I was nothing but a baby? Lucky for Doug, even at three, I had a forgiving nature, because we had some big adventures yet to come.

DETROIT

Chuga-Chuga-Chuga

The next year, Maw went away and, as Mother was "not well", there was no one to take care of us at home. Therefore, the summer of 1942, when I was four and Doug was eight, we were we getting ready to go to Detroit to live with our Aunt Phyllis and Uncle Roy for the next while.

"Come on slowpoke, you don't want to miss your first train ride. Here let me tie your shoes and get into the car." As Dad tightened my shoestrings, I told him my feet hurt.

Dad said he had to put money in my socks for it would be needed in Detroit, where we had to stay until Maw came home. While there was a wartime restriction on the amount of money allowed across the border, for kids there was none, he explained. He also told me that I would be sitting down on the train, and my feet wouldn't hurt then.

When we arrived in Welland at the train station, we had to hurry along the side of the rail cars, which were so huge they seemed taller to me than the roof of our house. Doug wanted to see the engine, and tugged me along towards it, but it made such a big hissing sound that it scared me. I stopped completely when I saw its white smoke coming at me. Was it on fire?

Doug took my hand and told me not to be afraid; it was just steam coming from the engine, which was even more enormous than the cars and rested on a set of wheels that curved high above my head.

A man with a soldier hat on approached us. He had a gold chain running across his belly to a pocket on the front of his vest. My dad talked to this man, and then they shook hands. The man reached to put something Dad gave him deep into his pocket. The soldier-hat man called to a man with a tan face and a hat like a bus driver's. His white teeth sparkled as he took our suitcases and put up a step for us.

As he helped Doug and me onto the train, all of a sudden I realized Dad was not coming. I started to bawl. Dad gave me a short, brisk hug and told Doug to look after me. Then the tan man took us to our seats across from an older couple who seemed like grandparents.

When I looked out the window, I could see Dad on the platform, waving. I waved back as hard as I could, blubbering. The whistle blew, and I heard, "All aboard!" and the train started up: Chug. Chug. Chug a. Chug a. Chug a. Then chuga, chuga, chugachugachuga as it picked up speed, and Dad grew smaller and smaller through my tears

"It's okay, Billy. I'll take care of you," Doug said. "Pull my finger."

I did, and he made a farting sound with his lips. We both laughed.

As the train swayed and shuddered, some soldiers who were standing in the aisle tried to be very friendly, asking us questions. Doug and the grandparent couple cut them short. I was not to talk to strangers unless Doug said it was all right. He did tell me to be nice to the old couple. They were going to Detroit also, and they told us funny stories that helped pass the time.

We finally got to Windsor, just before crossing the Detroit River, and the tan man came to talk to Doug, and then said something to the older couple. Doug told me to pretend I was sleeping and to put my head on the woman's lap. She tucked her arm around me, rubbing my head as she cuddled me. It made me feel safe. I wished my mother would do that.

The train chugged across a long bridge, and then it stopped, and I heard a commotion. As I peeked up, I saw two funny-looking men with big shiny badges walking down the aisle. They halted at each set of seats. Doug slid over beside the woman and hushed me, and both of us pretended to sleep. One of the men asked the man and woman for their book, checked it, and then passed on, assuming we were a part of their family.

Just before we got off the train, Doug asked me to give him the money from my shoe. I was happy to get rid of it because my foot hurt. Why didn't he help me before?

He told me that in Canada we were not allowed to have "'Merican" money, and now he had to hide our Canadian money until we got back to Canada. Whatever Doug said must be right. I trusted him.

Welcome to Detroit

At the Detroit Station, a man rushed up asking if we were the Bates boys. He said his name was Larry Cody. He was a partner of our Uncle Roy's, and we were to call him Larry.

Larry took us and our luggage over to a van. I couldn't read, but Larry told me the lettering said, *AAA Refrigeration*, and that he and Uncle Roy owned it. Then we were off to Uncle Roy and Aunt Phyllis's house on Log Cabin Road.

At the door, Larry instructed us to take off our shoes. That was strange for me.

I asked Doug, "Will you help me tie them after, okay?"

Larry said, "better yet, I will teach you how to tie your own shoes. That way, you can be the boss of your shoes."

That sounded good to me.

Aunt Phyllis greeted us, and a little later Uncle Roy came home from work, and everyone had supper. Larry and Roy really made us feel welcome, but there was some tension with Aunt Phyllis. She pretended to be happy to have us, but after all the do's and don'ts she gave us, I didn't want to be there.

One rule was that we were not allowed in the living room. Unfortunately, after a couple of days I forgot, and I went to the couch and jumped up on it. Aunt Phyllis marched in, grabbed me up, and slapped me across the face. I was crying, and Doug took her on and started hitting her.

She screamed, "I didn't want you brats here. It's all your mother's fault. There was no other place for you to go. I was being kind. Now see how you treat me."

Doug and I went to our room and made a vow to stick together.

After that, we avoided Aunt Phyllis as much as we could and spent a lot of time with a gang of kids on the street. We all had scooters made of orange crates with broom-handles for steering and compartments that held our special possessions. That was our mode of transportation up and down our new Detroit neighborhood.

One day, the gang gave me a job. I was to stand across the street from the gas station at the end of our road and look out for cars and people coming. If I saw anyone, I was to bang the pot Doug gave me with a big metal spoon. Doug and a few other kids headed inside the gas station and started to bug the manager. He chased them out front, but they kept taunting him until he ran after them down the street.

Then I saw the older kids dart into the front of the station and come roaring out with a car battery that they crammed into one of the orange crates, before scooting down the street in the opposite direction to the kids who were running the other way, the gas-station manager hot on their tail. It was wartime and everything was rationed, especially tires and batteries. I do not know how much money they got for the battery. All I know is Doug and I had ample supply of candy for the rest of our stay.

Down the Drain

Aunt Phyllis took me down into the basement and guided me to stand on a metal drain in the middle of the cement floor. Although everything seemed clean, the room smelled musty. Small, high windows let shafts of sunlight in, and I could see the bare rafters above me.

Aunt Phyllis, with towel in hand, asked, "Are you ready?"

Ready for what? I wondered. Without waiting for my answer, she pulled on something, and a rain of water from a sprayer in the ceiling deluged me. I laughed and jumped up and down, splashing. After a few moments, she asked if I was finished.

I whined, "No," so pitifully, she said, "Okay. Just a few minutes more."

In a couple of minutes, the water got freezing cold, and Aunt Phyllis got mad at me. "Now you've made me use up all the hot water. Uncle Roy will be mad at me when comes home shortly," she shouted.

Then she dried me roughly with the towel and dragged me off to my room to change.

When Uncle Roy came home, he was not mad at all! He was proud that he had one of the few showers in Detroit, and he just wanted to know how I enjoyed it. Well, that was my first shower—and except for Aunt Phyllis being so harsh, it was fun! I never heard of such a thing in Niagara. In Niagara, it was a bath once a week: The adults bathed on Saturday night to go out, while the kids were bathed, usually in the laundry tub, on Sunday night, to be clean for school.

Trick Knot

Uncle Roy's partner, Larry, was as good as his word. He was very patient as he painstakingly showed me how to tie my shoes. There was only one problem: He smelled! The odor on him was just the same as my mother's and my aunt and uncle's perfume. (I later learned the name of this particular perfume was "Crown Royal.")

With Larry's kind, if smelly, help, I practiced and practiced until I could tie my shoes all by myself. He congratulated me and told me I was a big boy and a fast learner.

I felt so proud, and thought; "Now I can be the boss of my own shoes. Dad will be surprised."

***

Many years later, my wife asked my daughter who taught her to tie her shoes.

She proudly answered, "Daddy."

My wife replied, "That explains why they keep coming untied."

You see, the way Larry taught me was unique. The bows last for a few hours or so, and then they unravel. I call it Larry's trick knot.

To this day, Kelly Jo and I tie our shoes the same way. We have tried and tried to relearn with no success. Our only solution to the slippery trick of Larry's bow is adding a hefty double knot.

Between Us Men

Aunt Phyllis wanted us out of her hair. Doug went off with some friends, and I was able to go to work with Uncle Roy. Roy was kind, but he really did not relish me making calls with him. He made sure I understood that we would be taking the AAA Refrigeration truck into some bad areas. I had to promise to do whatever he told me. He also said not to ask any questions in front of other people. We could talk in the truck, but not while he was working. I understood and nodded solemnly.

One of our first stops was a bar. It was dark and smelled very funny—like Mom's perfume mixed with beer. Uncle Roy put me up on a bar stool, then went to the back of the bar with his tools. The man behind the bar asked me if I wanted a coke.

I said nothing.

He asked me again.

Again, I said nothing.

Finally, the bartender shouted at Roy, "Is this kid deaf or something? I asked him if he wanted a coke, and he just looks at me."

Roy laughed and said it was okay for me to accept the coke.

Uncle Roy finished up his repair job, and we got back in the truck. He thanked me for obeying him. Then he laughed and told me what a good kid I was.

We went to a few more places, and Uncle Roy let me carry some of his tools, then watch and hand him things when he asked.

At the last call, he said, "I really want you to stand back, watch, and be quiet."

We went up a dark set of stairs in a messy, stinky building. The walls we passed were full of writing scrawled on top of grime. Uncle Roy knocked, then pounded, on one of the doors until a big, fat, black woman let us in.

I was told to stand by an old, torn couch that looked like it was going to fall apart any minute. Uncle Roy went into the kitchen to look at the fridge and repair it. I was waiting patiently for him, looking at the stained cracks in the ceiling, when a really dark, really pretty, young woman came into the room with a sad-looking house dress on.

She was carrying some black stockings and said something, calling me "honey chil'." I knew she was talking to me, but I could not understand her. Besides, I was supposed to keep my mouth shut.

She moved me over and put her foot up on the couch where I'd been standing. She then proceeded to pull on one of her stockings. As she tugged the stocking on, I could see that the bottoms of her foot and hands were white. I could not help staring.

She noticed, and looked me right in the eyes. Her eyes were devilish, and then she gave me the strangest smirk as she rolled that black stocking up her black leg. She kept on going, sweeping aside her dress to expose her bare black thigh and black in-between. Then still giving me those devil eyes, she took her time pulling on the other stocking and exposing herself in the very same way.

When we got back to the van, Uncle Roy asked how I liked working with him. I said I really did. Then I asked about the white hands and feet. He explained that the people in the apartment where we had just been were called Negroes.

"They are just a different color than us."

I knew what he was saying, because we had some Chinese people in Niagara who looked different from us, too.

After a few minutes of quiet, Uncle Roy asked about the young woman's stockings.

I said, "They went way up."

"I know," he said. "I happened to see that."

Then he told me, in a way that made me understand, but feel comfortable about it, that some things had to be between us men. Aunt Phyllis would not understand, and if we told her, she might not let me go to work again.

I told Roy I knew. "Doug says that we have to keep it to ourselves. We always have to keep our mouths shut."

Uncle Roy said, "That's right. You are a bright boy."

I went to work with Uncle Roy a few times after that, and he always told me I was a good boy. But we never had another secret to keep between us like that first one.

That one trip to Detroit showed me many aspects of life I had never known before: I rode on a train for the first time; visited a big American city for the first time; witnessed my first robbery; took my first shower; became the "boss of my own shoes"; and met the first Negroes of my acquaintance.

I sure learned a lot that summer, but I was glad when Doug and I got back home to what I knew and loved: Maw, Donna, and The Store.

WAR STORIES

Meanwhile, Back At The Store

When Doug and I got home from Detroit, The Store was the same active, busy spot that it had been when we left. Bates Rexall Pharmacy was a place where children laughed, demanded, and cried. People came for medical help; local gossip was scooped up with the ice-cream; and newspapers, magazines, and "pocket books" were available for everyone. There were comic books for all the kids—and sly peeks at the nudists' *Sunbathing Magazine* for the older kids.

Only on late winter nights were customers sparse. But even then, the lonely would congregate around our coal-oil—yes, oil made from coal—space heater. This was conveniently located in front of the pharmacy to add additional heat to support the feeble furnace.

Mom was an important part of making the store a success. She was The Store's original marketing director, using her charm to beguile the army camp commanders into giving the store their support.

Bates Pharmacy and the army camp became trading partners. Mom and Dad had The Store, as well as U.S.

contacts, and the army (of course) had privileged, Government Issue supplies. Both the army camp and Mother and Father's U.S. customers had access to various foods not available to most Canadian civilians.

This meant that getting sugar and flour did not pose a problem for us. Also, doctors could prescribe pure grain alcohol as a medicine, and Dad could buy the 95% alcohol from the government liquor store, bypassing the need for ration book coupons.

The army camp, in turn, could submit the necessary paperwork to my father claiming that many soldiers had "eye problems" that required this particular 95% medication. Additionally, most of the diluted alcohol went back to the officers in return for hard-to-get rations. This win-win situation lasted until the camp closed at the end of the war.

Since The Store was a place for soldiers to spend chunks of their free time, the staff, including my mother, got to know the men before they were shipped out—too often to be badly wounded or killed. There was constant tension in the air which radio broadcasts and blackouts only increased.

Partly because of the way she had finessed her way around the rationing, and partly because of the personal magnetism she displayed to the outside world, the townspeople looked upon my mom as a movie star. And in some ways, she and my father lived the life of celebrities. They worked from nine in the morning until ten or eleven at night, and then, late at night (or earlier, if they could get someone to cover for them) it was release time.

For my mother, both her work during the daylight hours and her late nights of escape comforted her, quieting her fears and creating a diversion from her too-keen awareness of the nightmares of war.

Christmas Surprise

One afternoon just before my fourth Christmas, as I was chasing my cousin Donna into the back kitchen, we ran into my older cousins and uncle.

Hey! They were painting my shiny black kiddie train a bright enamel red. This was my special kiddie train car designed after a real 1930s locomotive; it had a wooden tube grip on top of the smoke stack that allowed me to steer in any direction as I pushed with my legs. Or used to.

"What are you doing to my train?" I shouted.

They informed me that I had outgrown it, and now it was time to let another child enjoy it.

Okay. I knew I never used it anymore, but still, it was mine, not some other kid's.

My uncle, knowing how disappointed I was, put a kind arm around me. He then slipped a candy bar into my hand. I accepted my fate—and the candy—with a big sulk on my face. Donna comforted me as we shared the candy.

By the time Christmas came, my sulk was over. Santa had brought us lots of presents! When we woke up, there were toys, books, and clothes waiting for us to tear into. I liked Santa!

After all the packages had been opened, Donna and I donned our new boots and mittens and went out to play in the snow. Soon, the neighbor-lady saw us and invited us to come in for hot chocolate. We were sitting at her kitchen table, when her little kid scooted right into my leg.

I looked down and saw the kid grinning up at me from his happy seat on his brand-new enamel-red locomotive train car.

I could hear my uncle's words echo in my head. "Billy, I want you to promise that you will not recognize this train should you ever see it."

I knew I would be in big trouble if I didn't keep my mouth shut, so I asked the boy, "Did you get that train for Christmas?"

Beaming, the little kid proudly pronounced, "Santa Claus brought it to me."

Wait! I knew that train didn't come from Santa. I swallowed hard. What did this mean? I couldn't even talk about this with Donna, because her belief in Santa Claus was the most important part of Christmas for her.

Later, when my brother Doug came home, I explained what happened and told him that I did not believe in Santa Claus anymore.

Doug's sage advice: "You have to believe or at least pretend to. You know all the gifts you got from Santa? Well, if you stop believing, none of us will get gifts from Santa. Keep your mouth shut and don't spoil Mom and Dad's fun. They need Santa Claus as a reason to buy all of us gifts."

Five years later, when I was nine, Dad reluctantly informed me that I was too old to believe in Santa any more, and he wanted to tell me the truth about where our Christmas presents came from. Surprise, surprise.

'Fraidy Cat

I shouldn't have been there. But I was.

Was no one looking out for me?

It was night-time, and a very young me was sitting in a lumber yard with my brother Doug's friend "Dodge." I was playing with his knife, plunging it into a stack of wooden planks. The space was dimly lit from above by pot lights. The wood was soft; the air smelled of damp sawdust. In the distant darkness we heard voices and then muffled running feet.

Dodge bolted. A primal fear propelled me after him. After running for about a half block, I caught up with him, and he hoisted me into the branches of a small tree and took off. Camouflaged by misty leaves, I clung to my branch for minutes, sucking for my breath. Then I saw a herd of soldiers stampede right by me, chasing down Dodge. They caught him, and after a good shaking he squealed on me.

I was taken home and roughly shoved into bed.

Where was Maw? I don't know. Only that she was not there for me.

War Time Uncles

Even though I was so young during the war years, I could sense the fear that permeated almost every situation. Everyone was tense. Everyone feared for the safety of their loved ones.

Those who were living today might be dead tomorrow. Throughout those war years, there was electricity in the air. People were anxious for news. Every day the post office was visited; the boxes were checked twice. Sometimes no news was good news.

The soldiers who visited The Store were no less anxious, even if they showed it differently. They knew better than anyone what could happen. When my own uncles went off to war, some of the soldiers who came to the house or saw me at the store "adopted" me, and, instead of just my two original uncles, I suddenly had a bunch of new "uncles" who came and went. These very young men, missing their own nephews or sons, would pick me up and throw me in the air.

When they held me close, they all smelled alike with their damp rough woolen uniforms and their bay-rum splashed faces. They hugged me as though I might have been the last little kid they ever got to hug.

Inside the Box, Outside the Box

Because Dad's store was a Rexall drug store, we got big wooden boxes from Rexall distributors. These boxes contained patented medicines packed in excelsior, which prevented them from breaking in transit. And they were big. Really big.

They were not so tall that we couldn't climb inside. They made fantastic storage boxes, but usually, before anyone was able to get to them, we kids would use them as forts and hiding places for hide and seek.

In 1940, I learned another use for those big boxes. One day, my father's friend Bluebird Freel set up three of the Rexall boxes in the yard and put chicken wire over the openings to form a cage. Then he built a little door to the cage, covered the floor with straw, and stocked the box/cages with a few very cute bunnies.

We thought they were our pets. We fed them every day, and once a week we removed their dirty straw to put into our victory garden, rabbit pellets and all.

Our victory gardens were a point of pride to all Canadians during the war. In these back-yard gardens, we cultivated all manner of vegetables for our own families in order to satisfy the demand for the produce that the bigger farms grew so that the food could be canned and given to our soldiers.

That made the rabbits, with their weekly load of pellets, contributing members of the war effort. But the bunnies had to eat, too, to keep up their pellet supply.

Fortunately, the Marino family, who owned Marino's Grocery Store, were happy to help feed the rabbits as well as the growing kid who took care of them. Whenever I went to Dad's store, I had permission to go by myself up Queen St. to Marino's. Sometimes Doug would go with me. However most of the times I wanted to go by myself. I considered that I was a big boy, besides I did not want to share the attention.

The aroma of all the different cheeses and spices, and the kindness of Mr. and Mrs. Marino, made their store a special place for me. Mrs. Marino would always say I was too skinny and take me back to the kitchen to eat some delicious Italian dish she had prepared.

Her husband, Pete, as he insisted I call him, treated me warmly too, telling me he thought I was "quite a boy." And while Mrs. Marino took me to the back for my meal, Pete would stay up front to tend the store.

When I had finished eating all I could, I'd go back up front to find that Pete had stuffed a flour sack with carrot tops, lettuce, cabbage leaves, celery tops, and any other food scraps that the rabbits would like to eat.

It was my job was to feed our furry pets, and I loved it. The rabbits repaid me with their attention and affection. Every time I brought them food, I felt like the sun was warming my soul, and I watched happily as the little bunnies grew into large rabbits.

One day I went out to say good morning to my long-eared friends. I found their cage clean—and empty.

There were no rabbits.

I ran crying into Maw. She consoled me, saying that rabbits are better off not being caged. "Would you like to live in a box for the rest of your life?" she asked.

Well, I could understand that, and maybe my rabbits were better off wherever they had gone.

It wasn't until I was an adult that I connected the dots. Because of the war, we had a hard time obtaining scarce items such as specialty cheese and fruit. And oranges, which were favorites of mine, were particularly difficult to get. Yet, somehow, all of these would magically appear on our table.

Ah! Cooked rabbit was an Italian specialty. The Marino's were Italian. They had a grocery store that stocked cheese and oranges. They must have been happy to barter with someone for difficult-to-get foods in exchange for non-rationed rabbit.

Truly, be I right or wrong, I am glad this did not occur to me until I was grown. The Marino's were my special people, and I want to remember them for the many kindnesses that they showed me.

A Pot and a Grate

In the wintertime, the big grate in the center of the house, close to the dining room and front bedrooms, was a community-collecting place.

When we came in from the cold, we changed over it and warmed up before continuing into the house, leaving our wet clothes above the grate to dry. In the mornings, we would race from our cold bedrooms with our clothes in our arms to dress near it. Dad stoked the furnace so that spot was always toasty warm. The women liked to stand over it to gossip, letting the warm current flow up their house dresses.

The grate also served as a place to pre-prepare rolled oats for our breakfast oatmeal. Hot water was added to dry oats, and the mixture was left on the grate for the night. In the morning, the oats were put on the stove for five minutes rather than the fifteen to twenty minutes normally required.

Because the upstairs received so little heat, we rarely used the small bathroom on the upper floor—mostly just the grownups did. Instead, we did what we needed to in our "toilet", which was really a pail set in one of the downstairs bedrooms. Whatever had to be done was done where it was warm. Number One remained for others to contribute. Number Two was taken up stairs by an adult to flush down the toilet. It was a scramble, coordinating up to ten people and just a single toilet, so the pot was always for the kids.

Excitement Next Door

There was a somber commotion at Mr. Young's next door. A white van was parked with its back doors flung open. Two men were wheeling a wagon towards the van, and Donna and I could see that someone was lying on top of the wagon with a sheet stretched all over him, covering him head to toe, even his face.

We watched as the men slid that the person into the back of the van and banged the doors shut. Donna asked me if that was Mr. Young. I thought it was. She asked me if he was dead. I told her I think he must be, because his head was covered. I was curious at the same time I was afraid. I had heard about all the death in the war, but this was the first time I actually saw a dead body. I could imagine Mr. Young through the sheet. As a little boy, I could not explain all of this to Donna.

We ran to find Maw. She bent down to tell us that our neighbor Mr. Young had died that morning. When we asked why he died, she explained that he was on the toilet, and apparently, he was trying to go Number Two and had a heart attack. Then Maw told us to go and play, which we did.

A few days later Donna shared that she had a funny feeling when she went Number Two.

"Me, too," I said. "I can see Mr. Young's face when I grunt."

Donna asked, "Are we going to die if we grunt too much?"

I assured her that Maw would warn us if that were the case.

Maw's Chili Sauce

In the fall, Greaves Jams & Marmalade created a chili so rich that its aroma perfumed the air over one full, square block, from Queen Street to Prideaux to Victoria to Johnson. When Greaves was cooking chili, the scent meant fall-and sniffing it on a cool autumn breeze gave me an unforgettable "I am glad to live in Niagara" feeling.

But as great as Greaves' chili was, Maw's was even better. When she was preparing her own chili sauce, the aroma of tomatoes, onions, and allspice, created a sense of warmth and wellbeing that permeated the house. Then came the moment when the soft Dempsey bread, dripping with the dense, aromatic, tomato-y sauce entered my mouth.

The only thing that beat that culinary experience was when Maw would grill cheese sandwiches on the hot wood stove: First, she would toast one side to a crusty brown; then she would flip it over and toast the other side—all the while watched like a hawk by my hungry eyes. It seemed to me that a watched cheese sandwich took forever to be perfect, but finally, she would remove the sandwich from the stove, slather her chili sauce on top, and hand over the plate.

Even at a young age, I could gobble two of them. That is, if my brothers weren't around to push me out of the way.

The Ming Vase

Maw's big white Victorian house was home for two or three families at a time. And all of those families agreed that the large upstairs was forbidden land for the kids. But as soon as the adults were busy outside, we would climb up the stairs to the first landing, listen to make sure we were safe, then proceed all the way to the top, where there were four big bedrooms, plus the small bathroom.

One afternoon, when everyone else was out in the yard doing spring cleanup, Cousin Donna and I saw our chance. We snuck up to the top of the stairs and started running around chasing each other, laughing, and just being silly.

My brother Doug heard us. He came and dragged us back to the bottom of the stairs. As he started to walk away, Donna and I scampered back up to the first landing. This landing had a fake (at least I hope it was a fake!) Ming Dynasty vase with a cluster of pussy willows sprouting from its neck.

Doug went to pull me down from the landing and knocked over the vase, sending it tumbling down the stairs, where it broke into many parts.

Under Doug's direction, we helped gather up the pussy willows as he picked up the shards of the vase and mopped up the water. We swore not to squeal, and he hid the broken pottery in the trash, telling us to do the same with the pussy willows.

We were scared and quickly obeyed, except that I kept one fuzzy little gray bud so I could finger its silky fur. When Doug and Donna went outside with the others, I slid that pussy willow bud across my face to feel its soft fur. I rubbed its softness to my ear. Then I shoved it right inside my ear canal where it fit as snugly as if it had been made to be tucked there for safe keeping.

Why, Oh Why, Can't I Fly?

Our Victoria St. house had a white railing around the veranda. It was a special place, warmed by the sun for most of the year. The wide green steps connected to an even wider plank floor, our playground for hide and seek, tag, ring-around-the-rosy, or tussling.

The Veranda

I delighted in climbing up the railing to the ledge. This ledge could be anything I wanted it to be. I could walk the plank along it. I could lie across it and swim through Tarzan's hazardous swamps. I could sit on it and shoot down enemy airplanes. I could practice flying by jumping to the veranda floor with a towel tucked into my collar—which bestowed upon me Superman's abilities. I could practice jumping from my crippled Spitfire using that same towel as a parachute.

Once, I was lying on top of the ledge, perfectly balanced. Suddenly, the world seemed like a dream. I felt I was truly capable of levitation. And then I found myself floating above the porch, rolling over and looking down at the little kid still stretched across the railing.

I wanted to comfort him, but I could not speak. I floated higher, and knew, in that moment, that in this world, nothing is impossible.

Was it a dream?

Maybe.

Broadcast News and Bedtime Bunnies

At Maw's house, we had a modern, stand-up, Philco radio with a small knob dial that turned the yellow station finder. The radio was as tall as I was and stood in the dining room as the centerpiece that everyone gathered around.

When supper was finished, Donna and I would play in front of the radio, as the whole family listened for war news on CBC. All the grownups were tense, and we had to play quietly. If one of the women started crying, Donna or I often were grabbed up and hugged and hugged.

It was confusing for us kids, and we heard only the edges of whispered discussions with double-talk references as to who was not coming home. Often Maw would get sad, lonesome tears in her eyes.

After the news, we had to get ready for bed. Bedtime back then was special because Maw would read the book *Uncle Wiggly* to us, which would distract us from trying to understand who was coming home and who was not.

Uncle Wiggly was a rabbit. He looked like a white version of the chocolate Easter Rabbit. And he never got in trouble. Our worries of the day disappeared listening to Maw tell us about his antics.

Learning Curve

When I was small, I would trail behind Doug, even when he told me to stay home. I was somewhat of a slow poke, and sometimes it took me quite a while to find him.

Once, I followed him down to the end of Victoria Street, to the vacant lot left where the famous 1869 Queens Royal Hotel had stood in all its splendor, until 1902.

This lot still had rubble from the grand old lady, and I used to collect pretty stones from the site. The weeds there were as tall as I was, and a path wove through them to the top of a small hill that led down to the mouth of the Niagara River, where there was a slight drop to the lake.

On this day, when I found Doug, he and another boy were bending over a half-naked girl on a flat, weed-less spot just before the bottom of the hill. I innocently asked Doug what he was doing.

He said, "Here let me show you," and told me I had to take down my pants and underwear and lie on top of the girl.

He said that if I was to tell on him, I was doing it, too. Therefore, I would be in as much trouble as he would. Even at this early age, my family had already taught me well how to keep secrets, so I knew I had to keep my mouth shut. But I can still close my eyes and see that girl's staring eyes penetrating me. Did she accept what was going on? Her eyes were blank. I could not tell.

DOWN ON THE FARM

How Are You Going to Keep 'Em Down in Niagara, Once They've Seen the Farm?

It was the summer of 1944, and once again I was being sent away—and once again, my mother was not there to say goodbye.

This time, I was not being sent off on the train with Doug. Instead, Dad packed my clothes and put up a lunch just for the two of us. He was driving me to his sister Ruth's small farm outside Schomberg, a few miles north of Toronto.

On the way, we stopped at the side of the road for a picnic. It was a treat to be all alone with my dad. At that age, my whole world revolved around him. While we ate, Dad explained that I would be with Aunt Ruth for a while, that Ruth would give me special attention, and that he himself would visit as often as he could. Then, to make me feel better, my father, who had grown up in an area not very far from Aunt Ruth's farm, told me some stories about his own boyhood. These included some about his father, a salesman for Raleigh's patent products, who drove his horse and buggy from farm to farm soliciting and serving customers.

We got back on the road, and it wasn't long before we arrived at Aunt Ruth's. When we pulled up, she was waiting at the door with my much older cousin Jean. The two women bombarded me with unexpected hugs and kisses. Since the only other person that gave me that kind of love was Maw, the warmth of their attention became too much, too quickly. I squirmed from their embrace and ran back to my dad, who just laughed, hugged me goodbye, and counseled me to be a good boy.

When Aunt Ruth, Cousin Jean, and I had waved Dad's car off down the street, they took me into the house where a plate of freshly baked chocolate cookies awaited me. The mouth-watering smell diverted me immediately. The only cookies I had ever known before this came from Niagara Home Bakery. Those were fine, but they didn't have the warm, chocolate waft that these homemade farm cookies did.

After washing up, I was settled at the table and given a big, cool glass of unpasteurized milk to go with the cookies. I took one bite of chocolate cookie and then followed that with a sip of the creamy, thick milk. Ahh. It was the perfect enhancement to my mouthful of cookie. I was already pretty certain I was going to like it there.

All of a sudden, my younger cousin Paul came bouncing in to join us. He may have been littler than me, but he was such a great kid, we had a lot of fun, no problems. With Cousin Paul, Cousin Jean, and Aunt Ruth, there was so much laughter and teasing in that kitchen that a trusting friendship was immediately born.

Unfortunately, Paul lived with his parents, my Uncle Wendle and Aunt Martha, on their own farm. He had only come by to make me feel at home, and I wouldn't get to spend much time with him until later that summer.

Still, Paul was there long enough to be the reason Aunt Ruth dropped the bomb: after cookies, it was time for a nap! Who ever heard of a six-year old having a nap? Cousin Paul could have a nap. He was still little. But naps were not for this big kid.

In her wisdom, Aunt Ruth told me she knew I didn't really need a nap, but explained she needed my help. If I did not go into my bedroom, Paul, who did need his nap, would resist lying down so that he could play with me. What if I took a picture book into my room and just read it on the bed?

I took two books with me, and right away, I enjoyed the pretty, clean room Jean had gotten ready for me. (I won't tell if I maybe did sleep a little bit. That is nobody's business but my own.)

Poop, Poop, and More Poops!

On the farm, there were interesting rules about relieving oneself. For Number One, I was invited to go to the back and pee on the ground. I had done this often when traveling or on an adventure with Doug. However I found it funny being told to do this at someone's home.

For Number Two, there was the outhouse. Aunt Ruth suggested it was wise to open the outhouse door for a few minutes before going in, to help get rid of the smell and the flies.

The first morning, when I was ready to go to the outhouse, I was given some half-sheets of soft tracing paper. Jean explained that on the farm, the adults used pages of Eaton's or Simpson's catalogues to wipe their bums, but she realized that would be too rough for a boy who was used to toilet paper. Since toilet paper was a new and expensive item that could only be purchased at a drug store like Bates, there was none available way out in the country. So tracing paper it was.

Further instructions were required, however, concerning the number of sheets to be used: Three half-sheets should be quite enough, I was told, if I carefully folded them as demonstrated. The idea was to make one swipe, fold, make a second swipe, fold again, and then make a final swipe. Additionally, I was warned against getting any poop on my hands.

Ruth said, "It is okay if you do the first couple of times. We will wash your hands well. Don't worry you will get the hang of it quickly. I gave you three sheets so you could practice."

Proud and prepared for my new adventure, I headed to the outhouse, which was about as big as a large broom closet. As told, I opened the door to let the flies and stink out. Right away, I noticed that light shone down through a screen near the roof, giving the outhouse odd, filtered shadows.

I jumped up to the first wooden step and was about to turn around to sit down, but, curious, I first peered into one of the two wooden-rimmed holes.

What I saw in the dim light was mesmerizing. There was a big mound of poop piled beneath the seat. I had inspected my own poops before, but they were never as varied as these! Some were hard, some mushy. There were big poops and small ones. Some were brown, some black, and some were a combination with colors in-between. Remnants of the wiping catalogue intermingled with the poop.

Even more interestingly, just below the top layers, all the mush was mottled brown and white.

But, regardless of the fascinating images below, I had to go. It was time for me to add my bit to the pile. I hopped up on the worn wooden seat and grunted and grunted, but without success. I had heard that if you block one nostril and blow through the other one, then reverse the process, it will get matters on the move. And it did.

Once the hard block had pushed its way out, the rest was easy. And I only used two half-sheets to wipe.

While I was sitting on the outhouse throne, I began to notice a good smell, the smell of wood all around me, above the smell of all that poop. After a minute, I began to notice the sounds of the crickets and other little country animals scampering around outside.

And then I spotted the catalogue. I became so engrossed in all the stuff the magazine held, I forgot where I was. A loud knock penetrated my deep thoughts. Aunt Jean's voice came through the door.

"Are you all right, Billy?" she asked, anxiously.

I quickly dismounted, pulled up my pants, and emerged proudly, waving my remaining half-sheet.

Professor Dickey

After my first outhouse adventure, I got to help cousin Jean feed the chickens. I tried to catch them, but they were too wise and much too fast. I could hardly believe my eyes when one actually flew up into the air and landed a few yards away.

"Hey, Jean, I thought chickens couldn't fly!"

"They can fly, but only for a short distance," she said, adding with a smile, "only when they want to escape someone like you."

Then she led me into the small, haphazard, wooden shack that housed the hens. Inside, it was warm and stuffy, but the hay and the chicken-laden air smelled good, and there was a whole lot of clucking going on. Even though most of the birds were outside, those that remained inside were not happy to see a stranger—never mind having one reach into their nests and take their eggs.

Jean showed me how to tell which eggs were for eating and which ones were hatching. She told me to take eggs from the back of the nest, because the chickens would always lay more eggs to keep the nest full.

"So as long as we keep taking one or two a day, they will keep laying," she said.

That made sense to me, and, besides, Jean was the chicken expert.

After eggs, it was lunchtime, then a short nap, which I didn't resist. I awoke to the sound of Jean talking to someone at the backdoor. She was saying, "Paul had to go home."

I jumped out of bed and ran to see who had come over. There was a kid just a little older than me standing there, dressed in something like a cross between jeans and a bib. Jean introduced him as "our neighbor Dickey Jones who has come over to play."

Then Auntie said, "Billy, I have a surprise for you. If you go out to play in those shorts, you will get your legs all scratched up by the burrs and thorns."

She handed me an outfit that was just exactly like what Dickey was wearing. They were called "coveralls", and all the farmers wore them. When I put them on, they sure enough "covered all" of my legs completely, but even though Aunt Ruth said they fit, I felt as though there was too much room inside. If Dickey had not been wearing a pair of his own, I would have rebelled.

When Aunt Ruth produced a pair of rubber boots, my transformation from town kid to farm kid was complete.

Dickey looked me over, nodded, and said, "Let's go."

Once we were out of the house, Dickey plucked a blade of grass with seeds dangling off the end and stuck it in his mouth to chew on. I followed suit like an old pro, but even though I may have looked the part of country boy, I was still wet around the ears.

Spying a tower with a ladder on the side, I ran for it and started to climb up.

Dickey screamed out, "Stop! Don't do that!"

"Why not?" I asked. "I've climbed ladders before."

"See that windmill on top?" Dickey said, pointing. "If you climb up there, and the wind starts blowing, the paddles will knock you off. If you fell down, you would be squished dead."

Hey, I thought, this kid is smart. I had better stick close to him.

Over the next few weeks, I did stick just as close to Dickey as a country burr, and he gave me a fine country education.

From Dickey, I learned that if you prick both pointed ends of an egg with a safety pin, and then blow into a hollow straw stuck up tight against one of egg holes, flop, the whole egg vacates its shell. This was fun just on its own, but then Dickey showed me to put the empty shell back in the nest to fool whoever gathers the eggs. I bet we gave Jean a surprise.

He also taught me about cow pies. You don't step in the dark, wet ones. The dried, gray ones are okay. Dickey knew more about cows than just their pies, though. For instance, in a lesson about milking cows, Dickey told me that cows can kick backwards, but not forwards. Then he showed me how to lie under a cow.

When I was in position beneath her big bag, Dickey squirted my face with milk. I squirmed as the warm milk filled my mouth, but the creamy taste reminded me of warm ice cream, and I just lay there, gulping the treat of a lifetime.

Professor Dickey then importantly informed me that "udder" was what the women called the cow's bag and nipples, and men called them "teats."

"All female animals and women have them, he told me. "It is just that the animals have more."

Another fascinating lesson had to do with outhouses. According to Dickey, a full one would be picked up by a tractor and moved to a different spot, where it was gently placed on a new hole, and new pails were put inside. Dickey also explained that some farmers emptied the big pails and re-used them, but if you could afford them, new ones were better.

After the outhouse was relocated, the old pit, including the pails, got sprinkled with white stuff called quick lime. (Oh, I realized. That must have been what I saw in the layers the first time I looked.) When a good dousing of lime has been completed, the old hole is covered with lots of dirt.

Some of what Dickey taught me was just a lot of silly fun, like "feeding the pigs." In Dickey's version, we climbed up into the loft by the pig stall, then pulled down our pants, put our bums over the railing, and defecated down by the pigs. Once we were done, we'd pull up our pants and watch the pigs fight to eat it. It was "bombs away" and "giggle, giggle!"

There were also mice to catch in order to nail them on the side of the barn; stones to throw at the pigs; and cows to chase. Professor Dickey also pointed out some facts of life: We observed chickens "doing it", dogs "doing it", and even saw cows trying, unsuccessfully, to "do it."

Yes, thanks to Professor Dickey, even though I had not officially started school, my learning was far in advance of my soon-to-be classmates. Heck, by the end of that summer, I probably qualified for an advanced degree in "grossology."

Uncle Wendle's Farm

Summer was almost over. It was harvest time. Dickey, who had been my constant companion, was kept at home to help with the harvest chores—and perhaps to separate us two mischief-makers! But I was not lonely for long, as we were all needed at Uncle Wendle and Aunt Martha's farm, where it was time to bring in the hay.

Uncle Wendle and Aunt Martha were my cousin Paul's father and mother, and getting to see Paul more than made up for the loss of Dickey.

Haying was a great experience. A team of two horses pulled a thrasher, which cut down the hay. The thrasher reminded me of a paddle wheel on a steamboat, only it was a paddle wheel turning on land, and it was powered by horses, rather than steam. Men followed behind the thrasher, pitchforking cut hay onto a big wagon that, in turn, followed them.

There were so many men working together, there were more than even three times my hands could count.

Paul and I were busy, too. We helped by bringing all those men water. We also got to ride on the wagons and up on the broad backs of the big horses. But even more fun was chasing the creatures that fled after the thrasher came by. Mice, rabbits, birds, and funny-looking animals they called groundhogs, all went scurrying, with Paul and me hot on their tails.

At breaks, we all stopped to eat sandwiches put together and carried out to us by the women, who were making sure their men were looked after. And towards the end of each day, everyone gathered up at the house for supper. Like all farmhouses in the area, there was no indoor plumbing, but at Uncle Wendle's, there was no inside water at all. Aunt Ruth at least had a pump at the kitchen sink, even if it was only cold well water. At Wendle and Martha's, even the wash-up water had to be pumped outside and taken indoors for heating.

That was just for the women, though. The men washed up outside, gathering at the well pump. Paul and I stayed with them, and before anyone could start washing, Uncle Wendle would always say a sort of end-of-day blessing: "The day's work is done. All sweat and arguments are to remain in the fields. All is well that ends at the well."

And then, all together, men and women, boys and girls, would join together at the table and partake of the good food and the good feelings that our hard work had created.

SHORT NIAGARA STORIES

C-A-T

The autumn of 1944 brought many changes. When summer—and haying—was truly over, my dad came to pick me up and drive me back to Niagara to get ready for my first year of school.

My new classroom was a single room just for first graders. We had our own building on Castlereagh Street, separate from the larger building that housed grades two through eight. All eight grades shared an out-building for our toileting needs. In order to go to the bathroom, I had to go across the play yard to the building with the washrooms and, sometimes, I had to negotiate past the big kids who were on recess.

Once inside, there were usually some older boys hanging out. This is where I was taught many words I had never heard before. The principal, Mr. Cromar, knew what was happening on his school's property, though, and he ran security on this area. More than once, he sent me back to where I belonged, but that didn't keep me from learning a few useful things from the older boys, things I hadn't learned, even from Doug or Professor Dickey.

Fortunately, from my teacher, I also learned what I was officially in school to learn. Miss Hutchison was in charge of all the first graders. She was wonderful. In fact, that year, I had another first: the first time I fell in love with an older woman—Miss Hutchison.

I gave Miss Hutchison my heart, and she, in turn, taught me how to spell "cat."

Fire!!

On Thursday night, November 2nd, 1944, the telephone center, where the Marino and Tonner girls worked the state-of-the-art cord-plug system, went crazy! There were two lines always available for emergency, one for the Police Department and the other for the Fire Department, but on this particular night, things were jamming up, wires were tangling, as Fire Chief Don Sherlock received frantic calls that the Tobe and Dietsch houses on Victoria Street were going up in flames.

That was at 11 p.m.

Two hours earlier, I was crying in my bed. Every time I lay on my right ear, the secret pussy willow bud I'd shoved into my ear canal that spring caused me excruciating pain. Maw came in and soothed the pain with warm eardrops, and, lying on my back, I finally fell asleep.

I was prone to nightmares, maybe because of the pain from my ear, or maybe because of the situation with my mother, but, also, like all of the kids I knew, I was afraid of the Germans coming to capture us and put us in the oven, just like the scary witch tried to do in the fairy tale about Hansel and Gretel.

My brothers had added to my stockpile of fear. First, they ordered me to give them all my lead toy soldiers.

When I asked, "Why do I have to?" they explained that the lead was needed to make bullets to kill those damned Germans.

They also taught me how to draw a swastika and to listen for anyone who said "winilla" instead of "vanilla." People who said that were the enemy, and the enemy could be anywhere!

Once, when I peeked out of the blackout blind, a light flashed in my face. Maw told me shut the blind, quickly, as the air raid warden had seen the light, and if the warden could see the light, so could the German's airplanes.

There were so many worries for such a small boy.

And then, on that November night, my nightmares seemed to all come crashing into one big terror when the screaming of the air raid siren woke me to the realization that my blackout blind had fallen down and in my bureau mirror I could see the reflection of bursting orange fireballs interspersed with blazing, rotating lights.

My whole room was pulsating in a bright, blood orange, and the fear these images created was compounded by the acrid smell of smoke, the intensity of the fiery heat, and the huge, flickering shadows.

I had heard stories of Hell. Surely this was it—and the Germans had brought it on.

I screamed out, which brought a huge, black monster covered in a black, shiny oilcloth, barging into the room. I caught only a glimpse of this alien, whose entire head was covered by a gigantic, dark helmet, below which, a strange hose dangled.

Was this a German? I wondered, and then screamed even louder as the monster grabbed me up and wrapped me in my "blankey." Talking softly to calm me down, the "monster" told me he was a fireman, and he was taking the rest of the families in Maw's house to safety.

Although I was still weeping, I listened carefully, and could tell the man did not have a German accent. He was not the enemy. I relaxed into the fireman's comforting, secure grip.

Out on the street the night air was cold, but the fire coming from the direction of the lake was a furnace, blasting heat our way. Carrying me in his arms, my friendly monster sloshed up the road through tangled hoses and shouted instructions to the other firefighters. He asked the crowd to make room so he could make his way further up the street to a friendly house where I'd be safe.

Upon entering, he placed me in the arms of a caring woman. The woman instructed her pajama-clad, twelve-year-old daughter to take me up to her room, while she herself went to see if she could help the others on the street.

"Be kind," the mother said to her daughter, "and comfort little Billy, for he is very scared."

But once we got to the top of the stairs, the young girl became hysterical; she was the one who needed the comforting. When we entered her bedroom, she began to strip off her own pajamas and then mine. Suddenly, I remembered her eyes as those of the young girl at the river, the girl that Doug had made me lie down upon so I would be in the same trouble as Doug and the other boys.

This memory scared me all over again, eliciting a new sort of anxiety from me as she led me into the closet and pulled the door shut behind us.

A sour, fear-tainted smell, like rancid oil, emanated from her pores as, in the darkness, she hugged and rocked me close to her naked body. She shook and mumbled things that I could not understand and, already exhausted, I simply sobbed myself to sleep.

The next morning, I awoke alone in the girl's bed, with my pajamas, top and bottom, back on, and my dad came to collect me. As it turned out, it was the Tobe's barn that had caught fire when their piles of war-effort scrap paper had ignited.

The barn burnt down, and the sides of both our house and our garage were badly scorched, but, thanks to the expedience and caring of the fire department, a much worse disaster was avoided.

As for me, my nightmares continued for another week. Finally, Dad got us an appointment with a Niagara Falls ear specialist. When the doctor irrigated my aching ear, the offending pussy willow popped out with a sort of a pow-whistle, right onto the tray.

The doctor held the bud up for my dad and me to see.

"Look at this," he said.

We looked. The bud had started forming roots and had a green sprout emerging from the soft, slimy fur.

I imagine my father wasn't sure whether to be happy for me or angry with me, but, for my part, I am pleased to report that my hearing has been excellent ever since.

Artists At Work

A few weeks after the fire, our cousins were conscripted to repair the damaged boards that blistered or were scorched because of the heat from the burning barn. Once repaired, they proceeded to paint it so the whole side of the house would look like new.

They were painting the house white, with green trim. Donna and I were playing in the driveway that ran beside the house and led to the garage. Beside the side door, was my brother Jack's bicycle. Right beside his bike were two gallons of house paint—white and green—and two paintbrushes.

Our cousins had gone inside for lunch.

In the time it took them to finish their meal, Donna and I had completed an amazing paint job—on Jack's bike. We were thorough! We even painted the seat and the spokes. We felt so grown up, doing just as we saw our cousins do. In our enthusiasm, we even got some of the side of the house partially painted as a bonus.

We were just standing back and admiring our work when the cousins returned. They hollered for Maw. When she saw what we had done, she let out a long sigh. Then they all started to laugh, which brought Jack running out.

To him it was not a laughing matter, and he started shouting at us.

Maw and our cousins shushed him. Then the four of them got out the turpentine and started to ruin our masterpiece. Thank God, the paint was still wet. It soaked off with ease, but we still had to promise never to do that again.

V-E Day

It was May 8, 1945. I was six years old, standing with Maw on Queen Street not far from The Store, when all of a sudden the church bells started ringing and the air raid siren was screaming and cars were beeping and, right in the middle of the street, people were crying, and hugging and kissing, jumping up and down.

Maw bent down, gave me a big hug, and through her tears, she sputtered out a joyful, "It is over."

Soldiers came over and shook my hand, and too many women wanted to smother me with hugs.

While it took many years for me to understand all the implications, on that day, I understood one very important thing: The Nazis were finished. I no longer had to worry about them coming to put me in the oven.

However, just three months after all the cheering on the streets of Niagara, on August 6, 1945, the United States dropped an atomic bomb they called "Little Boy" on Hiroshima, Japan, and everyone said the war was almost over.

On August 9th, the U.S. ended World War II with a second bomb, "Fat Man", dropped on Nagasaki.

I have remembered these dates my whole life, even though to the young boy that I was, one date seemed the same as any other, except for Christmas and my birthday.

These dates stand out, not only because they brought an end to a frightening war, but because they brought with them new fears: fears of atomic fallout; fears of atomic poison in the water, in the food, in the milk; fears that the Russians had the bomb, and would use it.

In the 1940s, there was always something to fear, something about which to pray.

What, Me Worry?

Pray. Pray. Pray.
There is a machine gun up on the town hall balcony.
Rat a tat-tat-a-tat.
There is a sniper in the clock tower.
Pow! Pow!
The Bren gun carriers are entering the main Street.
The firing noise is deafening.
Soldiers are falling down everywhere.
I hold Maw's hand tight.
The whistle blows.
It is all over, as the Marshall tells the fallen to get up.
This is the last practice before leaving for the front lines.
Pray for them. Pray for them.
Niagara's army camp is fully occupied with trainees,
Then it is emptied, only to be filled anew.

Pray for them.
Listen to the teacher.
Learn to hide under the desks.
Knees forward with hands clasped around the neck.
Keep praying.
The Nazis and the Russians are coming.
Pray.
The Russians are now our friends
They are beating the Nazis on the western front.
Now the Nazis have surrendered.
Thank the Lord.
More surrender came.
The Japanese have been blasted by the atomic bomb.
The war is over.
Pray prayers of thanks
But America has given uranium to the Russians.
A former German scientist working on the Manhattan project gave them the Fat Boy plans.
Now they have the atomic bomb.
Hide under your desk,
Place knees forward and hands clasped around your neck.
Communism is coming. Communism is coming.
Pray. Pray.
I am already so mightily afraid that I don't give a damn.
Me worry?
Should I?
Socialism is already here.
Pray for the conversion of Russia.
Pray.
Who has converted whom?

Pray for the Holy Mother, the Catholic Church.
I want the Church to be as innocent as the Catechism says.
I hope and pray.
Don't question the Holy Church.
Just pray for Her.
Don't worry.
Prayer will heal.
Heal whom?
Why do I pray?
Should I worry?
Why?
Pray.

All For One, One For All

My cousin Donna Hindle and I were like brother and sister. She was exactly one year younger than I, almost to the day. We were friends, playmates, confidants. Our mothers, wanting to strengthen our bond, made us do all the same things, even learn the same lessons.

When Donna took ballet, I had to do likewise. (After a razzing from Doug, I revolted. From then on, I would do boy things with Donna, but not that dance nonsense.)

When one of us was sick the other was thrown into the same bed. We had all the childhood diseases together: mumps, chicken pox, measles, diphtheria, flu.

The only disease I had without Donna's company was whooping cough, because I caught it when I was still in the crib.

So when Donna got a sore throat, it was natural that I would go with her to the hospital. At the Niagara Cottage Hospital, a small hospital with one operating room and only two wards, I was told to undress.

"Why?" I asked.

It was because I was going to have my tonsils out with Donna.

The next thing I remember was the doctor putting a mask over my face and telling me to count to ten. First my head was filled with ten thousand flickering little lights—then darkness.

When I woke up, I was in a hospital bed next to Donna. She was sipping on ginger ale. A nurse brought me some, too, putting a straw in my mouth and telling me to sip slowly. My aching throat didn't seem so bad when Donna comforted me by telling me that in a while we would get ice cream.

X-Ray Vision

For Donna and me, getting new shoes was a special event. When the time came, our mothers took us to Billings Shoes, across the street from Greaves Jams & Marmalade, on the corner of Queen and Prideaux Streets. Billings was a store right out of the old west. Its big, glass-front windows welcomed us, and, inside, it had hardwood floors, high ceilings, wooden shelves, and even a wooden showcase with glass fronts.

Besides loving the specialness of getting new shoes, Donna and I liked the store for two other reasons. First, we could run and play tag without getting scolded because Mrs. Billings understood kids. Her own son was unable to speak due to some developmental problem, so she was extra-kind with us.

But what made Billings Shoes exceptional was the X-ray machine. X-rays were a relatively new, modern, medical development, and no self-respecting shoe store would be without one.

When Donna and I tried on our new Buster Brown shoes, we'd get to stick our feet into the X-ray machine and wiggle our toes so everyone, including us, could peek through the viewfinder to see if the shoes were a good fit. While our mothers were busy looking at shoes for themselves, Donna and I would take fascinated turns watching our toes wiggle. This game would last until our moms said we had to leave. And sometimes, when Donna and I were at Dad's store across the street, we would run over to Billings just to have our feet checked.

When the store finally had to remove this modern miracle, we lost one of our favorite toys. Of course we complained, but were told the X-ray machine was not safe. As usual, when we were faced with the inscrutable decisions the adults of our world made, while we did not understand the reason, we accepted the outcome.

Accidents Will Happen

Like all children, I had accidents. I'm not talking about the types of accidents like falling down and skinning my knees, though I had plenty of those. No, I'm talking about the types of accidents that were embarrassing. Perhaps, even smelly.

Once, when I was in Grade Two, I had dressed myself, made my own breakfast and made it almost all the way to school when I had to turn around and return home. My mother, hearing me enter the house, woke up and came asking what was wrong.

I told her that as I was walking, I thought I had to fart—but I had to do more than fart.

After I washed myself and changed my underwear, my mother recited this rhyme: "Thought, thought that he had to pass a little gas. But what Thought, thought was not what he passed."

Her moral. Be careful what you think. It's better to be sure. A wry sense of humor, limericks and sayings often substituted for real communications.

How Holy Am I?

When I was seven, I attended summer school, where the kind Loretta nuns from Niagara Falls introduced us to the Baltimore Catechism.

One afternoon, the sisters took us on a picnic to Queenston Park, which had the closest wading pool. While playing tag with some of the other boys, I decided to climb a tree—thorn tree. Of course, I got a huge thorn rammed deep into the back of my right hand, just below the knuckle of my middle finger.

Hearing my cries, one of the sisters came to my rescue. She saw where I had been stabbed and tried to remove the impaled thorn, only to have it break off in her hand. Treating it the best she could with iodine, she told me to be sure to show it to my dad when I got home. But it stopped bleeding and didn't hurt, so I forgot all about my misadventure.

Thirty years later, I went to the doctor with a sore knuckle. "What is that round, dark spot?" he asked, examining my hand.

"It is left over from an old wound," I said, remembering my battle with the thorn tree.

He probed it, stared at it through a magnifying glass, and stated, "This has to come out." Then he froze my hand, cut open the black spot, and removed the rest of the thorn. Once it was out, he said he had never seen a thorn like that, and wondered where it had come from.

That made me curious, and I did some research. It seems that legend has it that when Jesuits came to Niagara in the 1600s, one had either the seeds or a cutting from a thorn tree from the Holy Land. From that start, the priest cultivated a grove of thorn trees in Niagara, where they grow profusely to this day—trees which, the story has it, are a direct descendant of the ancient tree that gave its thorns to crown Christ.

Could it be that Jesus and I share a little something? Maybe? But if that's the case, I do think I should be quite a bit more Christ-like.

"Cousin" Pat

Pat was a couple years older than I was. He was adopted, and "adopted" me to be his "pseudo-cousin." We went to the same school, church, and summer school; made our first communions together; were confirmed together. But more than that bound us together.

Like me, Pat had a difficult childhood. He was always in trouble, and his father never spared the rod. We both lived trapped in fear. I guess that is why we became such tough, strange friends.

But there was a difference between us. Pat was more of a bully than I. The town knew Pat as a tough, unpredictable kid who went looking for trouble. He did crazy things; he just never seemed to stop to think. While his reactions were quick, both in forethought and in the ability to take responsibility for his actions, he was slow. It was as if he was operating in a mental fog.

Still, at times he would open up and ask for understanding. And if someone else was in pain, and was not a threat to him, he would give to them with compassion. (On the other hand, if someone threatened him, beware!)

When we talked about heaven and hell as they were being taught to us by the Catholic Church, Pat revealed that he sought a true spiritual understanding.

Yes, he was weird, unpredictable, spontaneous, irresponsible, and irrational, but my friend Pat was struggling. Looking back, I'm willing to bet that the cemetery of his mind contained even more monstrous secrets than mine.

Picture This

In 1945, Cousin Donna, pseudo-cousin Pat, and I had our pictures taken twice, because we had both our first communions and our confirmations in that same year.

In the photographs, Pat and I were dressed in suits bought for these occasions, while Donna wore a white dress and veil. The Toronto Bishop only traveled to our town, an outpost of his Diocese, every five years. That was why the two sacred events occurred in the same year.

While I cannot remember who my sponsors were, I do know that Peter Marino and Harry Sherlock were involved. On the other hand, dear Aunt Phyllis was named my godmother when I was baptized, and she never let me forget it.

Donna and I for First Communion.

Ride 'Em Cowboy

Jack Green owned his own livery stables, and his horses were a fixture in town. I learned to ride—sort of—because Jack offered some of us the chance to exercise his horses for free.

The first horse I rode for Jack was named Queenie. Once the stable-hand helped me up onto Queenie's wide back, she calmly followed the lead horse as we proceeded the short distance to the Commons, then up to John Street by the River Road. Queenie was quite happy with our leisurely pace, but I wasn't. We were falling farther and farther behind. I tried jockeying in my seat and yelling, "Giddy-up," to no avail. Queenie just kept slow-moseying—that is, until we turned around.

Once the leader turned back towards the stables, Queenie, who knew she was headed to her dinner, wanted to run. I kept pulling back on the reins, but the big animal barely felt my young hands on her mouth.

Even with the lead horse blocking her to slow her down, we still made good time back to the giant, sliding doors of the livery stable.

Once she was home, though, just as calmly as she had left the barn in the first place, Queenie brought herself to a halt.

Even though I hadn't done very much myself, I emerged with a smile of accomplishment. After a couple more rides, I was an expert in my own mind. That's why, when Bluebird Freel's son Burley asked me if I wanted to get up on the back of his horse, I felt entirely confident in my abilities.

That adventure had started off as a beautiful springtime drive with my father, my mother, and Maw, through the Niagara countryside. We took a favorite route, along the River Road up to Queenston, marveling at the cherry, peach, and apple blossoms on the way.

When we came upon one of the Freel boys exercising his horse, Dad, who was good friends with the boy's father, stopped to talk. I took the opportunity to get out of the car and pat the horse, a sleek, tan-brown beauty.

Even though I could tell this horse was perkier than any of Jack Green's horses, when Burley Freel kindly asked if I would like to sit on his horse, I said sure, telling him all about my experience riding Jack Green's horses.

Burley boosted me up into the saddle, which was different from the ones at Jack's, having a small horn at the front of it. Smiling encouragingly, one hand on the bit, Burley led the horse forward while I held the reins.

I felt so big, looking down on Burley and my dad. I was like a real cowboy. Heck, Burley could let go of that bit any time, I thought.

And then a passing car beeped its horn. This scared the horse, who reared up and broke free of Burley's grip. I was so surprised I dropped the reins, and as the horse took off galloping down the road, I just hung onto the little saddle horn for dear life.

Dad, Mom, and Maw were chasing me with their car, and someone picked up Burley in another car, and he joined in the chase. Dad tried to head off the horse, but this just spooked him off the road and onto the grass, where he ran faster to get away from my dad's car.

On and on my bouncing body went. My hands were pinched beneath the saddle, but there was no way I was going to let go. I had no thought of appreciation for either the thunder of galloping hooves or the fresh scents of spring that we were flying through. I just held on for everything I was worth.

After what seemed forever, Burley's horse cut down a gravel road, turned off on a lane, and raced into a barn. Then, he simply braked to a dead stop. Instead of soaring ass over teakettle, as my hands were torn from their grip on the saddle, I slammed—balls first—into the horn.

Once the brigade caught up, Burley took charge of the horse, and Dad lifted me down. When I grimaced with pain and held onto my crotch, Dad understood what had happened. He took me into the Freel's house, where Mrs. Freel got me some ice-cold cloths.

Dad had me pull down my pants so he could apply them, while Mrs. Freel gave us our privacy. After a couple of minutes, Dad checked me out and said there was no swelling or danger of getting blue balls. I recovered quickly enough to tell my whopper of a story to everybody when we got home. I may not have been the cowboy I thought I was, but to my family, for one day at least, I was a hard-riding hero.

King George's Bum Spot

I wondered about Jack Green's placid horse Queenie. Was she named Queenie because she had pulled the carriage that carried King George and Queen Elizabeth on their 1939 visit? I knew that horses can live as long as thirty years so, with her good manners and pleasant nature, I could well imagine that this was the case. (As opposed to Burley Freel's hot-blooded horse, who would have been a menace to the Royal couple's safety!)

But whether Queenie had pulled it or not, it was common knowledge that the Royal Carriage was collecting dust and cobwebs at the back of Jack Green's stable. We kids would sneak back and climb up on its leather seat which, despite the dust, was still in good condition. We took thrilling turns sitting on the exact spot where the King's bum had sat.

Maw told me that I had seen King George and Queen Elizabeth in person when, in my infancy, I was taken to the parade held for them, which appropriately proceeded down King and Queen Streets. Being only in my first year as their loyal subject, unfortunately, I can't remember that event. I do not know whether or not I waved, but I do know that I did not get to shake his Royal Hand. Still, for me, sitting on his Royal Bum Spot was the next best thing.

Jack Green's Livery and Philosophy

In many ways, Jack Green was central to my growing up.

My first-grade school, Niagara Public, and my last-grade school, Parliament Oak, were both just a block from Jack's Livery, which we passed on our way to and from school. Certainly, he looked kindly on me, perhaps, because he really liked my cousin Jimmy Goode who still visited Jack for their heart-to-heart talks, when he came to visit from Detroit.

But for all of us kids, Jack's stable was a great place to go, especially when we got bored on school holidays. There was always something interesting at Jack's, and he talked to us in a different way than any of the other grownups in town did. Heck, he just was different than the other grownups.

To start with, he looked like a cowboy extra in a movie. He was unkempt with perpetual beard stubble and missing teeth. He had a cigarette in his mouth at all times and looked "horse-smelly." But instead of the boots and denim you'd expect him to wear, Jack dressed in regular, if rumpled, work pants, street shoes, and a variety of shirts and seasonal jackets.

Oh. And I understand that he had a Ph.D. in literature.

Whenever one of us kids asked him about this degree, he'd only say, "Life is much more than education. Life is the only education." Another of his sayings, which further illustrates his down-to-earth doctrine: "I would rather owe it to you than cheat you out of it."

For me, Jack was an enigma. Gruff but kind, unkempt, well-educated, living his livery-stable philosophy every day, he was no different with one person than he was with the next. Jack Green showed me something important that has stayed with me all these years: It is all right to be your own man.

Haunted Legacy

Adding to his mystique was the fact that Jack Green owned a haunted house. Or he and his brother did. The exact details of ownership were in dispute. But one thing was clear: The house, located on Regent Street just past Prideaux, had once belonged to Jack's father, Mike Green.

According to an article by my brother Lenny's friend Jim Smith, Mike purchased the house from its original owner, Tom Blane. At the time, it is said, it was one of the best-kept houses in Niagara, landscaped with beautiful, blooming flower beds, shapely shrubs, lovely, towering trees, and a wide, well-trimmed yard that spoke of wealth and pride.

When Mike's first wife died, Mike remarried a woman who did not want anything to do with the Regent Street house. When they moved to their new house at the corner of King and Center Streets, the Regent Street house sat vacant.

Jack and his brother were raised in the new house, and when Mike died, the brothers' dispute over the ownership of the Regent Street house went unresolved. So, for many years, that once-lovely house sat empty: weeds overtook the flower beds, shrubs grew into menacing-looking trees, the lawn disappeared under fallen limbs, and layers of leaves and rot became such rich, black soil that it was dug out by local garden enthusiasts.

Soon, the paint was flaking from the exterior, the seasons of leaf-fall piling up on the veranda, and the dirt covering the large-paned windows that formed the "eyes" of the house, combined to create what seemed to us a genuine haunted house.

For a while, we little kids ran by this house so the ghosts could not get us.

Then the older kids explained that the ghosts only came out at night, so we did not have to be frightened. Still, when we had to pass that house, we ran. We were not taking any chances.

One day, when I was (as was so often the case) tagging after Doug, we met up with a group of Doug's friends. By the time we reached the corner of Prideaux and Regent Street, there was a lot of pushing and shoving and daring among the six or seven bigger boys. Then the final dare came: "I bet you can't break into the haunted house."

The challenge was on.

Our small troop ran for the veranda, crushing damp leaves, trampling small saplings, and galloping up the front steps to the locked door. One of the older kids took out a set of skeleton keys. The first and second keys didn't work, but on the third try, the lock turned.

We all paused. Now that the door was unlocked, were we really going to go in? I could feel the heat of the daring bravado emitting from the other boys. No one was going to chicken out, I could tell. Besides, it was daytime. What was there to be afraid of—except the police?

Somebody turned the door knob and pushed, but the door was swollen shut. Two young toughies made short work of that, slamming their shoulders into the wooden door until, with a painful creak, it swung open. Everyone stood back. No one wanted to be the first to enter. Then someone shouted, "Charge!" and we all shoved through the door.

But there we stopped, our scuffed footprints anchored into the dust that puffed up around us.

What an eerie scene. Everything in the house was exactly as if someone lived there. The only difference was the inches of dust that covered everything and the grimy windows visible behind the musty velvet drapes. In the half-light of the foyer, a mirror topping a coat rack gave us back a spooky, scratchy reflection of our gang. If there were ghosts in that house, they might well look as we saw ourselves in the old, worn mirror. But such haunted thoughts did not deter the toughies.

Standing beside Doug, I looked up and saw what I thought was the ghost of one of Santa Claus's reindeers—even though I no longer believed in Santa—its antlered head sticking out of the wall, and its large, glassy eyes staring right at me.

All of a sudden, I heard a chilling "Oooooooohhhhhhh," and found myself lifted up and propelled towards the moth-eaten creature. I was shaking with fear, but realized, when the other boys exploded with laughter, that I was not being carried aloft in the arms of a ghost. No. Doug and one of his friends had lifted me and swung me through the air. I felt like a fool in front of all those older kids. But, on the bright side, I did get my first close look at a stuffed deer.

As the muted laughter echoed off the walls in a dampened, hollow chorus, we proceeded forward, entering into a huge, dimly lit dining room. There, the sun fought bravely through the filthy windows. Piles of plates and platters and bowls still filled a grime-laden china cabinet. Behind me, some of the boys were rifling through the sideboard drawers, making silverware chime as it thudded to the floor.

A what-must-have-once-been-sparkling chandelier hung above the large table. I asked Doug if I could have one of its prisms. Doug retorted, "You might as well, before someone else gets them all," and I scampered up onto the table, yanked off two grimy crystals, and shoved them deep in my pocket.

I stuck tight to Doug as the gang headed into the kitchen. It was darker than twilight (and much scarier), back there. Someone lit a match, which created weird, flickering shadows. I wanted to get the hell out of there, but I knew if I ran, I would be branded a chicken and never allowed with Doug's gang again.

As I took a deep breath to calm myself, I noticed the strange odor mingling with the sulphur of the match. I recognized the smell from The Store when my dad poisoned rats.

Another match was lit. Then, one of the guys cried out, "Oh, shit! I just stepped on a rotten, dead cat."

By the illumination of the single match, one of the boys found a door to the basement. He opened it, and the match flickered and went out as a cool, putrid breeze ebbed from the basement. Bravado notwithstanding, the kid slammed the door shut and the whole troop of us stampeded back to the front stairs.

A roar of false laughter echoed around us as we climbed the creaking stairs. The bedrooms were faintly lit by what little sun could penetrate the windows. Shadows were cast on the filthy, papered walls. While the dressers and mirrors were intact, for some reason the mattresses were piled up against the wall.

The room was cool, but I could still smell the adrenaline heat rising off the other boys' skin as we crowded together. We herded ourselves from one room to another. There was the sound of opening drawers, the smell of moldy clothes, and the whisper of denim pockets as prizes were stealthily slipped inside.

Bam! then, Crash! then, Boom! came like thunder from somewhere deep in the bowels of the old house.

"Get out!" was the echoing cry, and we stampeded back down the stairs and out the front door, me grasping Doug's hand as tightly as I could.

"What the hell was that?" one of the guys asked, as we stood panting on the veranda.

The boy with the keys said, "I don't know, but whoever it is—or whatever—is going to be locked in there." He pulled out his set of skeleton keys and re-locked the front door.

Then, trying to look as though we were just happy-go-lucky kids, we strolled casually away from the scene of our crimes. On our way home, Doug instructed me to keep my mouth shut. I could keep my prisms, he told me, but I had to swear that I found them in the garbage on the street.

Of course, once we had breached the haunted house, more break-ins followed, and the old place became increasingly decrepit as the wreck became everyone's playhouse.

Soon, ropes were strung from the upstairs windows so that all of the Niagara Tarzans could swing down to fight off the wild animals in Niagara's jungle. As needed, the house could become a gang hold out, a pirate fort, a mob house, a spy house, or the setting for the story of any movie that happened to be playing at the Brock Theater.

Sometimes, when we were bored, we would throw stones, bricks, or boards at the house to continue the damage it was undergoing due to our rough play. It is amazing that the fires that we lit to keep warm never did more damage. I moved out of town before the house was reduced to rubble.

***

Some of what occurred in Niagara's haunted house belongs only to the memories of those who were there. Whether these memories surface as pleasant dreams or as nightmares, as far as I know, in the wildest of our play, no one was ever killed—or even seriously injured—at the haunted house. All of our fun took place without the interference of unions, safety supervisors, the health department, or the fire department.

Yes, until Jack Green's death in the 1960s which took the house from the kids of Niagara, we got along just fine, thank you, without the help of the Government. Once Jack died though, all of his inherited properties were sold. The haunted-house property was divided to accommodate three separate dwellings, while the stone livery stable that was across the street, was converted into a picturesque architectural prize.

The Songs of Regent Street

The year I was eight, Dad purchased our house at 157 Regent Street, two doors down from Prideaux, for $2500. My parents were happy to have a home of their own. I was happy to be living kitty-corner from Jack Green's haunted house! Also, our new house was just one block from Queens Royal Beach and from Dad's pharmacy (and all the treats I wanted).

The Regent Street House

The Regent Street house had a unique, Dutch-style roof line. Under that roof, my two older brothers, Jack and Doug, got their choice of the two kids' bedrooms—of course. I had to take what was left over. But there was something special about my room: In what once was a very small closet, there was a secret compartment where a loose board allowed me to hide treasures.

Also, all of our bedrooms faced the large backyards of Prideaux properties, giving us views of beautiful, well-kept lawns and gardens and towering pine trees that whispered their "hushes" into the wind. And more importantly, from my window, on calm evenings, I could also hear ripples of sound wafting over the border from the U.S. side.

My room was my refuge, a place of sanity in my sometimes insane world. Many hot, still, summer nights I would be lying in my bed, windows wide open, while I wished for the nonexistent promise of a breeze and instead, what blew through my windows were the clear, distant notes of a bugle coming from Fort Niagara, New York. Those notes knew no borders. They glided that half-mile right into Canada, into my waiting ears on Regent Street, Niagara-on-the-Lake, Ontario. The night-time melody, only twenty-four drawn-out, haunting notes would resonate inside me for minutes afterwards, calming me like a peaceful, melancholy, bedtime story.

In bright contrast, on some very clear, early mornings, a raucous tumble of cavalry charge-notes would gallop through those same windows. That blasting morning song made me stuff my head under my pillow so I could snooze the last half-hour before the alarm went off. But even that song made me feel befriended.

I learned much later that the evening melody was called "Taps", and the morning melody was "Reveille."

These two songs and the memories of comfort that they hold have become a permanent part of my history—a history inside a history. Now whenever I hear the twenty-four simple notes of "Taps", the nostalgia wells up in me, all the way to my eyes.

Missing: One Appendix and Two Kittens

When I told my mother I had a bellyache, she sent me to my room to lie down. I dozed off, but was jolted awake by a sharp punch of pain in my stomach. I thought I was dying. I called and called, and at first no one came, but as my groans increased, my brother Jack rushed in to find out what was wrong.

I had doubled up trying to avoid the pain. Jack wanted to look at my belly so he could see what was happening. He tried to help me straighten my legs, but I let out such a blood-curdling scream, that Jack shouted, "I think he has appendicitis!"

Someone fetched my dad from the store, and he drove me straight to Niagara Falls Hospital, where the surgeon took me in immediately. The next thing I knew, a mask was planted over my face, and I was counting backwards to the now-familiar anesthesia light show—and then it all went dark.

I was released with the instructions to take it easy for a while—no school and no roughhousing—but I did have permission to walk. The weather was nice, so I walked up to The Store to visit Dad who sent me down the street to the Marino's to get a head of lettuce. At their store, Mrs.

Marino showed me their new kittens. They were so cute, especially one little tiger-striped puss that I promptly named Ginger. Mrs. Marino offered the kitten to me. Back to my dad's store I went, with a nice head of lettuce and a sweet little Ginger cat.

Ginger was a wonderful playmate. The entire time I was recuperating and not able to go to school or play with my friends, the days went quickly as I taught her to chase a string and allowed her to rub and purr all over me.

After my first day back at school, I ran home to see my Ginger, but she was nowhere to be found. I asked Mother if she had seen her.

"No."

I asked Jack if he had seen her.

"No."

I asked Doug if he had seen her. And Doug, in his sage voice, informed me that kittens wander away, get lost, and are unable to find their way back home. I went back to Mrs. Marino to see if Ginger had returned there, but she had not, and Mrs. Marino had given all the rest of the kittens away.

The next spring, when the Marino's cat had another litter, Mrs. Marino again let me take my pick. I chose a kitten that looked a lot like Ginger and named her "Tiger." By now, I knew that to train a kitten you had to keep it in a box until it was old enough to know its home.

But despite my precautions, I had Tiger for only a couple of weeks when she, too, escaped and ran away.

Doug said, "Don't worry. I asked Dad for a dog. They do not run away."

I had had it with unreliable kittens. A dog sounded like a great idea.

***

It wasn't until I got older that I learned what happened to Ginger and Tiger. My mother could not abide having cats in the house, especially with my new-born baby brother, Lenny. On Mom's instruction, my loving brothers had put my both my kittens into burlap bags and thrown them into the river.

I also learned that my appendix scar suggests the emergency medical care I received might not have been absolutely first rate. During a physical exam in my later life, the doctor asked, "What kind of an accident did you have to get a scar like that?"

"It's from having my appendix out," I told him.

"Well," said the doctor, "the butcher that did that should have had his license revoked."

Raise a Glass To Prohibition

Officially, Ontario was a dry, no-booze, evangelist-Billy-Sunday-blue province. But while the temperance movement tried its best to completely totally quash the drinking of alcohol, there was always a way to party. Ife Stevens, seven miles out of Niagara-on-the-Lake, had a bootlegging gourmet restaurant in St. Davids that he kept open till the wee hours in the morning, making it a perfect spot for Mother and Father to head to after The Store closed.

Another popular drinking and eating spot was just across the border, in Lewiston, New York, where prohibition had ended in 1934. To get to Lewiston was simple, too. All my parents had to do was drive the few miles to Queenston, cross a rickety, wooden swing bridge, drive down a hill, and they were in the heart of the village, where both rationed food and alcohol were legal and easy to find.

So the trend was set: work, party, sleep—in that order—and "Meet you at Ife's (or Lewiston)" was the evening cry, with both destinations only a short drive away.

All this drinking and driving was not a problem, either, because 1) there were no insurance companies to worry about, and 2) since Ontario was dry, there was no law on the books dealing with drinking and driving. Also, the U.S.-Canada border was practically a "free border", with families on both sides having relatives living on the "other side."

In fact, the customs workers either knew or were actually related to most of the people who traveled back and forth to work, live—or eat and drink!

Small-Town Canada

Even though we were pretty sophisticated when it came to partying, some people after the War called Niagara a backward town. Some, from St. Catharines and Niagara Falls, even looked down on us as hicks.

To be fair, getting in or out of Niagara-on-the-Lake by bus or car was a fairly treacherous undertaking. Our roads were inadequate and hard on the vulnerable tube tires of the time. The potholes and scrap nails that plagued the main roads were a constant threat to those traveling any distance. And if someone was coming from Toronto, they had a difficult time getting past the lift bridge at Burlington.

Even if the bridge proved no problem, Burlington's steel mills and scrap steel particles proved another threat to their tires.

There was another lift bridge over the Welland canal at St. Catharines. When that bridge was up, you could wait for as long as twenty minutes to cross it. (The locals were used to cursing at it.)

Sure, compared to other better known spots, we were a small town, with only a handful of stores: the drugstores; three or four family groceries; and just a few clothing stores. With such a limited selection, we often had to order clothes from the Eaton or Simpson department-store catalogues, and then pick up our things at one of their small, local offices.

Of course, the best shopping was to be had in Buffalo or Niagara Falls, New York, where we'd go, then smuggle back our ill-gotten goods.

But we did have the means to bring goods to us, when we needed. Buses and trucks conveyed much of what was needed, and, in the case of large commodities, we counted on the Michigan Central railroad.

The train stopped near the corner of King and Queen Streets with goods for our main-street merchants. For materials destined for the basket factory, Shepherd Boats, or the Town itself, "The Dock" was the official delivery spot.

Niagara-on-the-Lake also sent goods, especially the fruit in season, to market via rail. In the summertime, the magnificent boat The Cayuga, which held up to twenty-five cars, complete with drivers, and a couple of hundred passengers—and was also used as a troop-transport for the army camp—carried produce from our region to the Toronto markets. And, as an added bonus, for pleasure trips, passengers from either Toronto or Niagara could ride up and back to Toronto on the same day.

For Toronto folks, Niagara's main attraction was the Falls.

For us hicks? The main attractions were the Toronto sights and the Toronto Exhibition.

The War Is Over, But Not the Rationing

Not only was I personally short one appendix and two kittens in 1946, but there was also a general shortage of coal, butter and sugar, which were still being rationed in Canada, while England recovered from the War. The English were getting our allotment of rationed goods, and we were importing English candy made with sugar.

With a restriction on these basics, we resourceful Canadians found various ways to make do. One way we did so was by simply using less of the hard-to-come-by goods. The *Niagara Advance* gave suggestions for canning with less sugar. (The trick was to use more salt, mix corn syrup with the sugar, and add a little vinegar to be sure the jars did not spoil.)

Also, Oleo Margarine, which came in a plastic pouch accompanied by an orange "button" of food coloring, was introduced as a replacement for butter. To make the ghost-white lardish contents a more buttery color, we had to break the orange button and hand-mix its contents by squeezing the pouch until it became a more natural, orange-ish hue. This replacement lasted for years while the dairy industry protected their butter market. My small hands often cramped with all the mixing required. We looked on this duty as a hand exercise. However, in a time of rationing, living in Niagara suggested other solutions in addition to restricting our consumption of the rationed supplies. You see, it was only a short ride to the U.S., where the A&P Grocery Stores and some of the drug stores had margarine that looked and tasted more like butter than our Oleo Margarine. Also, in the U.S., while sugar was in short supply, it was not rationed and could be obtained—if you had friends.

On the other hand, unlike us Canadians, Americans had a ten-percent luxury tax on jewelry, perfume, cosmetics, and anything that was not considered a necessity, which created a wonderful situation in which friends on two sides of the border could create a comfortable balance during hard times. Thus, our U.S.-Canadian barter system was fully mobilized, and, as the owner of Bates Pharmacy, my dad was in a great position to make the system work.

Friendly customs officers would just ask, "You do not have anything to declare do you?" and across he went.

There were times that the Canadian dollar was worth more than the U.S. Legally, merchants could receive American money, but were to give Canadian change in return and take the U.S. dollars to the bank for deposit. The people of Niagara may have been considered hicks, but we were not stupid, especially not my dad!

Instead of depositing the U.S. dollars he received at The Store, he would simply take the U.S. dollars across the border to Lewiston, New York, and exchange them for the more highly-valued Canadian dollars at the restaurants there. Of course, there was an official limit on how much money you could bring across the border, but no one I knew was ever searched.

Gun Running

War having ended, at the almost-deserted army camp, the abandoned government buildings looked like so many aging rectangular boxes. Their clapboard sides were a worn white; their trim was a sun-faded green; their roofs were covered in a deteriorating, gray-green tar shingle. And with only a few maintenance personnel readying the properties for sale, there was nothing to keep us out.

Two cars full of boys—including my brothers and me—and another five or six boys on bikes formed a parade as we quickly covered the couple of miles to the rifle range on the outskirts of town by the two-mile pond. A large padlock on the fence was designed to keep intruders out, but the lock was no deterrent to Niagara kids. It took only one blow of a tire iron to make it spring; then the gate opened, and we dashed inside.

What we found was a boy-treasure heaven. There was a trove of shell casings, including a brass mortar shell. Spent bullets were begging to be carved out of their targets with our jack knives. I got my share just by picking them up as the others pried them loose and flipped them to the ground.

Then one of the gang spotted a building that was more securely padlocked than the gate had been. We knew this meant that there must be something really great behind that door, but the lock was tough, even for us devil-makers. After several tries with the tire iron, it still would not budge. But in numbers, there is genius. One of the toughies said, "Wedge the iron between the lock, and pound its neck with a large rock."

We did. It took several blows, but the lock finally gave up its guard.

We swung the door open and crowded in and, in the dim light, found an arsenal that was meant to supply an entire company of troops. There were rifles neatly stacked in rows and a shelf full of pistols. Everybody was helping themselves to the artillery. The rifles went into the cars; the pistols were stuck into the belts of the bicycle riders; and I picked up the smallest handgun I could find, for they were all heavy.

We all swore an oath of secrecy and then took off.

When I was dropped off at home, I made my stealthy way directly to my bedroom and stashed the gun in my secret hiding place. But I was not afraid. I was elated. I had been accepted by the gang.

A couple of days later, I was playing at Jack Green's when I heard my dad calling me to come home. Once I got there, Dad led me into the living room where Chief of Police Lou Warner and an army officer I did not know both sat on our couch staring holes into me.

Dad sat beside Lou Warner and beckoned me over.

Now I was frightened.

My dad put his arm around me. "Chief Warner says you are not in trouble, but we have to know where the gun is."

I tried to play dumb, but guilt must have been written all over my face.

The Chief said, "Billy, we have recovered the rest of the guns. The one you took is the only one left. The other boys did not think you took any. However, we know differently. Please get the pistol so we can forget all about this."

Okay. The jig was up. I scurried up the stairs, got the pistol from its hiding place, and brought it back downstairs. I sheepishly handed the gun to Dad, who passed it to the army officer, then scooped me up and gave me a big hug—bringing another Niagara saga to a close.

Tag, I'm "It"!

The paved roads that wound throughout the empty army camp were lined with faded army buildings, and, at night, streetlights continued to illuminate the ghostly streets—at least the streetlights that had not been shot out with sling shots or rocks.

On the King-Street side of the camp was a spot that must have been built with the kids of the town in mind. There, a half- track tank-training area had been laid out that was perfect for drag-racing (once that idea came to mind!), and the track was surrounded by streets that, while officially government land, were out of the jurisdiction of the Police Chief and his constable.

All of this combined made that the best darned car-tag track in the world.

When my oldest brother, Jack, turned fourteen, he applied—to a friend of the family—for a dispensation to get his driver's license. The trumped-up reason he gave was that he needed to be able to drive to make deliveries for the drug store. Of course, his application was approved immediately—one of the perks of living in small-town Niagara.

Next, Jack conned Dad into getting him a Model A Ford, complete with the rumble seat that made it the most sought-after car of university-bound kids. One of the boys in town happened to owe Dad a sizable debt, for which Dad took the Model A in payment, making Jack's first car a repo—which just added another layer of cool to the car's image.

One late spring night—I was still just eight—Jack shouted to me, "Hey, Billy! Want to come for a ride?" This was out of character for Jack who, different than Doug, mostly considered me a nuisance.

No way was I going to pass up a chance to hang out with my biggest brother, so I immediately ran to the car and hopped right in. Before I could get settled, though, I had to slide over a couple of hockey sticks that had their blades removed and both ends taped making them look like pretty tough weapons. I didn't know what these particular weapons were for, and I wasn't about to annoy Jack by asking.

Without another word, Jack revved his engine, and we rumbled to the entrance of the deserted army camp where we met a half-dozen other jalopies. The rules were established: In car tag, one of the cars was designated as "It," and everyone else would take off racing away from the It car, down the road to the half-track training area.

Jack's instructions were that in the event that we were tagged and became It, I was to take one of the taped hockey sticks, hang out the window, and bang on another car when we were close enough.

It was only moments until another car crept up beside Jack's Model "A" and whomped his fender. Jack peeled off and came alongside another car that was following us.

He said, "Billy, lean way out of the window and whack that car." I was so excited that I hit the car with all my might. I hit so hard that I almost fell out the window. I hit that darned car so hard the reverberations shimmied all the way up my arm. And, proudly, I held onto the stick.

Once car tag got boring, someone suggested a drag race.

All the cars lined up and beeped their horns: "Ooga! Ooga!" bellowed the Model A's horn.

I can't tell you who won the race because Jack took off so fast, I slid right off the seat and onto the floor and could not get back up until the race was over. (No seat belts back in the forties.) But even though I wasn't looking, I knew I was having a real-life experience that rivaled anything I ever saw in the movies.

Gainfully Employed

Even as the war (and the lives of so many) was ending, my own life was moving ahead. During the year I turned eight, my father had decided to try to keep me out of trouble by putting me to work in The Store. I'm not sure if his goal was met, as I still got into plenty of trouble outside of working hours, but I did love our store. To me it was a beautiful and important spot, the center of the grown-ups' world, and a place to pick up real information about how that world functioned.

One educational feature was the public, pay, phone booth. Situated just inside the front door of Bates Rexall, once its glass-paneled, folding door had shut on the single adult the booth could accommodate, the door was supposed to create privacy for the phone-callers. The phone demanded copious coins. The callers had to shout at the operator and then shout at the one they were calling. This meant it was not private to me. I could easily sneak up to the end of the soda fountain counter, lean an ear close and listen in. I was instructed not to eavesdrop, but I found strangers' lives so interesting and informative, that I ignored the no-eavesdropping rule in favor of a well-rounded learning experience.

Over the next couple of years my soda-fountain duties grew, which sometimes acted as a cover for my pay-phone snooping, took place behind a counter of Brazilian granite, its dark jade green streaked with veins of pure white. In front of the counter, five chrome stools stood sentinel and behind it was a stainless steel cabinet which protected a variety of Neilsons' ice-creams in their deep paper tubs.

Most importantly, atop the counter was the device that made it a soda fountain: Two taps dispensed the fountain elixirs; one provided flat water, the other, the soda water that provided soda water for cokes or for sodas, sometimes called floats, which were created by dropping ice cream into a glass partially filled with soda water or pop. (This magical fountain was like other family drug stores of the time. Ours was a "Mr. Potter-style fountain," which was memorialized in the 1946 movie *It's a Wonderful Life*, when the young Mary Hatch whispers into George Bailey's deaf ear, "George Bailey, I will love you for the rest of my life.")

In addition to the stools at the counter, we had three green, wooden booths that could hold six people if they squished. The high backs of those booths allowed for giggling and private discussions-more private than the discussions held in the telephone booth!

On our big soda fountain mirror, we listed the variety of sundaes, ice-cream floats, and sandwiches we made. Our simplest sundaes consisted of a standard ice cream flavor topped with whipped cream and a cherry. More exotic were the confections known as the Banana Split and the David Harem. My personal favorite was simple vanilla ice cream drenched in chocolate sauce with a maraschino cherry on top, but I loved experimenting. I created new sundaes like other people created works of art. Some of our regular customers actually ordered my creations.

In addition to these delicious cold treats, The Store also sold bacon and eggs for breakfast and sandwiches, including grilled cheese, ham and cheese, Westerns, and BLTs. To make the grilled sandwiches, we used an almost-prehistoric flat grill. The grill lid took two hands to lift. The early morning jobs were 1) put up the coffee in the huge Bunn coffee maker, and 2) fire up the grill—which might have taken quite a while to heat up, but once that thing was ready, beware! It was hot, as my many burns did testify. At a young age I paid the initiation fee to become a short order cook.

To cool our customers down, we had a red pop cooler, adorned with the famous Coca-Cola logo that required ice to keep the drinks cold. (Even though this was a Coke cooler, our two biggest sellers were Niagara Dry Ginger Ale and Niagara Cream Soda.) We got our ice from the ice man, who carried a block of ice on his shoulder in a canvas sack—a block of ice that could weigh up to fifty pounds! Fortunately in Niagara, up until June, the water was freezing cold, so we only had to buy ice in the heat of summer and early fall.

We also sold *Kleenex, Toni Home Permanents* and, very intriguing to a young boy, unmarked packages of women's necessities that were usually displayed in front of the pharmacy. But as interesting as these were, it was the newspapers that were most special to me because of my dad's great interest in the information they held.

The papers were important to most of our customers, as well. When the *Toronto Star* increased the price from two cents to three cents, there was a hue and cry that the robbers were getting a fifty percent increase. The consensus at The Store was that they could give away the paper and still make money; with all the revenue they got from advertising, so why charge their loyal readers more?

My favorite early store memories consisted of Dad talking about current events. He was an avid reader, and I could listen for hours as he explained all the political intricacies. At lunch and dinner in particular, he would discuss the news of the day, taking care to make sure to lay out all the many details. He would cite the great journalists of the day and talk about propaganda, parading as news.

As I grew, I learned of important happenings. My father discussed such wide-ranging topics as Roger Bannister breaking the four-minute mile; the amazing Dr. Fredrick Banting's discovery of insulin in Toronto; Alexander Fleming's discovery of penicillin; and the Korean War. Whether historical or current events, Dad delivered information in a way that made me feel like I was there, living the events as they happened.

I'm not sure I understood everything my father shared back then, but I do know that I inherited his love of trying to figure out the truth of what was being purveyed to me by the media.

In The Money

During the summer of 1947, things at home were much the same, except that now I was old enough to get out of the house when Mother got angry with me. I recall eating at The Store or a better variety of suppers at Club 19 and at Gene Ing's restaurant, Elite. It got so that I could just pay for my suppers there or, later, at The Thistle and Shamrock. The best was when Doug would come with me and pay. (Also, Anderson's Hut across from the park was always good for a lunch that replaced breakfast.) Most of the time I just wanted to be out of the house.

I turned nine that summer. This was the year my baby brother was born. Even though I was in the way at the house, I was not sent away, I did spend some time at my cousin Donna's house. This was arranged so that I would be out of my Mother's way. My dad had made a deal with Uncle Wink to supply me with food, especially milk, to offset my growing hunger. But this arrangement only lasted a short while because my Aunt Frances was just as bad as Mother—except that Frances was not a drinker.

Dad was working eight to nine hours a day; he was at the store seven days a week. He decided the best way to keep an eye on me during school year was to have me working alongside Doug at The Store. Because the full time help looked after the soda fountain, I was put to work dusting the large, heavy bottles called "Winchesters", which contained liquids used to compound medicine. These included cherry bark extract, vanilla extract, balsa oil, tincture of iodine, mineral oil, castor oil, peppermint oil and, worst of all, cod liver oil.

In the winters, my brothers and I would have to line up to down a tablespoon of this disgusting cod-liver slime, chased by an orange or a lemon coated with soda bicarbonate. We all held our noses, but I still gagged on it every time. My dad had his dose along with us, and big brother Jack took his like Dad. Jack called me a sissy because I had so much trouble with the dose, but Doug said, "It's okay. I used to gag when I was your age."

Working, of course, meant more pay. I started out the year before at ten cents an hour and quickly learned the value of money. This year I got a raise to fifteen cents an hour I stashed my earnings in my piggy bank and received a raise when the price of a chocolate bar went from five cents to eight cents.

Even after a big chocolate-bar boycott, staged by Canadian kids who were protesting a sixty percent increase in chocolate prices, dialed those costs back to five cents, I kept my increase and was still paid twenty cents an hour. This was great! I would work for four or so hours, make Eighty cents, then have twelve cents for the show—and still be able to buy a five cent Long John pastry at Niagara Home Bakery with the money left over. Since I did not have to pay for ice cream, pop, or milkshakes at the soda fountain, I was a rich kid. And to top all of this off, I was able to eat most of my meals at The Store.

Breaking News: Summer, 1947

In what was called "The Five Cent Chocolate War," kids that protested a forty percent increase in chocolate bars I read their story and saw the many pictures in the store's newspapers and when we went to the show they were in the newsreels. True to form big business and the unions could not tolerate a bunch of smart alec kids drawing too much attention to politics. They became movie star heroes. The little kids lined up on their bicycles boycotting the giant corporations. Eventually their civil actions were called off, when it was suggested that the protests and boycotts were linked to forces of communism.

It was announced that the Niagara Public School would be replaced in the autumn of 1947 by the new Parliament Oak Public School in Niagara-on-the-Lake, and high school students would be bused to Stamford High, outside of Niagara Falls. (Mr. C.E. Brunton was named Principal of the new Parliament Oak School, replacing Mr. Commar "Crow Bar", who acted in that same capacity at Niagara Public.)

Dad's friend Noel Haines was digging a new foundation, his truck fell into a secret tunnel, sparking a lot of discussion about the fact that some of Niagara's earliest houses had tunnels—and what their intended uses were. Some suggestions were that the tunnels were meant to be escape routes in the case of attacks from the Americans;

that the tunnels were employed by rum runners avoiding the authorities; that smugglers used the tunnels to transport goods that were difficult to obtain or were banned in Upper Canada or the U.S. The least acceptable explanation I like is that, as in England, servants and trade service people were regulated to an unseen private entrance, which often meant secret tunnels.

The excitement I enjoyed occurred during the leveling of the property for the new school, when a new source of fire was discovered by the children of Niagara. We youngsters quickly discovered that the slate shingles strewn across the property would spark—like old flintlock guns—when we struck them on iron. We traded and horded this treasure, using the slate to create sparks to light off firecrackers.

While, generally, the kids took the announcement of the new school in stride, the walls of Niagara Public I would be greatly missed as a marble-shooting gallery. Historically, in the safety of those walls, marble players had found it easy to protect their games from "famfobbling" marble thieves.

The oil-retro-fitted S.S.Cayuga returned to Niagara on May 14th, and all Niagara townspeople were invited on a free ship-ride to Queenston and back. All my friends and I took full advantage to create mischief by harassing the adults.

On June 26th, it was announced that the Niagara army camp would become a designated National Historical site. As of June, 2012, this designation has still not been approved. So much for government declarations.

The roof of Fort Mississauga, which is a designated National Historic Site, was mysteriously destroyed by fire. I still wonder about this.

Diving

I had tagged along with my brothers and cousins as they made their way down to the lake. While standing on the shore with my younger cousins, I could see the older gang standing out on the first sandbar, so I just decided to walk on out to them.

The only problem—I couldn't swim.

As I was bobbing up and down, out of my depth, my cousin Frank shouted the obvious: "Hey! He can't swim."

They dragged me back to the shore where I'd started, only now I was flat on my belly retching up lake water. For the next couple of years, I was not allowed near any body of water unless accompanied by my brothers. And then one day Jack and Doug told me to get my bathing suit on. We walked down Front Street to King Street, and then took the railroad track over the bridge at Delater Street.

I had to take giant steps, as the railway ties were spread wide apart. Doug told me not look down—he was holding my hand—but I was still scared I would fall through. The tracks took us past fishing shanties owned by some of the Niagara families. In the off-season, these shanties were neat hideouts and came to hold many secrets that I dare not tell.

Finally, we arrived. My brothers had brought me to the Cayuga dock. Jack dropped back, but Doug walked me closer to the dock, where he had me to take off my shoes. He did likewise and, holding tight to my hand again, told me look at Fort Niagara and take a deep breath.

S.S.Cayuga

The next thing I knew I was in the water. Doug had pulled me up to the top, and there were four or five older kids swimming around us. Doug let go of me shouting, "Swim like a dog!" Everyone around me was dog-paddling to show me how. With all the support, I did not have time to panic; I just splashed with all my might.

The current carried me the few yards back to Jack and his friends, who guided me to the small beach at the edge of the dock. Everybody cheered and then they tossed me back into the water to paddle again and again. At some point, they showed me how to swim like a frog. It took a while, and my lessons continued for some time, but I became a proficient swimmer with the help of my brothers and their friends.

View from the S.S.Cayuga

I would also go to the dock with the bigger boys when the Cayuga was in, but I would stay back while they dove for money. They would shout, "Toss down your money folks," to the crowd on the boat deck, and I watched how they would duck-dive to get the coins.

One day, after the boat had pulled out, my swimming lesson focused on treading water and duck-diving. I learned to suck in a deep breath and, once under the surface, release the air from my lungs slowly. This way, they explained, I could stay under longer and would not feel the urge to try to catch a breath under water. Little did I realize that this technique would one day save my life.

After a few days of practice, I graduated and was allowed to dive at the boat. There were rules, though: I was to stay close to Doug at all times. When a coin came near me, I was to dive and try to get the coin, and even if I didn't grab it, I had to pretend I had and mime putting it in my mouth. Then I was to shout, "Thank-you."

(Of course, I missed most of the coins, so Doug or a friend would dive below me to retrieve my missed catch. Nevertheless, I do remember the thrill of getting some of them. And my brother would share a little of their money with me, too, while encouraging me to do better on my own.)

From below the surface, the water was a cold green, yet when the sun shone through, it became a fairy world. When coins were thrown with force, they would hit the water and sparkle down a few inches. Then they would start to zigzag, back and forth, as they slipped towards the bottom. On the way down, they reflected any available light, reminding me of a silvery fishing lure.

I and a couple of other young ones were the big attraction because the crowds liked to see us little ones get the better of the big kids. The people on the ship wanted us to "win" what they saw as a competition, and would even try to get us away from the big kids so they could throw closer to us. The more involved they got in the outcome of this "competition", the more money got tossed—and I learned my first business lesson: People will part with their money if you give them a reason to justify doing so.

Occasionally, one of the passengers would toss down a fifty-cent piece—or even a silver dollar. When they did, the result looked like sharks in a feeding frenzy. There were usually five to ten kids in the water, and we river rats were focused on the large coin as soon as it left the thrower's hand. The race would be on! Every boy for himself, the water boiling as everyone aimed for the coin. There was pushing, shoving, ducking, and hitting, but I soon realized that, in such competitive confusion, some of the stronger ones would almost jump out of the water to grab the prize, when, most likely, it would be knocked out of their hands.

Doug taught me that if I dove deep beneath the foray, my chance of being first to the coin, as it was knocked through the greedy, grabbing, rough crowd, was dramatically increased. Because of the frenzy, most of the divers were short of breath as they competed for position. I could afford to take a very deep breath and wait patiently several feet below them and grab the missed coin if I was smart enough to be in the right spot at the right time.

Once, though, I arrived seconds too late, and the coin, a silver dollar, had already tumbled far below everyone. I chased that prize down and down and down, the pressure on my ears building, until, when I finally retrieved it, I realized I was at the bottom, almost twenty feet down.

I pushed off from the river bottom as hard as I could, and slowly let out the air I had been holding, as I had been taught. My lungs were screaming; I thought I was going to pass out when I finally broke through to the surface and sucked in the fresh air!

I held my trophy high as I heard the applause from the dock. Then I swam to the shore with just enough strength left to drag myself out of the water.

Peep

As planned, in the autumn of 1947, the new Parliament Oak School, did in fact open on King Street—even though the opening was two weeks late. The school was named for a legend that has the first session of the Canadian Parliament being opened by Governor Lord Simcoe under an oak tree. The legend then widened to include the idea that the very oak tree that grew on the spot where the school was being built was, in fact, the famous parliamentary tree. (I suspect this last was just an instance of Niagara's romantic imagination.)

When the school was finally completed, there was a grand opening ceremony with all the important citizens of Niagara present to have their say. The parents and some of the kids were excited about the new school and the new teachers, but my friends and I just took it all in stride. I was entering Grade Four, and if I thought about it at all, I felt confident that I was going to get on just fine.

Our new building had the only underground wiring in town. It boasted easy-to-clean terrazzo floors; large windows that cast light on our innovative green chalk boards (complete with roll-up maps of the British Empire); and fluorescent lighting that made seeing the work on the board easier—not that this helped me to learn.

With its water fountains, asphalt playground, and a field for soccer, football, rugby, and baseball, the school was the pride of Niagara. That is, for everyone except me.

We had just settled into our new classroom a few days after the opening. This is when our new teacher told us she had to leave the classroom for a few minutes. On the way out the door, she turned and said, "I do not want to hear a peep out of anyone."

True to my inner self, I took that as a personal challenge. Just as soon as she had left the doorway, and I figured she was out of earshot, I called out, "peep." As the other kids began to laugh, the teacher came marching right back into the classroom, yanked me out of my seat and dragged me up to her desk. My stunned face was turned toward the class when I heard a drawer open, and she produced a short, leather, razor strop that I learned later was a Board of Education issue.

She grabbed me with vise-grip force and growled at me to open my hand. Then, with a baseball pitcher's force, she wound up, and with all the pent-up anger inside her, she smashed that strap full force onto my tender ten-year old hand.

When she had landed ten hard whacks on my outstretched left hand, she commanded me to hold out my other hand.

"Are you stupid?" she yelled.

"No," I cried. *However I must have been because I held out the other hand.*

In the dead silence of that classroom, with an audience of scared kids, she gave my right hand ten whacks, too. Before that incident, I had thought she was pretty, but through my tears that day, she looked like a witch. It took ten more whacks before all her frustration was released.

I sniffled, groaned, and wiped my tears with swollen hands. I had just started to my seat, when I was saved by the bell for recess. As I left the room, no one acknowledged me. I was a leper. As I darted towards the boy's washroom, one of Doug's closest friends followed me.

Disastrous news travels fast; he had heard what happened. He took one look at my hands and turned on the cold-water tap. I put my throbbing hands into the cool water. It felt good.

This older kid was a pro. He said, "The pain will go away. The skin isn't broken." Then he added that to do such a thing, the teacher must be bleeding.

"Bleeding," I sobbed. "I thought I was bleeding, not her."

"No," he said. "She must be having her period."

Then I understood what he meant from selling menstrual supplies at The Store. But understanding didn't make it any better.

I didn't know what to expect when I returned to the classroom, but my teacher acted just like nothing happened. Instead of giving me an apology or showing any remorse, she just wore the air of a conqueror, nose high and a sneer on her face.

This was when I understood that fear does not teach students anything worth knowing. In my case, all I learned was to be more careful when I was breaking the rules.

(Almost) Forbidden Fruit

At The Store, the magazine rack butted up against a glass showcase of lighters, pipes, knives, playing cards, dice and "flat fifties," small, flat, metal boxes that held fifty cigarettes. Behind the counter, a rack held brand-name cigarettes, including *Players Navy Cut, Export, Black Cat, Buckingham, British Counsels, Cameo, Craven "A",* and *Sweet Corporals*. There were even medicinal cigarettes for asthma and menthols for soothing the throat.

While these all came in a pack, some of the stores sold individual cigarettes for two cents, which made them affordable for kids. The smoking age was fourteen, but it was not strictly enforced. And anyway, if anyone wanted "cigs", the older kids would get them for us. Usually, though, my own stash came from my mother's purse.

Yes, the cigarettes and other paraphernalia of manhood drew the boys. For the littler kids, though, there was a different sort of temptation. Right beside the cigarette showcase was the candy display. Its glass case had to be constantly cleaned of tiny finger and mouth prints.

Fire at Fort Mississauga

In 1947, I was one of a group of kids that had slipped past the wooden door—with its long-broken lock—that guarded the entrance to Fort Mississauga. We entered into a dim, large room, where we saw both an entrance to the basement and a set of stairs leading to the second floor.

Up we went. We found an opening out onto the roof, through which some of the older kids scrambled so they could walk around. It must have been amazing to look out over the landscape from the roof, but even from the safety of the "window", which is where I stayed, the view of the lake and the river was spectacular.

Once everyone was done with sightseeing and had crawled back inside, the real fun began. We piled scrap wood into the huge, open fireplace on the Fort's second floor and lit it to create a roaring fire. Everyone was smoking, telling stories, and flipping their cigarette butts against the Fort's walls so we could watch the sparks bounce.

When it was time to go, in a final salute to a great day, together we extinguished the fire with our small, personal fire hoses.

It wasn't until the next day that we learned that the roof of the Fort had been destroyed by fire, a fire that was attributed to vandals.

Donnybrook

I had just finished having my supper and was cleaning up the dishes when Dad called to Doug and me to get into the car; we were off to the dock to see what was going to happen with the attempt to shut down the Cayuga.

Dad pulled out into a parade of cars, and we proceeded up Queen Street, turned around at the dummy policeman, and headed down King Street past the park where buses, jeeps, and trucks had parked, crowding the side of the road. We maneuvered around the back way towards the dock, finally parking by Balls Fish Market, and then walked to Lockhart Street almost to the slip. The crowd was dense, but we were able to make it most of the way to the Riverside Hotel.

There was electricity in the air. The townspeople were talking about the possibility of a donnybrook. As the seven o'clock boat signaled its approach to the wharf, the voltage of the crowd rose to a static mutter. Several out-of-town policemen disembarked from three cruisers parked in front of the hotel, billy clubs at the ready. They forced their way through the crowd—quite a few of whom had baseball bats in hand—towards the landing dock. Then I lost sight of them.

Even though we were getting to be pretty big kids, Doug and I both held onto one of Dad's hands tightly.

From what I could tell, the Cayuga had slowed to a bump stop. I could not see the lower part of the ship from where we stood, but I could envision the heavy docking rope being looped over the pylon and the press of passengers trying to get down the gangplank, but being blocked by the mob. A roar broke out, and I was shocked to witness one man club another across the back of the head and shoulders. The victim crumpled just like a scarecrow without its support, blood matting his hair and shirt.

With that, Dad commanded, "It is time to leave."

As we were working our way back to the fish market, I watched as three sinewy, tattooed thugs lugged a heavy chain behind one of the police cruisers, looped the chain around the car's rear axle, and attached it to the hotel building post. Dad hurried us along around the corner, but some part of me wanted to stay and see if the car fell apart like in a Keystone Kops movie.

Thanks to my father's protective good sense, Doug and I missed most of the violence. But there was plenty of information about the riot and the conflict that caused it in the news for some time to come.

I read the following *Niagara Advance* historical record on microfiche at the Niagara Public Library:

June 10th 1948: Clubs Swing Away; Strikers Attack Steamer at Dock.

A large crowd of passengers on the Canada Steamship Lines S.S.Cayuga, and many who were at the wharf to see the seven o'clock boat pull out for Toronto, found themselves in the midst of an exciting ten minutes when strike trouble developed at the dock.

Immediately after the passengers disembarked or embarked, as the case happened to be, a car, jeep, and truck pulled into the wharf and unloaded some thirty-five alleged members of the Canadian Seaman's Union (CSU), which organization went on strike Saturday.

The auto carried a loud-speaker unit, and, through this, the crew of the Cayuga was ordered to leave the boat in five minutes time. The crew, composed of members of the rival Canadian Lake Seaman's Union and non-union workers, refused to abandon the ship, with the result that the strikers, armed with baseball bats, attempted to board the steamer.

Some did get on the boat, swinging their clubs, but the Cayuga crew had hauled out the fire hose and proceeded to turn streams of water on the attackers. Anticipating trouble, Toronto policemen were aboard the Cayuga, and Chief L.A. Warner and Constable E.H. Ball of the Town of Niagara, also did their best to break up the riot.

One of the attackers, in being forced off the boat, stumbled and plunged into the river. He was grasped by Chief Warner and hauled to safety, but not before some of his opponents had shoved him under the water several times. In the meantime the Cayuga got underway and started to leave the wharf.

Those of the attackers who had not yet been driven off the boat rushed down the gang-plank to the dock. The battle ended when the boat pulled out, with union members on both sides hurling threats at one another. The attackers left in their vehicles, and as far as the <u>Advance</u> can learn up to the moment, it is not known where they came from. No arrests have been made.

The strike was called after the companies refused to renew their contracts with the CSU and instead signed agreements with J.A. "Pat" Sullivan's Canadian Lake Seaman's Union. Prosecution of the CSU, authorized by the National Labor Relations Board, is still pending in the courts.

Harry Davis, president of the CSU, said the seamen would fight to defend their picket lines and jobs. He said the strike would spread as the vessels touched port.

On Monday, some fifteen Provincial police were on hand at Niagara wharf in the event of further disturbances, but the strikers failed to put in a second appearance.

Further reports from that summer included the news that, on July 1st, while Seaman strikers demonstrated on the wharf, seven passengers were taken off the S.S.Cayuga with what appeared to be ptomaine poisoning—although no one could ascertain what caused the food poisoning.

Then, on July 29th, a union picket line at the dock ended with fifteen CSU members arrested and placed in Welland County Jail with their bail set at $2000 each. (In this case, not only were CSU members on the picket line, but they were joined by placard-carrying women and children who chanted, "We shall not be moved," as they marched.)

Subsequent to the arrest of the CSU members, police raced to Queenston, following a tip that another huge picket parade was planned there. Once the police arrived, however, all was quiet. The only men on the docks were fishermen.

It was the talk of the Store that in September that a fire broke out on the Cayuga while she was at that same

Queenston dock. The fire was minor, and quickly extinguished, but, as with the food-poisoning of passengers in July, the cause of the fire was never determined.

**

For the businessmen of Niagara, the Cayuga was their summer lifeline. As they attempted to create a tourist destination of Niagara after the death of the army camp threatened the town's survival, the Cayuga, which carried passengers back and forth from Toronto, was of the utmost importance.

But it is difficult for a passenger ship to be profitable in a three-month season. Even though Canada Steamship Lines had repaired the ice-floe-damaged Niagara and Queenston docks at great expense, the strikes, the fire, and the traveler intimidation seem to have started what ended up being the downhill slide of the iconic S.S.Cayuga.

Because of all the strife, Canada Steamship was forced to put her up for sale in 1952: "We will be prepared to sell the S.S.Cayuga on reasonable terms to anyone interested in going into such venture," their statement read.

I Am Here

In early spring or in the fall, when the weather conditions were just right, the lake and the river would fog over at the same time, and I would hear the foghorn—which was located on the golf course near Fort Mississauga—blow until the fog burned off.

I am what is called "monotone deaf", but even to my ears the eerie sound had an almost mystical quality. It would moan its deepest tone, BEEEEEE-Ohhhh, which sounded like, HERE IS DANGER, at intervals of thirty-five seconds, until the fog lifted.

BEEEE-Ohhhh. HERE IS DANGER. BEEEE-Ohhhh. HERE IS DANGER. BEEEE-Ohhhh. HERE IS DANGER. Until the Cayuga or another large ship approached the Niagara River and sang out her own song: I—AM—HERE; I—AM—HERE," forming a memorable, romantic chorus with the foghorn, the horn moaning every thirty-five seconds, the Cayuga blasting its own warning every thirty seconds.

HERE IS DANGER! I—AM—HERE.

HERE IS DANGER! I—AM—HERE.

HERE IS DANGER! I—AM—HERE.

Today, along with so much else that was special to my growing up years, the foghorn no longer exists. First it was replaced by radar, then by infrared equipment. With it went an era of unforgettable Niagara memories. The foghorn first to go, the Cayuga second—their historical romance never to be duplicated.

Technology to the Rescue

By the 1940s, communications technology was well on its way to transforming the denizens of even small towns into world citizens.

First, of course, had come the telephone. In Niagara, early on, we had the old-fashioned type of service that required users to check to see if a stranger was on the party line. While the polite thing to do, if you heard someone speaking, was to hang up and try later on, if you were less polite (or just very curious), you could listen in on their conversation. Once it was your turn, you turned the crank handle and waited for the (always female) telephone operator to answer.

While the telephone connected us efficiently one-to-one, it was radio that delivered the news of the world with an immediacy that outstripped even the daily papers. The adults gathered around their living-room radios to hear the most urgent happenings of each day. We kids preferred the shows about our heroes the Green Hornet, Superman, the Lone Ranger, Hopalong Cassidy, the Shadow, and "Fatty and Skinny," as we called Bud Abbott and Lou Costello.

We also went to the movies, which we called "the picture show", on Saturday afternoons. We had to go by ourselves, as no adult could ever stand all our screaming and shouting. A loyal mob, we would shout out warnings to the Lone Ranger: "Look behind the rocks! The Indians are about to get you!" Likewise, the serials that always ended with the heroine at the very point of being killed. Of course, those heroines, like the Lone Ranger, evaded death, and returned to the show the following week having been miraculously saved.

The majority of the movies we watched back then were in black and white (it was a big thing when Technicolor movies came to town), but that didn't keep them from seeming real to us. One of our favorites was *Our Gang*. We tried to copy all of their stunts, with varying degrees of success (and bruises), and the pirate and cowboy movies gave us great ideas, too, for hours of playtime.

In the late 1940s, my family cashed in war bonds and bought a small, black and white, RCA television encased in a large cabinet. At first, the only available television station went on the air just a few hours a day, and we needed a special antenna to pick up the signal, which transmitted from Buffalo, New York. Eventually, we could get two Buffalo stations, and much later, we could receive signals from Hamilton, Ontario. In the late 1950s we installed a rotary antenna and could actually get a Toronto station!

The early television sets had tubes which had to warm up before we could watch a program, and would burn out if we watched the TV for too long. When that happened, we had to go to the main street to Fry's, the store which sold radios and televisions, and hope that they had just the right tube to replace the one that had burnt out.

Often, I would buy several new tubes. Then I would take out all the tubes from the back of the set and eventually, by trial and error, find the exact one that had expired, replace it, and return the good ones to Fry's for another time. It was a happy day when someone invented a stand to test television tubes and set it up right inside the store. This way I could carefully extract a series of tubes, take them to the store and find the ones that needed replacing.

Phew. Technology to solve the problems of technology.

Drugstore Confidential

Because of my father's occupation as a pharmacist, the men and woman who came to The Store spoke freely to him about even the most personal of their ailments. They also spoke in whispers to one another about other aspects of their lives. And, sometimes, they spoke about confidential matters directly to me. All of this almost-secret dialogue was woven into the life of Bates Rexall Pharmacy—and I was truly a part of it.

I heard stories of various operations and their outcomes; about customers who were taking placebos for their nervous conditions; and about those who needed laudanum (an opiate my father kept locked behind two doors, which required two separate keys) either for their great physical pain or for mental torment.

I learned who had to go away for a few months to "visit an aunt", and learned what that meant, too. I was warned by some of our army-camp customers to think with my "big head" and not with my "little head." I might believe a girl is "clean", they told me, but I should learn from their mistakes. Look at what happened to them, they said, holding up the sulfadiazine my father had just dispensed to them. (Of course, it did not take long before the whisperers told exactly who the suspect girls were.) And once, an older boy came to Dad to buy *Sheiks* and acted so comfortable, as though I was not there. Did he know that I knew his girlfriend?

Under my father's tutelage, I was privy to so much of the intimate portions of our customers' lives. I came to understand that each one of us inhabits our own personal jungle, and that the territory of each of our jungles changes with the seasons of life. Those men and women placed their complete trust in my father, and, to honor that trust, I had to keep all that I learned in The Store to myself. Whether or not these were truly secrets, they were our customers', not mine, to tell.

The Store Was My Living Classroom

When I first started in the store (in my official capacity), I dusted the bottles. Later on, I graduated to putting away stock. Then I was allowed to close out the cash register at night. Finally, after I demonstrated my competence, I was allowed to help Dad in the dispensary with the medicines. I was growing up.

At first I was only allowed to mix the salves together and spatula them into a jar. But after I proved myself capable of that task, Dad showed me how to grind medicines into powder with a mortar and pestle, take half-capsules, tap them full, and close them up with the other end of the capsule. When I mastered that, Dad taught me how to pour ingredients from a large bottle into a smaller one without spilling.

He said it was similar to carrying a cup of coffee to a customer across the store in one of the booths. "Remember," he said, "You just look where you are going, because your body will automatically adjust so you don't spill. But if you look at the cup, you're more likely to slop."

As my father showed me these different skills, I felt like a grown up; I was contributing to people's health with professional techniques. Almost always, when I asked, Dad showed me what he was mixing and what it was to be used for.

For instance, I learned that cough medicine was basically a mixture of fruit-flavored alcohol and codeine, and that extract of wild strawberry was great for diarrhea.

From my dad, I learned that women and girls get their menstrual periods approximately every twenty-eight days, and that is why they are called monthlies; that when a woman is menstruating, it is a sign that she is not pregnant; that different women have different flows, and that was why we carried three different colored boxes of unlabeled sanitary napkins.

For menstrual cramps, my father recommended baking soda and acetylsalicylic acid, commonly known as aspirin, unless a woman had a doctor's prescription that allowed him to add a half grain of codeine to her mixture.

On the other side of the coin, the *Sheiks* and *Ramses* we carried were brand-name prophylactics used to prevent the transference of venereal diseases and unwanted pregnancies. In one father-son moment behind the counter, Dad made sure to let me know that these "safes" were far from foolproof. I took this as a warning.

For those who had not avoided trouble, I helped Dad mix up a blue ointment for the venereal infestation known as crabs. Since the ointment virtually burned out the crabs from the pubic area, I heard a lot of cursing from the guys using it.

Much worse than crabs, though, was gonorrhea, which we also called "the Big Drip." A terrible venereal disease, to fight it, Dad had to mix up a solution of sulfadiazine which was to be inserted up the penis while the infected area had to be scraped clean.

Yes, I got a well-rounded education at The Store. But as much as he taught me, Dad was an introvert. He did not seek me out to further my pharmaceutical education. No, I had to go to him. When I was in his domain he took time to explain to me, but this was probably the only time that he and I had anything even approaching intimate discussions. He was always full of information, but very short on communicating feelings.

At the time, despite the huge amount of knowledge that he shared with me, I would have said that my dad was aloof and disinterested in me. It took years, and the raising of my own children and grandchildren to allow me to see the truth: My father was showing me his love and teaching me what he knew with every patient instruction that he gave me. Now, I cannot even measure the amount of wisdom and savvy I received from him.

Not the Girl for Me!

I was at my soda-fountain post, saying goodbye to two of my classmates, when I heard the giggling. Gladys, by far one of the prettiest girls in the school, was coming towards me, not dressed in jeans, like most kids our age, but cute as could be in a pleated, tartan skirt and a starched white blouse. She almost sparkled with clean, her long black hair flowing over her white collar. And she giggled.

I felt a twinge of insecurity as Gladys hopped up on one of the chrome stools and looked me right in the eyes with the full force of her school-girl charm. With her disarming smile, she said, "Now let me see. I think I will have a sundae."

I thought I would melt. Instead, I asked in my most professional voice, "Which sundae in particular? Would you like a banana split or perhaps our popular David Harem?"

Gladys twirled around on the stool a couple of times, long black hair swaying, and said words that made me think she might be my life-long love: "You know, I think I will have just a plain vanilla."

"Would you like some whipped cream and a cherry on top?"

"No, Billy, I will just have a plain vanilla please."

I was starting to flush at her attention, but didn't understand how "just plain vanilla" could be a sundae. "What would you like to drink?" I asked.

"I think a cherry Coke would be nice."

I nodded, and lovingly, I scooped out two large balls of the creamy, white ice-cream. Looking into her eyes, I said, "Here you go, just special for you."

At this, Gladys performed another twirl on the stool.

I turned away to prepare her cherry coke, picking out the two most perfect cherries with special care. But when I turned back to set the Coke on the counter, I was horrified by what I saw.

Gladys, the maybe love of my life, had dumped catsup all over the pure white mounds of the vanilla scoops and was spooning into the bloody sundae.

She may have been one of the prettiest girls in school, but right then and there, she had lost my heart.

How could she?

When Reasoning Stinks

It was an unusual year for skunks. They were a plague, like locusts. They just kept on breeding and appearing out of nowhere. We could not drive down River Road without gasping from the stench of the numerous gaseous skunk road-kills.

We kids had a heyday, shooting at the black-and-white striped offenders under the street lights down by the golf club. The summer visitors had locked up and gone home, so we could take our time getting in position up-wind. If we were patient, in the mild fog we could take out two or three skunks a night.

While the stink was terrible (there was a run on tomato juice to spray down most of the dogs in town), the big fear was rabies, and we took that very seriously.

It seems that the Ontario Government noticed just how serious the situation was, as it issued warnings in the *Niagara Advance* about being careful to not mistakenly poison pets and livestock, trying to get rid of the pests. In the same warning, we were sharply reminded that skunks are fur-bearing animals and, as such, could only be trapped or killed by those carrying a special government-issued license.

At The Store, we had a poison book. Anyone wishing to purchase poisons, such as the strychnine used to kill rats and mice had to sign it. Of course, strychnine worked well at killing skunks, too, but they were protected under the fur-bearing law.

One day, during the worst of the skunk scourge, a loyal customer I'll call "Mr. Cannelloni" came to me and said, "I want to buy some strong poison."

I was pretty certain I knew why he wanted to the poison—and how to get around the obstacles the government had set up for the situation.

To Mr. Cannelloni, I suggested strychnine would do the trick. "But," I said, "You will have to sign the poison book first."

"Okay," he replied cooperatively. "Where is the book?"

Before handing Mr. C. the book, I carefully explained that fur-bearing animals were protected, and he could not use strychnine to kill them.

"Thatsa okay," he said. "I gotta get rid of skunks."

I pointed out that skunks were fur-bearing, and so they were protected. "But if you sign for rats, I can sell you what you need," I told him, with what seemed like perfect logic.

"My wife, she keep a clean house," he said, offended. "I don't got no rats. I got skunks."

I tried again. "I know a lot of farmers have the same problem. But the law says we cannot sell you strychnine unless you sign the book saying it's for rats."

By now, Mr. Cannelloni was getting mad. "Hey, kid. You your poppa's boy. I thought you were smart. Let me say again, I got no filthy rats. I got stinky skunks!" With this he huffed off to the dispensary and called out to Dad. "Mr. Bates. You know me a longa time. I like your kid, but you should teach him something."

"What is the problem?" my dad asked from behind the pharmacy.

Mr. C. said, "I keep telling Billy I got no dirty rats. My wife keepa clean house. I tell him I got smelly skunks, and he keeps saying I got rats. Teach him good, okay?"

Now it was Dad's turn. "Mr. Cannelloni, you know that beaver and muskrat are fur animals."

Mr. C. nodded. "Yes."

"Well, skunks have fur also, and they are protected under the fur-bearing law, just like the beavers."

This was the final straw for Mr. Cannelloni. "I never heard of such a thing. You mean they make skunk coats? Rats got fur. What? Are they too small for coats?"

Dad could see he was getting nowhere, so he convinced Mr. C. to send his neighbor Tom to come in to The Store. "In meantime, here are some mothballs. Put them where the skunks are," Dad said, handing over a box of the odorous spheres.

"Will they kill the skunks?" Mr. C. wanted to know.

My dad explained that while the mothballs wouldn't kill them, skunks don't like the smell, and it might get them to go away. "Oh," he added, "do please ask Tom to come in tomorrow."

The next day Mr. Cannelloni's neighbor Tom came in and asked, "What's all this about skunk coats?"

Dad explained the rule: Strychnine could be bought to kill rats, but not skunks.

Understanding dawned on Tom's face. "I get it," he said. "I got rats. Where do I sign?"

English, What a Strange Language

A woman rushed into The Store. She was slightly older, perhaps twenty-two, and wore her long, sand-colored hair in a ponytail that seemed to dance. (In fact, this lovely young woman looked so much like the Jennifer O'Neill in the movie *Summer of '42*, that when I saw the movie many years later, I recalled the same feeling of a gulping heart that Hermie has when he first sees O'Neill as the beautiful Dorothy. But back in the 1950s, I didn't have this reference. I just knew she was older, and she caused my throat to pulse.)

I had worked at The Store long enough so that I wasn't embarrassed when the woman asked me where the napkins were. In a professional manner, I took one look at her and sized her up as a blue box. Since pink was for girls, and white was for older woman, I just knew she was a blue.

I sauntered over to the feminine napkins, John-Travolta style, where all the boxes were wrapped in plain colored paper for discretion, and confidently tugged the correct box from the shelf. Then I sauntered back to the cash register, where I proudly served this movie-star beautiful woman her blue napkins, placed them into a bag, and rang up the sale.

I felt so sophisticated.

That is, until I saw the perplexed look on her face. Had my stammering heart showed in my blushing face? What was confusing her?

Then the Jennifer-O'Neill look-alike took the napkins from the bag and proceeded to open them in front of me. Once she got the package open, she started to laugh. "No, no," she said. "I want napkins."

I was dumb-founded. Napkins were what I had handed her. Then the light went on, as I caught her American accent. "Napkins like table napkins?"

She smiled. "Yes, of course."

No longer sauntering, I crossed the store again, and picked up a package of serviettes. "Is this what you want? We call them 'serviettes' in Canada."

"Of course," she sighed, and then asked, "Do I have to take the other napkins now that they are open?"

I said that she didn't, because the girls who worked in The Store would appreciate them. And besides, "It's my fault," I told her.

"You sure are a cute kid," she replied, handing across the money for the serviettes. As I took the coins from her hand, I could feel a new blush rising to accompany my quick breath. Then with pony tail bouncing, she swung out the front door, leaving a sweet memory behind that would last me for life.

You Are Not My Boss

I did not like my Uncle Austin—and not just because of his exaggerations. What really annoyed me was that he thought he was my boss. If I had to work with him on his shift, Uncle Austin would order me around.

The tension between us escalated until, one day, we got into a fight. "I do not need to take your crap," I told him. "If you want to shout, you can shout at yourself." With that, I banged out of The Store and left him there alone.

I'd blown off steam, sure, but I wasn't sure what I was going to do next. Fortunately, I met up with my friend Neil. Neil said. "Let's go pick cherries at my aunt's farm on River Road and John Street."

"Isn't that the funny farm for retarded kids?" I asked.

He replied, "That's okay. They are harmless. Besides, it is other people who do the picking." And off on our bikes we went.

The first day, I ate far more than I put in the basket and was paid very little. That night, I evacuated most of the sweet treats I had so gluttonously consumed—and then I dreamed of leaves and red cherries and more leaves and more red cherries.

The second day, I actually picked some baskets-full. At the end of the day, I was disappointed to find that I was paid less than I made at the store in that same amount of time, and cherry-picking required much greater effort than being behind a soda fountain.

The third day, Neil showed up pulling a wagon behind his bike. I didn't think much of it at the time, but after we were paid, Neil doubled back towards the farm with me right behind him. We parked our bikes and crept into the orchard. There we saw many baskets chock-full of the gleaming red fruit—and no attendees.

Two by two, we carried the full eleven quart baskets out of the orchard and placed them in the wagon. Then we went to the summer army camp down the street. The soldiers proved an easy market for ill-gotten fruit. One heaping handful brought us a quarter. With more than ten handfuls to an eleven-quart basket, and fourteen baskets, we had an easy heist—over thirty dollars' worth.

But this was not a performance we could repeat. So now what?

We were preparing to leave the camp when the cook called us over. "Hey kids, do you want a job?" he asked us.

What a stupid question.

I asked, "How much does it pay?" When the cook told us it was over double what I made at The Store, I said, "When do we start?"

"Right now. Go over to the crock and mix up the fruit salad," he told us.

"Where is the ladle?" I asked.

"Use your God-given hands," he said.

"Where do we wash up?"

"Right in that crock," he told us, pointing.

"Anything you say," I said, laughing at how odd this seemed. But we did make money.

I know Dad felt I had let him down, but he said nothing about it to me. I think he actually appreciated my independence and was proud when I showed him how much I was making. All good came to an end, though, when I cut my hand on some not-so-hygienic glass in this supposedly sterile outdoor kitchen at the camp. I got blood poisoning and had to go to the new Niagara Hospital.

I did not really mind spending two weeks there, for I was still being paid by the army. Also, while I was in the hospital, this kid a few years older than me came into my room. He asked, "Do you want to see something?"

Of course I did.

He pulled down his pajama bottoms and I was staring at two, huge, black baseballs.

"What happened to you?" I chirped, already feeling his pain.

He told me he was a cadet at the camp and that he had tripped over a rope that held up one of the tents. He landed balls first, smack on top of a large tent peg.

Ouch!

I never had to worry about doing that myself, though. After I was discharged, Dad said to me, "I think you had better come back to The Store and work your shift with me."

I did. I could not refuse Dad.

New Life?

News-flash from the *Niagara Advance*: Welcome Reverend Major Weaver of Port Colborne. Reverend Weaver, a service Chaplain of WWII, will be pastor at Niagara's Saint Vincent de Paul.

Saint Vincent de Paul

    The parishioners were excited. My father was pleased. Change was afoot. "We may get new life for our church," my dad told me. This was the fall of 1948. Old Father Kelly had retired, and Father Kailey had been transferred to Malton. Our new priest—who was to bring that "new life" to our Catholic community—had been a Chaplain in World War II, which would make him a Major. Reverend Major Weaver. Dad liked this.

    At the time, I couldn't see how one priest's departure and another's arrival could affect me all that much. But before too long, I was to find out exactly what sort of "new life" Father Weaver had in mind for me.

Blood Brothers

Except for my girl cousins, I was all alone the year I was ten. My brother Jack was at St. Jerome's boarding school, and Doug had been sent to our Aunt Ruth's to live in Lloyds Town. So every day after school, I went to The Store to check in with my dad.

One day, as I hopped up on a soda-fountain stool, Dad came over to say, "I want you to meet our new employee, Mrs. Simmons."

Mrs. Simmons gave me a warm, caring smile and said, "Please do not call me 'Mrs.' Call me 'Ma'." I had only called one person Maw before, but the way she said it, I was not offended. At her request, I did call her Ma, and from that day, there wasn't anything she wouldn't do for me.

After our introduction, Ma Simmons turned to a young kid who was looking at me from behind the corner of the pop machine. She introduced him as her son, Mike, and asked if I would play with him after school when she was working.

What the heck? I thought. A younger kid is better than no kid to play with. And that was the beginning. (I guess Mike needed me as much as I needed him, because, as it turns out, Ma Simmons and Mike's dad were either separated or divorced. Although his father was the chef at the Oban Inn, Mike seldom talked about him, except to deliver a message from his mom or to try to get some money from him.)

There was a shortage of kids in Niagara, so the more adventurous ones hung around with whoever was available, even if the age difference might be three or more years. However, although Mike and a couple of others were the crux of our gang, whenever it was possible, Mike made sure it was just him and me. And from that time on, some people in the town thought of us as Tom Sawyer and Huck Finn; others said, "Here comes trouble looking for more."

I'm not sure what we were really like, but I do know this: Mike had courage. He would accept a challenge, but he also had a knack that I did not have. Different from both me and, certainly, Cousin Pat, when Mike smelled real trouble, he backed off—leaving me to test the rules.

I was told that Mike was part-Indian. Whether or not that was true, we did what we thought of as an Indian ritual. Just like in the movies, we each cut one of our own palms, then rubbed our bloody palms together, spit on the blood, and smeared the spiritual contents together one more time. We swore to be friends for life.

We were blood brothers.

Potential Fathers

Father Weaver was such a pompous priest. One Sunday he ranted about how it was the duty of Catholics to have children, saying that was the primary reason for marriage. "Condoms, *Sheiks*, *Ramses*, all are the work of the devil," he shouted from the pulpit. "They are evil. It is a mortal sin to use them."

I had to serve Mass that day, and Mike, who went to the United Church, often came around to St. Vincent's to wait for me. I told him all about Father Weaver's sermon. It gave us an idea.

The next day after school, we were at the store, as usual. And, as usual, Dad tried to keep Mike from just hanging around. He had found that if he allowed Mike to help me dust or unpack boxes, I would not be so fidgety and try to leave early.

So Mike was helping me, when, as if by God's orders, we found ourselves unpacking two large boxes of *Sheiks*.

I looked at Mike. He looked at me.

I went into the dispensary and carefully grabbed a half dozen straight pins.

Without speaking a word, Mike and I pulled out an entire roll of *Sheiks* and rapidly inserted a tiny pin-prick into each one of the individual foil packages. Laughing at our new variation on a Bob-Hope joke, we giggled, "A prick for a prick." But we knew to chuckle quietly.

Carefully returning the damaged *Sheiks* to their original box, so no one would know they had been opened, we pricked our way through two full grosses, two hundred eighty-eight condoms. We were well on our way to meeting that goal, when Dad called out, "Hey. No playing back there. Get the job done."

Shushing each other, we finished the second gross and put everything away neatly. When I asked Dad what we could do next, Mike burst out laughing.

Dad just ignored us. "Silly kids," I imagined he was thinking.

***

If you were born in Niagara sometime between 1951 and 1952, Mike and I just may be the ones to thank for your existence. If so, I guess you will either love us or hate us for our escapades.

We Owned the Water

We owned the water. Whether it was at the dock, the slip, the river, or the lake, the natural beauty of the ever-changing seasons spoke most fervently to us of God's glory at water's edge. There, Mike and I spent countless hours, accompanied only by my dog Perky.

We made secret caves, consisting of small holes, hidden and just large enough to reach into. We would smoke, swear, spit, and tell dirty jokes. We roasted bees' nests with flaming, "lighter torches" that I appropriated from The Store. (I learned that if I was putting pressure on the can and lit the resulting stream we had a flame thrower, but it was crucial not to let the flames come back to the can!)

These were places where we were glad to be alive. In them, we were free, having escaped the adults control and manipulations: no fears, no depression. The lake and the river were there as if water had poured out for us from Eden.

In those hours, no one owned us. We were free.

Ice and Escapades

When the sun shone on the frozen lake or river, they became our fairy-tale play lands. To us, the ice sang an irresistible melody that wafted on sweet, cool breezes right into our souls. We became restless, and commitments such as school, work, chores, or serving Mass made us gripe and swear.

Sometimes it seemed like the whole world wanted to keep us from our winter fun. But as soon as we were released from obligations, we would race back to the frozen water.

Usually, at the lake, the shore ice froze into uneven hills and valleys, but at special times, God would create a perfectly smooth, bright, sunlit, skating surface just for us kids—the ice a skin atop frosty-blue water, Fort Niagara seeming so close, I felt I could hit it with my slingshot. Only the muffled quacking of passing ducks broke the cold stillness.

With the start of spring, new miracles occurred. In the river, as the shore ice started to melt, large lumps of ice we called "icebergs" would appear. These would wash up near the shore and freeze together at night. Sometimes they would split apart into huge, separate chunks again in the warmth of the day.

These chunks, which originated in the springtime break-up of Lake Erie's winter ice, would eventually cascade over Niagara Falls into Niagara Gorge, where they would freeze back together and form ice jams.

It was a jam like this that tore down the Honeymoon Bridge, not long before I was born, destroying numerous docks, including the fortress-like Cayuga docks at Queenston and Niagara-on-the-Lake.

Occasionally, a jam would be so extensive that the daring would chance taking a walk along it from Niagara Falls, Ontario, clear across the frozen river to the American side.

When the jams were this big, a strong wind would usually force the ice back up the Niagara River and shut off both falls, leaving a wall of ice where pounding water should have been. And, in extreme cases, if an ice jam occurred at the mouth of the Niagara River, demolition experts had to be called in to place their sticks of dynamite and blow up the obstructions.

Generally though, the ice situation was not that extreme. Most of the time, the ice would simply break up as it travelled over the falls, then glue itself back together into our local "icebergs."

The larger of these icebergs could easily support two preteens, such as Mike and me. Never ones to let such an opportunity pass, we would clamber aboard a likely 'berg' and with the help of a long pole or driftwood board, turn them into rafts, or boats, or even a space ship, if that is what we declared them to be.

One fine day, Mike and I were aboard an iceberg that we had pushed farther and farther out into the lake, when suddenly our pole snapped. As we drifted away from shore, we shouted, but no one heard us. We tried waving for help, but the motion made the 'berg teeter-totter and sent water washing up over the sides. We started to lose our balance and knelt down on the ice for stability, soaking our jeans in the process.

By that point, we were many yards from shore—and no way back that we could see. Church-going boys, kneeling on that chunk of ice, we began to pray: Never, we swore, would we ever do such a thing again. And from then on, we promised God, we would even obey the adults in our lives. We were that desperate!

We might as well have kept our promises to ourselves; it seemed at the time that God wouldn't give us even the slightest breeze to confirm that he had heard us.

Of course, if it had been summer, Mike and I would have just stripped and swum to shore, but that day, the temperature of the ice-chunk-filled water hovered just above freezing. After some debate, we decided that if we were going to die, we might as well die trying: We would stick together and swim, if need be.

There were other icebergs close by, so we successfully hopped on the two closest making it a few feet closer to shore. But our third jump failed, and dumped us both into the bone-chilling water as the 'berg broke into smaller pieces. I had gasped a lungful of air and started to swim before I realized Mike was actually standing up.

The water was past his waist, but he was walking. I followed suit.

As we ploughed our way toward shore, the cold became numbingly unbearable. Our legs were as frozen as if they had been anaesthetized. In gasping breaths, I swore at Mike for being so stupid as to suggest this in the first place. He countered my curses.

To keep each other from giving up, we avowed that we were super-human, that we were immune to the cold, that no amount of ice could stop us!

In this way, taking one cramping step after another, we emerged to knee level, which, while it elevated our scrotum above the icy water, offered them little relief—they were frozen into a state that was beyond pain. Finally, though, balls, legs, arms aching, we were able to crawl up onto the rocks that lined the sun-warmed shore.

Once we'd confirmed that neither of us was mortally injured, we knew we had to get out of our freezing clothes. As Cubs Scouts—and river rats—we were prepared for recovering from getting cold and wet. Scrambling to one of our secret caves, we dug out a stash of matches and lighter fluid that had been buried in a large cookie tin. Quickly, we piled up drift wood, soaked it in lighter fluid, and set it alight. In seconds the fire was roaring.

Shaking hard, we managed to strip and hang our wet clothes close to the smoky fire. We emptied our rubber boots of water and wrung out our socks. We placed hot rocks into our boots, and began to dance around the fire naked, to keep warm.

Through chattering teeth, we discussed which lie to tell our parents. While we hadn't drowned, we might still die of pneumonia. We considered this sobering thought, and then laughed, deciding that if the Eskimos and Norwegians could swim in icy water and survive, so could we.

Finally, dressed in our steaming, still-damp clothes, we high-tailed it to Mike's house. Ma Simmons was working, so we didn't have any explaining to do. Instead, we stripped to our dry underwear, placed the rest of our clothes close to the oil heater, made mugs of hot chocolate to warm our insides—and fell fast asleep on Mike's well-blanketed bed.

Looking back, I believe God did answer our prayers. We made it home safely, having had an adventure to remember all of our lives. I don't think it is too late to thank God for helping us to survive that day and, for better or worse, many other days like it. Now a father myself, I imagine that He understood that we were young and forgave us for not following through with our promises.

Car Skiing

While weather conditions in the winter in Niagara could vary, with many freeze-thaws, when we got a good snow, it would pack hard on the road on Main Street. Then it was car-skiing time. Mike and I were experts at this sport, which required a very nonchalant approach. First, keeping out of the driver's line of vision, we would carefully meander up beside a parked car just as it was about to pull away from the curb. The driver had to proceed cautiously so as to avoid spinning its wheels.

As it was moving from its parking spot, with commando-like prowess, Mike and I would squat-run, grabbing hold of its back bumper and "skiing" behind it on our smooth-soled rubber boots. Once the car reached about thirty miles-per-hour, we would release our grip on the bumper and slide a fair way before stopping. Of course, more often than not, we would end up on our backside—

which was fine. It was the face-down landings that were not so good.

The most advanced trip—about the equivalent of a black diamond trail on a ski slope—was the five blocks down Queen Street to Mississauga. The cars had to slow down before turning towards Virgil, so it was an easy slide to the side of the road. There, at the stop sign, we would pick up another pull right back to the store! (Ski lift, anybody?)

Because there were no snow tires at the time, there was a lot of slipping and skidding which gave the effect of being on a zigzag carnival ride. When a car used chains on its wheels, though, it made for a rough ride—but we were up to the challenge.

The townspeople were aware of our antics, and drove very carefully. I imagine our parents must have known too, but they only scolded us for losing so many mittens and wearing out our boots so quickly.

With the advent of the town snow plow, we had less opportunity to put our car-skiing skills to the test. Finally, it was the sanding of the roads that conclusively killed our fun. But it's good to remember that, when the "ski conditions" were right, unlike most ski bums, we did not have to pack up our gear and travel far away to get our kicks. Back in my day, we got our thrills right on the main street.

Enamored

By Grade Seven, the strap had faded to just a memory—for me, that is. However, I am afraid I had already developed somewhat of a reputation for being a trouble-making brat, so the girls I liked in my class gave me a wide berth, as most of their mothers protected their precious ones from the likes of me. (I suspect they learned too much about me at The Store.)

It was the style then for the younger "Old Town" boys to have a special friend who was a girl. While I had my cousin Donna and her girlfriends as pals, that was different. They were friends, but not "mine."

Then Holly made her liking known. Sweet, tiny, and one year younger than me, beneath her short, thick, black hair, Holly had the biggest, brownest eyes I had ever seen. Sometimes her face looked all eyes, but then she would flash her quirky, slanted smile and light up her face—and mine. She would also make a little skip when she started to speak. Another part of her charm, this made it seem as though she was hopping into the conversation.

Holly's father was an accomplished furniture- and boat-maker. Her dad and mine were business friends. And, respecting each other, they extended that respect to each other's children. This meant that Holly and I could be friends with little parental interference—which might be the reason we were able to stay good friends through our teen years.

Fortunately, since Mike was my blood brother, Holly, who really was not a tomboy, did not object to doing things with Mike and me. Mike had his own girl "friend", too, so we often made a five-some that consisted of Mike and his friend, Holly, and me, and, of course, my dog, Perky. On our best double dates (plus Perky), we explored the lake or played at Jack Green's.

Once, though, Holly came to get just me to go sledding. More like a real date, leaving even Perky behind, we took her toboggan to the great, long hill behind Fort George. That ride took us over two or three jumps and stopped just short of the River Road at Navy Hall and the Niagara River. I had ridden that same slope often with Mike and my cousins, but with Holly, it felt different. (Or maybe what made it different was the way Ma Simmons and my dad doted over us when we went back to the store for hot chocolate. I guess we were pretty cute!)

Another time, I took Holly to the show at Brock Theatre, and we actually held hands. This was a strange experience. Her hands were tiny and very warm, but still, my hand got tired, and even after it started to cramp, I kept holding her hand. I thought that was what was expected. I bet she did too. Not only was Holly's the first hand I held in a romantic fashion, hers were the first lips I kissed with passion, our kisses lasting four times longer than the little pecks I gave to my cousins.

In return for her affection, I am afraid I introduced Holly to a very bad habit. I stole some cigarettes from my Mother's purse and talked Holly into going behind a neighbour's shed to indulge. I took great care to teach her how to light up and draw in slowly so as not to choke. Mom's cigarettes were not my brand. Mild and filtered, they were definitely made for women; I only resorted to them when I could not "borrow" some "real" ones from Dad or The Store.

Normally I would not have been caught dead with those sissy smokes, but sharing with Holly was different. To complete my air of machismo, I would tear off the filter and put the other end in my mouth lighting the formerly filtered end. Very impressive, no doubt.

In her teens, Holly worked in Dad's store. Sometimes, we even worked the same shift. As we got older, we did quasi-date a couple of times, but there was no spark between us, so we just remained friends. I lost touch with Holly when I left Niagara. I hope she gave up smoking, as I did—and I wish her a good life.

A Red Hot Lesson

It was May, and the fireworks were in: cherry bombs, lady fingers, sky rockets, and Roman candles. These incendiary devices were a great help to us boys as we re-enacted World War II. Cherry bombs were grenades. Lady fingers were machine guns. Roman candles were bazookas.

We aimed the fireworks at each other, but were so adept at twisting and dodging that we were seldom hit. Anyway, the explosion of the shot was intermittent at best. There was always time to run. That is, unless someone got in the way.

One day, a few of us were firing Roman candles at one another, just out front of The Store. I was so caught up in our game I didn't notice that Linda, a girl I happened to like very much, had stepped out onto the sidewalk and right into my line of fire. I had launched the fiery red ball directly into her new, pink wool coat—a new, pink coat that now had a burnt, black hole scorched into it.

Scared into uncontrollable crying, Linda wouldn't let me console her, but just ran straight home. It wasn't very many minutes before her mom was on the phone to my dad.

The upshot was that I had to buy Linda a new coat, and I had to work for two weeks for free to do so. It was a pretty nice coat. I have always suspected my dad of making up the difference between my meager two-week salary and the cost of nice wool coat.

The other loss was Linda's good will. If she were ever to read this, I hope she would be willing to forgive me.

Father Weaver Serves Me Peppers

I had served at Sunday Mass on that particular warm, bright August day, and Father Weaver asked, "Bill would you like some lunch?"

We had fasted for communion and cleaned up when Mass was over. It was well after twelve—of course I was hungry.

In the garden at the back of the rectory, I saw a variety of freshly ripened vegetables. I recognized the tomatoes, but not some of the other vegetables. "What are these?" I asked, pointing to some I had never seen.

Father Weaver said, "These are peppers. The little ones are hot, and the big green and red ones are sweet. The red ones are the sweetest. Would you like some tomatoes and peppers for lunch?"

I said I would, and thanked him, and we went into the rectory. It was my first time there, and I could not get over how clean everything was. The sun shone brightly on the hardwood floor, and the house smelled of fresh polish.

The housekeeper greeted us, asking whether I would prefer a ham sandwich or peanut butter.

I told her, "Ham, please," and then followed Father Weaver's directions to the washroom. In it, the sunlight shining through a wonderful stained glass window created a kaleidoscope-like swirl of color on the walls. It was as if the sun and the breeze blowing through the trees outside were painting God's spirit inside this holy house.

I felt good in this house. There was the beautiful vegetable garden and the brilliant beauty of the stained glass, but also, the rectory was different in another way from our untidy, neglected Regent Street house: The rectory smelled clean; it smelled good—not of beer and stale cigarette smoke.

I made a vow that someday I would own a house like this, and then returned to the kitchen to ham, tomato, and lettuce sandwiches—with those fresh sliced peppers on the side—awaiting Father Weaver and me on a table decorated with a vase of fresh flowers.

The housekeeper asked if I would like chocolate or plain milk.

I said, "Plain, please," glad for my mother's instructions in etiquette. But when the housekeeper handed me a linen napkin, I wasn't sure what to do with it. I had used napkins before, but this one was bigger than a diaper, more like a towel.

She must have guessed I was puzzled, because she directed me to fold the huge napkin across my lap.

Father Weaver said a quick grace, and I picked up my sandwich. Along with the soft yeastiness of the white bread, I tasted a mingling of the juiciness of the ripe tomato, the saltiness of the ham, and the clean crunch of the lettuce.

Then Father said, "Try the red peppers."

I bit into the crunchy sweet slice and liked it instantly—and still do to this day.

It's funny. Nothing that happened afterwards with Father Weaver ever took away my taste for the particular sweet flavor of fresh, ripe, red peppers.

Ready, Aim, Fire

I got my first pellet pistol at the age of twelve. Knives for throwing, followed. A Wham-O Slingshot was next. Then I obtained a professional hunting bow and also managed to procure a World War II paratrooper's survival long-barrel pistol that boasted a 22-caliber barrel on top and a 410 shotgun barrel underneath.

I shared my weaponry with Mike. He added his Daisy Red Ryder BB gun to the armory, creating an arsenal that was just what every twelve-year old should have.

Or was it? Oddly, no one ever asked how I obtained all of my weapons. No matter how sly I thought I was, my friends and brothers knew what I had. I could not keep anything hidden from them. Weren't these items awfully expensive and awfully professional for a boy my age?

The answer to that is, Yes. Yes they were expensive! Even though I had saved money from working, how could I have purchased all of them? I could not have. I did not. My source was part of an even bigger secret.

But despite the manner in which I came by them, I did use and enjoy every piece in my collection. The slingshot and air pistol I took to school to have ready for hunting on the way home. They also held threatening enemies at bay. The BB gun we used when playing with the other boys on the weekends. The under-and-over pistol was for pheasants and rabbits—we had to bike out to the farms or the river a couple of miles from town to stealthily do our poaching.

Once the game was killed, Mike—or whoever else was with me—and I dressed it ourselves and could usually get my dad or Ma Simmons to cook it for us. Once we tried to cook something Boy-Scout method over an open fire, but ended up with undercooked, meat that was too tough to eat.

While we did shoot a lot, none of what we did seemed out of the ordinary for our time. Not until, that is, the day I killed a rare Arctic Owl. Perhaps I just made a mistake—but it showed me something about myself that I needed to understand.

It happened like this: Mike and I were meandering through Simcoe Park on the way to the dock, when I spotted this great white bird perched on a branch. It was just looking at us. Rather than appreciating the beauty of the bird, which I probably would have done just a year before, instead, I put a pellet in the chamber of my gun, pumped it up, pointed and fired.

The majestic bird tumbled to the ground. It was dead.

As I looked at the corpse, I knew in the very pit of my being that I had done a stupid thing. Mike knew, too. Shooting was for sparrows, for ducks, for target practice—not for exotic birds.

We took off running all the way to the dock, as if we could outrun what I had done.

While I knew I had done something I would always regret, that day, I did not understand the psychological trap I had been caught up in, snared in a way that would take me decades to unravel. But in the meantime, my captor had armed me, literally. And shooting that owl—with a gun he'd provided—allowed me to feel a bit of a false release.

Finders, Keepers

We tried caddying (and when I say, "we", it could mean me, plus any or all of the following: Mike, or Neil, or Pat, or Jack or any of the other urchins that hung around with me). Caddying was too difficult. It tied up at least two hours when we should have been having fun. On top of that, the effort was not worth the money. Finding golf balls was much more rewarding in every way.

One approach we had was to "find" a ball before it was lost. To do this, we might strategically place ourselves in an area where most right-handed golfers would slice over the hill or into the lake. We would watch them slice, and then, if the golfer asked us if we'd seen his ball, we would enthusiastically misdirect him, pointing to an area twenty or more yards away from where we knew the ball to be. The golfer would give up after a quick search, and once he was out of sight, we would retrieve it.

Another method required one of us to dress in a bathing suit and position himself below the hill as the ball came flying over. The bathing-suited entrepreneur would then pick up the ball and throw it out into the water beyond easy retrieval.

When the golfer looked over the hill and saw one of us by the lake's edge, he would invariably ask, "Did you see my ball?"

"Yes," was the reply. "It bounced out into the lake."

"Would you get it for me?" the frustrated golfer would ask.

"Certainly . . . for a quarter."

But as much fun as the dive-and-deliver method was, the real fun was the second hole. Niagara had to have had the only golf hole in the world where the golfer had to stroke an iron blindly over a moat, because the green was right in front of Fort Mississauga.

Smart golfers, prepared for this challenge, would send up a spotter to the top of the hill to watch for their balls. But on busy days, with players backed up behind them, it got too time-consuming to have someone run down the moat, then back up the hill, then back to take their shot. So, instead, most golfers would try to bank their balls off the Fort and onto the green. But the Fort was rough, and the trajectory was anybody's guess.

This is where we came in. Off to the left of that green was the Fort's powder room, complete with covered tunnel. With its broken gate, this was a perfect spot to get out of the rain, as well as a great place for lovers, and, I suspect (because of the smell of urine that began to be evident in the 1950s), a safe haven for the homeless.

Despite the fact that we shared this spot with others, we were convinced the antique establishment had been created just for us. At the entrance of the powder room there was a circular brick tunnel that acted as a buffer wall to protect the gun powder. Once inside, we could stoop-walk through the tunnel from one entrance right around the outside of the powder room to the other. That second entrance was an ideal hiding spot that offered a great vantage from which to see where those tricky golf balls landed.

Then, we could either permanently "borrow" a ball, retreating into the tunnel with it, and not emerging until the golfer had given up looking for his ball. Or, we could trade out an old ball if a new one came flying our way. Then, from inside, we would listen to the arguments about whose ball was whose.

The most humorous events were when we took the furthest ball and put it into the hole, which led to too many holes in one.

Sadly, the Pro Shop figured out what we were doing, even though they could not catch us. The club responded by putting out a warning, suggesting golfers always have a spotter up on the hill.

Boy, those adults sure did know how to spoil our fun.

More Balls and More

I was slumbering soundly, when I heard the crack of gravel at my window. It was 6:30 a.m., and the sun was just coming up, but Mike was waving me to come on down. This meant to use the knotted rope hidden under my bed—and the gloves. I had already learned my lesson about sliding down a rope without gloves leading to major rope burns. The first time I tried that trick, I had to let the ropes go and jump, almost breaking through the basement's bulkhead door!

Mike was in a hurry. It had raged and stormed for the past two days, and the lake's turbulent six-to-eight foot waves had now quieted to glass. At the golf course, Mike aimed for a spot near the Fort. It was as if he had a sixth sense for where the balls would have ended up.

Sure enough, we swam out about thirty yards, and duck-dove right into what seemed like a treasure trove of golf balls, all swirled together into a golf ball nest—so many, that we needed to hide them before getting a sack to take them home. Before we left, I led Mike to another prime spot right beside Fort Mississauga. We dove again, this time among the wooden piles that were sunk into the lake that we called "ramparts."

We hit the jackpot again! Some of the crevices around the posts held three or four balls, but most held at least one. It took us several trips, with our bathing suits full, to get all those golf balls back to our hiding place.

As great as that day was, Mike's lost-and-found skills proved to extend well beyond golf balls. One afternoon when I was working in The Store, Mike burst in looking very excited. Dad gave us his famous "work comes first" look, but even this could not stop Mike. As I finished up with the customer I was helping, Mike produced a soggy wallet. The bills inside were so wet they were pasted together.

"Where did you get that?" I asked.

He told me that he had been looking for balls in the water (of course!), when his foot squished into what he thought was a huge rag. When he dragged it out of the water, he discovered it was a pair of pants. He lugged the pants to the rocks and went through the pockets, where he found the wallet.

Mike was an honest kid; he wanted to find out who owned it, but he was smart enough not to try to pull it apart and risk ripping the papers—including the money—inside.

Although many suicides (or murder victims) went over Niagara Falls, the rapids and rocks were more than rough on the bodies, and they usually remained dressed in their tattered clothes. Therefore, although bodies were certainly not unheard of, a lonely pair of pants with its wallet intact was unusual.

My dad and Ma Simmons thought we should call the police, but first, Dad carefully dried the open wallet. Eventually, he was able to extract the driver's license, and find a phone number to call, a Toronto number.

When the owner answered, he was very pleased that his pants had been found. He told dad that he and his wife had been walking along the ice when she fell in. She panicked, he stripped off his pants, jumped in to rescue her, and—minus pants—they got back to nearby friends, who helped them dry out. A few days later, the man came to retrieve the wallet and gave Mike twenty dollars. That is a lot of golf balls.

But Mike's luck—or talent—didn't stop there. Another time, Mike found a purse on the side of the road and brought it in to The Store. Dad was just opening it up to find out who it belonged to, when the phone rang. The woman was inquiring about her purse, as she had put it on the roof of the car while she put in her parcels and forgotten it there. This time, for his honesty, Mike was rewarded with profuse thanks and a couple of dollars.

Much More than Balls

Some summer days were definitely dog days. Even if I could get away from The Store, if it was too hot for golfers, there would be no new golf balls to seek out—and since the old balls had already been found, and just swimming or lying around was boring, we would have to resort to treasure hunting.

Our "treasure hunting" was really more like archaeology or geology—even though we wouldn't have known then what those words meant. We would start by digging into the slimy blue clay out in front of the Fort using our pocket knives, or flattened wooden sticks or, best of all, trowel-like rocks as tools. Sometimes we would just roll the blue clay into marble-sized balls, bake them beside a fire or dry them in the sun, and then shove them into our pockets for later use as slingshot ammunition.

Other times, though, we would discover actual treasure.

Once, Mike and I were digging and uncovered something made out of metal. When we cleaned it off, we saw we'd found a musket ball. We were not the only kids who found relics from the War of 1812—nor was this the first we'd found ourselves. What made this special was the place where we'd found it. Usually, cannon balls and shot were discovered either in the water or much closer to the fort, not as far out front of it as we had situated ourselves. As you can imagine, we kept our site a secret. And we kept on digging.

After Mike found that musket ball, I uncovered a bone, then a soldier's button. We dug on and found more bones and more rusted, deteriorated relics. Some crumbled in our hands as we tried to extract them, but we kept digging, imagining eventually we were going to find gold—or at least some sort of coins. No such luck.

Finally, we covered up all the evidence of our excavation, split up our treasure, and went our separate ways.

When I showed my finds to my dad, he cautioned me, saying that the Fort was on Federal Land; that the golf course only leased it, and that there were history buffs who might not take kindly to kids excavating historical artefacts!

While he believed the bones were probably from animals, he was not able to say what kind of animal, only that he didn't think they came from either pigs or cows. But what he did think was that we'd uncovered an old dump that had been established just outside the Fort's perimeter.

Dump or not, Mike and I weren't telling about our new treasure-hunting site. But Niagara is a small town, and secrets are hard to keep. Soon we learned that other kids had found quite a few more relics there. I even saw a musket in reasonable shape that had been uncovered by a much younger kid who sometimes hung around with us. (In fact, as of this writing, I know of one person who still has a collection of pieces from that site—including some cannon balls which are in very good condition.)

Despite the competition (and the government!), Mike and I snuck back to do further "research." We sure made a lot more blue-clay sling-shot ammo, but, sadly, we only recovered a few more relics that summer. What we did find included a knife, some more buttons, a much-rusted bayonet, and many clay pipes. All of those we took with us. But, although we found quite a few more of them, we left the bones.

I still wonder about those bones. Recently, more and more bodies that date from 1812 have been uncovered. So many years later, in my mind's eye, I can see a 19th century surgeon tossing away those body parts.

Like so much of what I found as a boy growing up in Niagara, the treasures I found with Mike were traded, lost, or stolen, leaving me with nothing to show for them but memories of digging into cool blue clay on a series of dog-day afternoons.

It's probably just as well. With the 200th year anniversary and re-enactment of the war between Britain and the U.S., I suspect that Mike and I would have had to give any that we still owned to the American Historical Society, because they would probably claim the relics had originated in the States and had just gotten lost in Niagara.

This would accord with the widely-held understanding that, since the Fort itself was not built until 1814, it could not have been fired on by the U.S. Of course, strictly speaking, the yet-to-be-erected building of Fort Mississauga could not have been fired upon. However, the battery fortification on Point Mississauga did receive intensive fire from U.S. ships as they passed the Point to land a party not far away. Their mission was to revenge the burning of Lewiston.

On December 10th, 1813, Americans did set fire to the Town of Newark (now, Niagara-on-the-Lake). And since a fort can be defined simply as "a fortified position stationed with troops," I suspect history will eventually show that the relics Mike and I and many other young treasure hunters found are as a result of that invasion, which is known as the Battle of Fort Mississauga Point.

Ye Olde Spring

While Niagara-on-the-Lake had many attractive attributes, its town water supply was not one of them. In the 'forties and 'fifties, the waterworks housed in The Old Pump House—which was built in 1891 and was state of the art for its day—pumped water directly from the river. The filtration system was only capable of removing solids through a sand filter and adding some chlorination. Later, carbon powder was added.

It wasn't until the 'sixties that activated carbon was perfected, which would remove a wide variety of chemicals. In the early 'seventies, while working for a chemical company, I introduced Niagara to special activated carbon to remove most of the chlorinated chemical by-products which were being dumped into the river by the chemical plants. These were upstream at both the American and Canadian Falls. This left Niagara in the 1950s with what can only be called "unique-tasting" water.

But people from out of town, not familiar with the reasons for the water's taste, would have a cup of coffee in Dad's store and rave about it. They would ask to buy our house-brand coffee—and then be disappointed to learn that our house brand was just Maxwell House and could be bought anywhere. It was our water, our lump-free, complex -chemical abomination, which was our secret ingredient.

The townspeople did have a source of great tasting water, though. It came from a spring that was located very close to Queens Beach. When we got thirsty after swimming, we just ran down Decatur Street to a short distance across from the Elliot house. Here we had ourselves a delicious cold drink. From just below the railway trestle, the spring flowed from the side of the hill, into a horse trough alongside the road. The overflow would pass underneath the road and appear as a stream on the other side.

Trestle and Horse Drinking Trough

Every kid fisherman knew this stream on Barry Wright's property as a great place to ferret out the crayfish that silver bass hungered for. All you had to do was gently remove the small rocks that they hid beneath and grab them before they could flip into a new hiding spot. Although the point was to catch the little shellfish to use as bait, I do believe that Mike and I had more fun catching the crayfish than we did using them to catch silver bass.

Ye Olde Spring was a part of Niagara's history. When you sipped that refreshing, cool water you were literally drinking in Niagara's past—both the good and the bad! Dad nicknamed the spring, aqua vita, the water of life. But maybe it should have been called, aqua mortem, the water of death. The stream was ultimately condemned by the Health Department because, after its origination in the commons, it trickled past all the privies that had been used for the many army camps since 1812. Then it flowed through two graveyards, mixing truly historical DNA particles into the sparkling elixir!

Still, people would line up on weekends with pails, pots, milk cans, and glass milk bottles to carry away this fresh spring water, while we kids just used our hands to get our fill.

In our house, we knew that winter was definitely over when Dad would go to Ye Olde Spring and gather mounds of watercress for a spring salad—complete with a few centuries-worth of local DNA.

Breath of Life, I Have You Back

Pat and I had just finished diving and were on the dock watching the Cayuga prepare to depart. The gangplank was already up, and the ropes were being released, when Pat shouted," Follow me!" Without hesitation, I jumped over the railing at the first gangplank hatch. The crew was busy checking equipment. We had snuck on before, and the crew had just seemed to ignore us, those feisty brats, so, as the boat made its way from the dock, churning full force against the current, we fully expected to hitch a ride to Queenston.

What we did not know was that the sailors had been told not to let us on board like this, that we needed to come aboard with a pass, properly attired, like all the other passengers. So we were surprised when we heard the crew hollering, "Get off the boat! You can't come aboard!"

Quickly, we hid behind a post. Minutes passed, and then we heard shouting and feet pounding. We knew we would be in big trouble if they found us, so we decided to get off before we could be thrown off. That was when we dove off the Cayuga in unison. I was sucking in a deep breath as I flew through the air, and, BAM: I hit the water and was sucked into a 4,300 horse-power tornado of water.

I was immediately pulled down, down, down, only to be jerked back up by the action of the turbo engine. At the top, I managed to grab a breath, only to be sucked back down again, rolling and flipping as the pounding, deafening, pulsations of the vibrating propeller pistons chased me, and I was torpedoed to the surface again. I was trapped in a relentless roller coaster of a fire-hose jet stream. I had no choice but to go with the flow as I was thrown up and dragged back down, back and forth, back and forth, intermittently catching my breath at the top of the ride.

In what seemed like forever, but must have been just a few moments, I was spit out into a calmer stream. The stream I found myself in was less violent, its wake less rough. This was the very same stream we often swam into for a roller coaster ride, and I was thanking God that my brothers had taught me to conserve my breath when they were giving me my duck-and-dive lessons.

That was when I noticed Pat bobbing up and down a few feet away. "God damn that was one hell of a ride!" he shouted. But it didn't seem like that kind of fun to me. I was scared to the marrow of my bones.

Eventually, we made it out of the water, and I went home, exhausted. Lying in my bed reflecting on the nightmare events of the day, I realized that through all that watery turbulence, I had seen a bright white light shining—even though my eyes were closed. Even as I emerged from the water, the brilliant glow shone through my eyelashes, wet with river water.

I never told anyone else, but I knew I had seen my guardian angel, Michael. Even with all my fortitude and stubborn bravado, I had to admit that I had come inches from being sucked into death that day. But mysteriously, I—we—had survived. Because we dove out as far as possible instead of jumping, because we leapt from the side of the ship rather than off the back, we didn't get caught up in any of the boat's dissecting propellers.

We survived. When I told my brother what happened, Jack's response was, "You dumb ass! That is how Leslie Price drowned. He was sucked into the propellers." While it's true that Leslie did drown, in my research for this book, I was not able to learn his exact cause of death. All I found was that his body was discovered at Queens Beach.

But, yes, I survived. My patron saint, Michael the Archangel, had my back again. And I returned from that adventure with a new sense of self-worth; somehow, my life was meant for something.

I could hear Maw saying, "Just listen and you will find your calling." Well, that afternoon, tossed by a force I could not control, I definitely felt the blast of the call. What it was saying, precisely, would take a few more years for me to understand. And today, I ask myself, if on that day I had drawn my last breath, what would have happened to my future family?

It took many decades for me to realize that many things in life are important. However, the most important by far is my next fresh breath of life.

Baby Death

It was a Thursday, and Dad and I were working in The Store. Dad said, "Father Weaver called today. He wants you to serve at ten o'clock on Saturday."

I had planned on going to the lake with Mike. "Why can't Father get one of the other servers?" I wanted to know.

"He asked specifically for you," my father replied calmly.

"Me? That's not fair. I have to work at four, and there goes my whole day. Mike and I had everything planned, and he's going away Sunday. Now because of this stupid Mass everything is ruined." I didn't hold anything back in my unhappiness.

My dad understood. "You can switch your shift to Sunday. Mass will be over by eleven, and then you will have lots of time. Besides, Father's been very good to you. You owe it to him, and he doesn't ask for much."

Well, that was that. I had been asked to serve at Mass many times, and always found it a long and boring process. I did not do well with Latin, but I had discovered that if I mumbled, like some of the visiting missionary priests for whom I served, I could get by.

However this time, I wasn't asked, I was conscripted, which made me mad. Damn it, I had other plans! I knew that for some reason Father Weaver had made me his favorite, but this was too much.

Begrudgingly, I arrived at the church in time for the ten o'clock service that Saturday.

As I was donning the surplice, Father Weaver said, "Thank you for coming. Now, I need you to be extra kind."

What the heck did that mean? I wondered.

As Mass started, I became aware of the cold, somber mood. Sure, it was a funeral Mass, but it was still much different from other funerals I'd attended. Then I saw the white shoebox of a casket that was being gently carried to the front. As it was placed by the altar rail with extreme reverence, I realized that this was a baby's funeral.

The cold feeling I had sensed was the hurt, the lack of hope, and the despair that the parents, grandparents, and other relatives were feeling.

Everyone came to the rail for communion. When I placed the paten under their chins, I saw a strange, numb, look in their wet eyes as they fluttered them closed while receiving the host. As Mass was ending, Father Weaver grabbed me by the arm and whispered, "You carry the box. I will carry the incense."

The "box" he meant was the tiny, white casket.

I was to carry it by myself, just me, to the grave for last prayers. Why was it up to me to carry the casket? Had the parents requested a child pallbearer? I wanted to protest, but there was no way to do so. Besides, it was probably Father Weaver's idea. This priest was definitely different from those I had known before. Reluctantly, I responded by doing what I was told to do.

I was darkly afraid of being clumsy with this tiny, dead body. My dad's nickname for me was "Sloppy Willie." But the little casket was surprisingly light, and I managed to follow Father from the altar through the small, lean-to sacristy, through the back door, and down the three back steps without mishap. With everyone following us, we led the quiet procession the few yards to the gravesite.

Someone took the casket from me. Father gave me back the incense. Standing at the grave, I thought, "This baby must have been baptized in order to be buried, so he is guaranteed to go to heaven and not end up frozen in limbo." I focused on his little soul floating off to heaven and wished I could go with him. But in my limited state of grace, I would be going down, not up.

While I focused on the prayers for the baby, I accepted that some of them were meant for me.

As the body, in its tiny box, was lowered into the cold, damp ground, a cool breeze riffled through the tall pines surrounding the cemetery. The atmosphere was a mix of pine and incense, prayers and tears. For my part, I tried to blank out what was happening from my mind, to be tough, so I wouldn't cry.

Later as Father and I were changing, a man entered the sacristy. He awkwardly slapped an envelope into my hand and one into Father Weaver's hand. My envelope contained five dollars.

This was the first time I had faced death from outside the circle, but still been a part of it. I didn't want to remember the funeral, but it seems I had no choice. No matter what tricks I played in my own mind, I have never forgotten carrying the tiny casket to its grave.

***

If you ever visit Niagara-on-the-Lake, please visit the cemetery at the back of St. Vincent de Paul. Feel the presence of the tombstones and the departed beneath them. Smell the fragrance of the pines mixed with the mold of the earth. And imagine, if you can, a young boy swinging the incense in its censer, wafting away the smoke from the mourners' eyes, as he tries to comprehend the terrors, strains, and stresses of his young life. Then, if you have a moment, say a special prayer for that young boy who grew up to be me.

Jack, Bill, Doug

Resurrection

The phones were ringing. The streets were full of anxious gossip. The police were interviewing anyone who might have information. The prayer groups were praying. The hospital was on alert. The U.S. Coast Guard in Youngstown had been notified. Even the undertaker had been informed to prepare for the worst.

Earlier that day, many hours before the crisis which set all of this civic action into motion, Neil, Pat, and I were on the loose. We had finished diving at the *Cayuga* to a sparse crowd, but had earned enough to buy fries and a pop at the canteen. Still in our bathing suits and shoes, we wandered over to the slip to look at the minnows, rock bass, and frogs that lurked around the boats.

As was usual at the picturesque scene of boats, boat houses, and light house, several artists had set up easels and were busy painting. We noticed three brightly dressed women painters in huge straw hats and colorful smocks. To us, who were already in a giggling mood, they looked like something out of the funny papers. As we got close we could see that two of the paintings were progressing into pretty pictures, but the third painting looked all fuzzy and smeary. I said, "If I handed that in at school, I would get an F instead of my usual C."

The others burst into laughter, but when the painter turned around and gave us a dirty look over her granny glasses which would have made any teacher proud, we knew it was time to blow that place.

We ran along, picking up rocks to throw at the lake gulls and anything else that deserved to be heaved at. We meandered around the slip having a throwing contest, attacking anything we could grab or root out from the boards. When we ended up at Neil's house on Ricardo Street, we headed to the back where there was a big stone wheel, which Neil's dad used to sharpen tools. We took turns sitting in the seat, pedaling to make the stone go faster and faster.

Once we tired of that, Neil went into the back garden and picked two gray muskmelons; then, in his tiny kitchen, Neil opened a can of pork and beans. He split the melon into pieces and the three of us shared that and the beans, chomping with gusto and making our chests a sticky mess. When the eating was done, we raced back to the dock to wash off the sticky remnants of our lunch.

At the diving platform, we kicked off our shoes into the pile of clothes we'd left by our bikes when we'd been diving. Then we scampered up the ladder, pausing on the second level. When we were all in line, we shouted, "Last one in is a dirty bastard" and jumped in unison, hitting the cold, deep water as one.

Finally, tired, we went to lie down in the sand. Here we played "blue balls." This game required a stick to be placed upright in a sand pile. Each boy had to sweep away some of the sand until the stick fell. The boy that made the stick fall had to jump back into the cold water. When our bodies were hot from the sun, the shock of the cold water reverberated all the way to the testicles. The result? Blue balls.

This game got boring, and someone suggested we explore the underside of the dock, which was anchored both to the shore and to the bottom of the river, some twenty feet down. We slipped into the cool green river near the dock's edge, where we found that the underside was a crisscrossing maze of huge posts, wide planks, and the iron rods that fused it all together.

We could see that the streaks of filtered light that lay along the surface were snuffed out by the dark water deeper down. It was spooky under the dock, and the quiet lapping of the water made it feel even spookier. We first heard—then spotted—a gang of huge river rats splashing into the water from the shore.

We scrambled into the open river, laughing and calling each other "chicken", while breast-stroking up-river against the fast current. Soon we had fought our way past the lighthouse into the mouth of the slip beyond the customs dock. The water there was stagnant, murky, and distinctly warmer, and gave off the rotting smell of lake weed and vegetation.

Inside the enclave we found a perfect play world, complete with tied boats whose dangling ropes we could swing on. We swam halfway down the slip to a boat whose front hatch was partially open. Up the rope we hoisted ourselves, landing on the boat's deck and slithering across the smooth, white deck into the galley.

We pulled the hatch closed, locking it behind us. In the small room where we found ourselves, the curtains were closed on tiny windows, allowing in enough soft, filtered light to let us see a pair of white vinyl benches and a small table. We could barely stand up, but the benches were comfortable to sit or lie on.

It took Pat only a few minutes to find the stores of beer and girlie magazines. At twelve, this was everything we could dream of. We relished our foamy, warm beer, as Neil explained that was the way the English drank their beer. When we uncovered a stash of crackers and nuts, our party was complete.

Time passed quickly. At some point, I glanced through the small window and saw the sun setting. I also saw a group of men using high-powered fire hoses to wash the sides of the slip. Muck and debris floated to the surface near the center. In a flat row boat, men were throwing three-sided, anchor-like hooks into the water and hauling them back out.

"I wonder what they are doing," I said.

Neil said, "It must be some kind of practice drill."

Then Pat looked out the other small window and said, "Holy crap, there are all kinds of people out there. We had better get out." But since we couldn't get out without being seen, we decided to wait until dark to make our escape.

Unfortunately for our getaway plans, at dark, big search lights from the fire and police vehicles lit up the area as if it were noon. We were starting to get scared, but decided that sooner or later everyone would go away. We just had to be patient.

A bit later, I heard a noise on the bow of the boat. I carefully unlocked the hatch and raised it enough to peek out. My friend Frank was sitting cross-legged on the deck, enjoying the spectacle.

I whispered, "Hey, Frank."

Frank turned around, startled, and said, "What?"

"Why the hell all are these people here?"

Frank asked, "Are the three of you in there?"

When I asked him why he wanted to know, his answer was, "Because you're all supposed to be drowned. They are searching for your bodies."

I made Frank promise not to tell, still thinking we could get out after everybody went home. Then I locked the hatch and went back to report the situation to Neil and Pat.

The beer started going through us, so we took turns going to the head, but it would not flush. By that time, our confined quarters stunk of rotting lake weed, urine, beer, and beer farts. We had other things on our minds, though, that made the stench seem unimportant.

Suddenly, we heard a harsh voice demanding, "Is this the boat that they are hiding in?"

Another voice answered meekly, "Yes sir."

The three of us fled for the head, closed the door enclosing all the rank perfume inside. I sat on the toilet seat with my two partners in crime packed on either side. Then a few rough voices demanded we open up. "Come out this instant or I will blow this lock off," someone shouted through the door.

Bystanders shouted, "Don't shoot. You may hit the kids."

While we huddled, shaking, in our quandary, we heard whispers, followed by a loud splintering sound. Someone had put a chain on the cabin door, attached it to his car bumper, and pulled the door right off its hinges.

We three, drained, slightly drunk, remorseful penitents were marched by the police, down the gangplank. Bright lights were everywhere. The flash bulbs blinded us, as we disembarked to shouts of "If he were my son, I would horse whip him," and "They should be sent to jail," and "Imagine all the worrying and trouble they caused."

My dad was there with Father Weaver. Dad gave me a hug as he led me through the angry crowd to the car. He said very little, but I could tell he was not angry.

At home, Mother, slobbering and also reeking of beer, greeted us with a slurred, "Thank God, you are alive."

Dad only said, "You had better have a hot bath and get to bed."

It wasn't until the next day that we learned what had caused the panic. The canteen owner, who had served us our French fries and pop early in the day, noticed our bikes and clothes, which we had left near the sand pile at the dock. Worried because he had not seen us for many hours, while our clothes were still there, he alerted the police. The three lady artists reported that they had seen us swimming to the U.S. With that, the search was on.

How they actually found us is down to Frank. After he left us on the boat, his mom wanted to know what was wrong with him, saying he looked like he had seen a ghost. He couldn't keep it to himself anymore, so he told her. She told the authorities, and they hauled us out of our cozy little hole.

On the recommendation of Father Weaver, I was sent away for the rest of the summer, both to keep me out of trouble and to avoid further embarrassment for my dad.

There was never a newspaper report of our "resurrection." It may well be that, since my father was a prominent business man, president of the Chamber of Commerce, and friends with the publisher of the *Niagara Advance*, the police chief, and the fire chief, once Dad paid for the damage to the boat, there was no reason to continue the episode further. So, at the end of the day, it was just an exercise drill, after all.

A Love Lesson

I fell in love so many times with so many different girls. These budding flowers sashayed into The Store in pairs, ready to practice their feminine wiles on me, the kid behind the counter.

First, they would approach the soda fountain with a smile or a slight, shy giggle. Then the serious witch-craft would begin. Using a combination of big eyes and pheromones, they would double-barrel me, and I would have to bring everything I had to stay afloat.

Once, a set of twin sisters from Buffalo came in and hit me with their double whammy. I responded to this pair with my best macho moves, and when I found out that they attended Mass, I bragged a bit about being an altar boy. That Sunday, they showed up at church. At communion, when I held the paten under their chins, both of them blushed, peaking at me through fluttering eyes.

I was making headway!

But after the service, Father Weaver, who had had his sharp eyes on what was happening at the rail, killed any chance I had with those cute girls.

He said, "I would caution you on what you are doing. Their father is a chief of police." And that ended that.

Looking back with less innocent eyes, I truly suspect Father Weaver destroyed those particular romantic dreams on purpose—and for a purpose.

Brother's Blood

Doug and I had the job of keeping the pop cooler full. If it was a hot July Sunday, this required constant running back and forth to the wooden cases of pop bottles stored behind the dispensary. This area was even hotter than the rest of the store, because not only was there no air circulating back there, but there was also a sky light, allowing the blazing sun to penetrate and intensify the heat. The pop was always warm when we grabbed it to take it to the cooler.

If the nights cooled down enough, the pop in its cases cooled, too. But in late July or August, when a heat wave would hit for a couple weeks, there was no cooling off. The pop, along with everything and everybody else, would stay warm—so warm, that the cooler could not keep up with the turnover of hot bottles for cold.

One hot day, we were almost out of pop and the delivery truck was nowhere to be seen. When it finally arrived, the driver remarked, as he wheeled in the pop cases that the reason he was so late was that his radiator boiled over.

While we had been awaiting the pop delivery, the iceman had filled the cooler's many vacant spots with lots of ice. It was ice cold in there. This would be a perfect place to cool the hot bottles of pop, right?

With our cold pop supply so low, Doug and I had to play catch up. Doug started with the ginger ale bottles which had just been wheeled into the storage area. He grabbed four, locking them in between the fingers of both hands. The first one, he stuck right into the fresh ice in the cooler—and it exploded with a blast that resembled a small bomb.

As the first bottle exploded, Doug dropped the other three, which also exploded when they hit the floor. Suddenly, from a peaceful, if hot, afternoon, we were in the middle of chaos: Doug's hand was bleeding; glass and ginger ale were everywhere; shards had flown like shrapnel all the way to the front door.

Off to the doctor, went Doug. I stayed behind to clean up the mess.

Here's my dad's scientific explanation of what happened: The pop had become extremely hot while the truck was broken down in the sun. When the dissolved carbon dioxide gas was heated it became unstable. The pressure of the heated gas exerted pressure on the bottle.

The extreme temperature difference between the very cold water and the bottle caused the glass to shatter.

Needless to say, everyone handling the pop from then on took great care not to toss over-heated bottles into the cooler—and not to shake up the pop, either. Of course, "everyone" was mainly me, as Doug's hand took weeks to heal.

Niagara, the Movie

The Table Rock Complex in Niagara Falls juts out over the Niagara River. It is the heart of Niagara Falls-where every year eight million visitors stand yards away from the thundering Horseshoe Falls.

This film *Niagara* was filmed in 1952 and has been credited with launching the film career of Marilyn Monroe. The film starred Marilyn Monroe, Joseph Cotten, Jean Peters, and Max Showalter. Filming took place in Niagara Falls, Ontario, at the Carillon Bell Tower, Table Rock, tunnels located behind the Falls .

Along with thousands, Doug, his girlfriend and I went to Niagara Falls to watch the filming at Table Rock. We found an elevated spot where we could see above the excited crowd. We could see in the distance that which we concluded was the movie set. We spied some actors which we later claimed were Joseph Cotton and Jean Peters.

We told the story many times including Marilyn Monroe, too. Heck I didn't know one actor from another. At the distance we were it could have been anybody.

Burning Springs, near Table Rock, was also a tourist attraction that provided another activity for those who came to see the Falls or to watch the filming. Doug, whose girlfriend worked there, had gotten us free passes to go into the hall that housed the attraction.

Once we got inside, we found a large stone well with a spring bubbling up inside it. In the guide's lecture, he told us that it was Indians who had first discovered this spring.

Apparently an Indian brave was walking past the site one night carrying a lit torch to light his way. He passed the torch over the little stream, and "Whump!" The whole spring lit up. After that, the Indians maintained the spring as a place to worship the gods of fire and water. Then, of course, the white man came and took it away. Eventually, it was discovered that natural gas, formed from behind the Falls, leaked into the spring and created the fiery phenomenon.

To prove the point, our guide took a glass, dipped it into the well, and then put a cigarette lighter to it. In the dim hall, the other sightseers and I watched in amazement as the top of the glass leapt into flames. Then, with a theatrical flourish, the guide blew out the flames and drank the glass of water.

I clapped with everyone else, but Doug just looked at me and laughed. The whole thing was a con, he told me. The well contained piped-in city water. However, gas was also piped in beneath the well by Consumers Gas. When the glass was immersed, the guide filled it with gas as well as water. Voila! No Indian braves were required for this magic, just the Provincial Utilities department cooperation.

I was stunned. "How could they get away with such a lie?" I asked, indignantly.

Doug laughed again, and said, "Everyone in Niagara relies on tourist dollars. Besides, the tourists need entertainment, so no one is hurt."

I've since learned that there are large deposits of natural gas all along the Niagara River and Lake Erie.

The Wonders of Niagara, indeed.

FIRST LOVE

Too Young to Love, Too Engrossed to Care

"CARLA COSTA," I LIKED THAT NAME

It was early in the summer of 1953. Carla Costa (not her real name) came to Niagara from the U.S. to stay in her parent's cottage for the summer. The first time I saw her, she was standing on the corner outside Fields Drug Store, surrounded by boys who were trying to get her attention. She was tiny and cute—and radiated what I thought was a blushing, innocent shyness—and I felt immediately challenged.

I had pulled up on my stallion (commonly called a "bicycle"). She glanced up at me with a look as penetrating as Elizabeth Taylor's famous violet-eyed gaze. From the intensity of her stare, I could tell that Carla Costa already knew who I was.

I patted my crossbar and commanded her to hop on. She did, and we sped away, leaving the other boys standing on the sidewalk, wide-eyed, and drop-jawed.

For our first "date", I took Carla across the street to Simcoe Park to "talk." What I learned in that "talk" was that first impressions can be wrong. Miss Carla Costa was not shy.

The next day, when I met Carla's mother, she mentioned the grass stains that had appeared on the back of Carla's new clothes the day before.

What could I say? Guilty as charged.

Safety First

When I first met Carla, I was struggling. I was trying to deny, if not forget, my past.

Maw used to say, "God works in mysterious ways." If this is the case, I guess God knew I needed someone to help me transcend the struggles of my past and move toward hope for my future—and that summer, maybe, in a strange and mysterious way, He sent Carla.

Before Carla, I had had many friends who were girls. I may not have had any sisters, but I did have Cousin Donna, and I learned a lot about girlish wiles in The Store—in particular, their varying moods around period time, as some of my co-workers were girls, and most of our teen-aged female customers were not shy about buying their feminine products from me.

I was a soda jerk and had some of the status that went with the job. Girls who liked The Store mostly liked me and found me a willing mark. With these early girlfriends, I learned to fast dance and slow dance and spent time practising various kissing techniques.

Even so, at just-turned fifteen, while I had always been advanced as far as getting into regular trouble, I had not gotten romantically entangled. But Carla was different. Our relationship was a deep, hormonal, puppy love. Very quickly we were committed and going steady. The only problem we had, as far as I could tell, was that while she was only five feet tall, I towered over her by almost a foot.

For us to kiss, she had to stretch up on her tiptoes, and I had to bend down to her awkwardly.

Then one day Carla whispered, "We do not have to always stand up to kiss."

Ah.

The couch, the beach, the lawn, anyplace we could make ourselves horizontal became our entwined playground. Although the throbbing down below corresponded to the throbbing in my heart, nothing was spoken. We would just keep on grinding.

Still, for all the heat that Carla and I generated, we were careful—very careful.

(Strangely, what I had already endured prior to my time with Carla did not interfere with my sexual blossoming. But our relationship did help confirm that I had turned a corner. A healing transformation had begun.)

My religious belief, coupled with the experiences I'd had at the drug store, kept me from crossing the final boundary. I had heard too many first-hand stories about how thinking with "the little head" could produce life-altering mistakes. I knew about venereal diseases and their painful treatments. Worse, I had seen older boys who had to quit school and go to work to support their babies. I knew of girls who had to go away to visit an aunt for several months.

But the most threatening of any of the checks on my surging hormones was Carla's too-comfortable closeness with her mother. Carla shared everything with her mother: not just some things, but everything—in detail.

So, yes, I made sure we were careful.

"Marty" and "Joyce"

When I was not working at my Dad's Drug Store, Carla and I saw each other at every available opportunity. At the very beginning, I included my close friends on our dates. Then, for a while, it was just the two of us. Finally, our two became four, as her parents joined us for most of our outings.

This seemed unusual to me, to say the least. It started when her parents told me to call them by their first names. Up until then, I had never called a married couple by anything but "Mr." and "Mrs." Older, single women were always "Miss." With single men, it was different. They almost always gave me permission to call them by their first names, and I did so comfortably.

At first, not calling her parents the more conventional Mr. and Mrs. Costa made me uneasy, but the payoff was worth it. "Marty" and "Joyce" treated me as a friend.

This led to the second arrangement I had difficulty accepting as normal: I could kiss Carla when her parents were present. I guess this was an off-shoot of Carla telling her mom everything I said and did, but it still seemed unusual. However, even this parental observation did not slow down what was going on between us!

What I realize now, is that this was not as outrageous as it seemed to me. Of course, Carla's parents were more liberal than was typical in Niagara at the time. But even taking that into account, it needs to be noted that this was an era when it was not seen as a failure for a young man to quit school after Grade Ten. He might quite respectably take on an apprenticeship to learn a trade, or go to work in one of the many factories on either side of the border. Getting a job was relatively easy after sixteen. In fact, farmers' sons, who were needed for work, could get their driver's license at fourteen and, with a "needed note", quit school after Grade Eight.

If you were headed to university, which was just starting to be an achievable goal for a greater proportion of young people, at that time, marriage would be postponed until the couple was in their early twenties. Otherwise, with adult responsibilities being shouldered by such young people, the acceptable age for marriage was seventeen for girls and eighteen for boys—or sixteen for both, if the couple "had to get married."

At fifteen, and bringing all the caution I could manage to my relationship with Carla, marriage was far from my mind. But perhaps that was exactly what was in the minds of the Costas.

"Bust"-ed

Soon after we first met, I took Carla on a golf-ball search with Mike at the Niagara-on-the-Lake Golf Club (which was actually the oldest golf club in North

America—not that that impressed us). We made our way to a spot where golfers would often slice a shot, just before the approach to the first green in front of Fort Mississauga. This was a perfect place to find balls, as they often disappeared into the underbrush on the steep hill or dropped right into Lake Ontario.

Mike and Carla climbed the hill, while I took to the water. When I emerged with a couple of balls, Mike hollered, "Throw up the balls you've got."

Since he was up fifteen feet or so, I hurled the first ball with all my might, but my aim was off. Instead of the ball smacking into Mike's outstretched hand, it slammed into Carla's right breast. As she clutched at her bosom, sobbing, I ran up the hill to her. But what could I do? I couldn't massage it. Finally, through her tears, she shook it off, and we took her home.

When I got back to my house, my mother, who was in an unusually motherly mood, having been told all about the incident by Mrs. Costa, confronted me with a litany about tender breasts and breast cancer.

I called Carla and apologized, but I figured I was on the outs. But I wasn't. I saw Carla the next day, and we picked up just like nothing had happened.

On the other hand, that was one of the last times that I got together with Mike. And that was the last summer that I hunted for golf balls or did all the things Mike and I treasured. Our friendship had drastically changed. I thought I had grown up putting my child hood behind me.

Custard

Later that summer, Carla, her parents, and I went for a ride in her father's big Desoto, Carla and I snuggling in the back. We traveled up the River Road to Queenston and across the Queenston-Lewiston wooden suspension bridge, which swayed and clattered as we rumbled over its thick boards, to the U.S.

After we passed through customs, we came to my favorite part of the journey. The road, which led past a rock wall into an extremely sharp turn, headed directly to the top of a hill and then plunged straight down into the village of Lewiston, New York.

As I was occupied with Carla in the back seat, I wasn't sure where we were headed. We entered the village near Schneider's Restaurant, and then passed my mother's favorite restaurant and bar, the Lewiston Restaurant, which was across from the Frontier House, continuing until we ended up at Hibbard's custard stand.

I'd never been there, and was surprised to see such a long line. Marty told me that this was the only custard stand for miles—there was not even one in Buffalo. I told him that I had never heard of this type of ice cream in Ontario. Then he informed me that "Custard is not ice cream. It is custard!"

When we finally got to the beginning of the line, and I got a chance to taste this new treat, I found it softer than the cones I made at the store, and not quite as sweet. To be polite, I told them that I liked it, which I did, but not as well as ice cream scooped by my very own hand.

Know-It-All

On another drive to the Costa's U.S. house, I found myself spouting every bit of knowledge I could find to spew into the conversation. As we drove up the River Road past the new Floral Clock, Joyce remarked on its beauty, but I quickly brought the conversation to the nearby Sir Adam Beck Generating Station.

I had visited the hydro plant with my class and did not hesitate to share the information I had gathered on that field trip. The Sir Adam Beck was a first-class plant running on 60-cycle compared to the old U.S. Schoellkopf 25-cycle, I claimed, feeling that the plant gave us Canadians bragging rights. (What I could not know, was that the entire U.S. Schoellkopf power plant would collapse into the Niagara River just a few years later, on June 7th, 1956, as the result of a rock-slide.)

We continued past the lower Whirlpool Bridge, then a short distance to the Rainbow Bridge, and paused to take in the activity in the area.

Someone must have pressed a button because I was off: Did they know that Niagara-on-the-Lake was at sea level and that millions of years ago this area was an inland sea? I asked, not pausing for an answer. Did they know that Niagara Falls was covered in ice just 15,000 years ago, and that the falls only started to form 12,000 years ago when all the ice melted in the upper lakes? Did they know that the original Falls were at Queenston and had retreated at an average of a foot each year to their present position?

They probably did know all of this information as 1) they were also brought up in the area, and, 2) it was more or less common knowledge. But they just listened and made me feel important. (I suspect there were smiles that I could not see.)

As we started across the bridge we had a full view of the falls. Marty said, "I never get tired of this view." We all focused on the powerful sight of the two smaller American Falls and the larger Canadian Horseshoe Falls, with it majestic mist framing its power. There was a lot of teasing about U.S. vs. Canada, and they reminded me that there were two falls on the American side and only one on the Canadian side.

I still had some go left in me, though, and I quickly retaliated, saying that from the States you can only see the Canadian Horseshoe Falls straight on, but from Canada you can see all three falls. I think with this final salvo I brought my two points home: Being Canadian is pretty darned special—and I was pretty damned smart.

Then we crossed the bridge and passed through customs into the U.S. I had been to Main Street many times before, but this was the first time I noticed the grime and dirt on the streets and the buildings. I also wondered about a peculiar marking that I saw repeated on some of the buildings.

Marty explained that, in the U.S., most public buildings with basements were designated as Atomic Air Raid Shelters, and the markings I saw identified them as such. We did not have these in Niagara, although I am sure an Air Raid Shelter would have offered considerably more protection than I was afforded by hiding under my desk at

Parliament Oak, which is what I was told to do during our nuclear-warfare drills.

On the other hand, from what I had seen in the newsreels about Hiroshima, an Air Raid Shelter would not offer much more protection than a school-desk, in the event of an atomic attack. If there were to be an attack, I decided I might as well hide in a closet like I did during the barn-fire when I was five—only this time, I would want to have Carla with me.

As we continued to Carla's home, we traveled past Goat Island and onto Buffalo Avenue. At this time, 1953, Buffalo Avenue was the only corridor through Niagara Falls, New York, and as we drove along it, I suddenly understood where all the grime was coming from. The route we were traveling was home to some of the area's biggest polluters—Olin Corporation, Union Carbide, DuPont, and Hooker Chemical (now Occidental Petroleum), later made famous by the toxins it dumped into the Love Canal—and I was choking on their output, the chlorine-rotten egg-ammonia-like fumes permeating the air.

Marty told us to roll up the windows. A slimy mist clung to the windshield and had to be wiped repeatedly so we could see. Marty explained that the chemical waste was in the sewers, and that the horrible gases came from the manholes as well as the exhaust stacks. Some days, he said, the manhole covers popped up in the air from the chemical pressure, so he had to be careful not to drive into an open hole.

For the first time, it clicked: When we swam in the Niagara River, we were swimming in a diluted chemical soup. Of course, I knew about the Manhattan Project; we had been taught that the chemical plants used cheap power to help win the war, and that chemical and metallurgical plants produced vital products that made the difference in defeating our enemies. And my dad had told me that nylon and vitamins come from coal; that oil and its chlorinated by-products were the basis of great modern inventions, including medicines, paints, plastics, DDT, insecticides, refrigerants, specialty lubricants, and rayon. I'd also heard that dioxins were manufactured there. But the way he said it, it seemed like these chemicals were war heroes—they were the good guys. I wasn't sure I was buying that, though. What I was beginning to understand on my drive with Carla and her parents was definitely not good.

***

As an adult, I saw the results of the pollution in the area when my wife and I purchased our Lewiston, New York, summer home in 1996. Our two bay windows were oddly hazy and needed replacing. We learned from our contractor friend John and our neighbor Jim that many of the windows in the area were etched by acid fumes, compliments of Stauffer Chemicals and Cyanamid. Sometimes, John and Jim told us, it was so bad when the wind blew across from the plants, that it hurt your lungs to breathe.

Pizza

When we finally arrived at the Costa's house, I was shown off to Carla's girlfriends and introduced to some of the guys. We took a walk by the grade school where she would finish Grade Eight, and then we returned to the house, where I was asked a puzzling question.

"Would you like pizza?" Carla asked.

"What is pizza?" I asked.

"What is pizza?" she repeated, as if she couldn't believe I'd never heard of this mysterious thing. You see, the Costas lived in an Italian area, where pasta, red sauce, and, particularly, pizza were very popular.

Joyce was quick to rectify this gap in my culinary education. She sent us to a pizza place to pick up a couple of pies for dinner. The restaurant was like a home, in that there were a few tables, but no counter or booths. There was a pop and beer cooler, and after Carla ordered a couple of pizzas to go, we shared a Coke.

Back at the house with the pizza pies, I waited for Carla to start so I could see how she ate it. She noticed me waiting and picked up a piece in her hand, saying, "Open your mouth," as she placed the slice close to my face.

I liked it from the first bite.

We left to go back to Canada after dinner; the trip back was lost in cuddling, giggling, and whispering.

Thunder in August

It was a warm summer evening. I had eaten at Carla's place, and after supper we went to Queens Beach for a hand-in-hand walk, just as I had seen lovers do. We sat on a wooden picnic bench up the hill from Regent and Front Streets, watching as the red ball of the sun started its slide down into Oakville and Burlington.

In front of us were the castle of Fort Niagara and the Niagara River; to the left across Lake Ontario was the faintest glow of Toronto, thirty miles in the distance. As it started to darken into a pitch-black night, a warm breeze came up off the lake, and I turned Carla towards the lake, holding her in my arms as the show began.

Streaks of sheet lightning, one after another, filled the horizon as if they were simulating a World War II sea battle. Then we heard simultaneous booms as the cannons fired and the big storm, still miles out, tumbled and rumbled its way towards us, while the warm breeze was fast becoming a tropical wind.

In awe of this natural showcase, enthralled by the explosions of lightning accompanied by the cannons' booms, Carla and I held each other, experiencing a thrill we had never felt before.

We could have stayed forever.

As it turned out, though, we stayed too long. Suddenly, the storm was upon us. Torrents of rain gushed down as though many thousands of sky gods released their bladders all at once.

We scrambled under the leaky picnic table and huddled tightly as what seemed like the "Charge of the

Light Brigade" crashed around us. Lightning to the front, lightning to the left, lightning to the right, and lightning—Boom! Smash!—behind us. What a show!

Instead of keeping Carla safe, as a good Scout should have, I had brought her to the best spot from which to watch, one of the highest spots I could find, surrounded by huge, lightning-attracting trees. We waited for a major electrical storm to come swooping in on top of us.

After the storm blew itself away towards Virgil and St. Catharines, all was dark, warm, and damp—and we were soaking wet. We took off our sopping shoes and splashed, laughing, all the way to Carla's house

Lenny, Nailed

I was supposed to be babysitting my six-year old brother, Lenny. I took him to Carla's house with me and left him outside, playing with some of the other kids, while I went inside to be with Carla.

Suddenly, we heard Lenny's terrified scream and went scrambling outside to see what had happened.

What we found was terrifying! Lenny, who had been sliding down the shed roof, had caught his hand on a big rusty nail, and was still stuck on it, hanging, shrieking for help.

I ran over and shoved on his small body, pushing him up and off that nail. His hand bled through the hole the nail made as though it was the start of a crucifixion. I quickly wrapped his hand in an ice-filled cloth, put him on my bike, and raced to the nearest doctor.

As I rushed Lenny in the door, it felt a little bit like we were entering into enemy territory. This doctor did not support my father, did not send his patients to Bates Rexall Pharmacy. But there was no time to get to one of the other doctors. My baby brother needed immediate help. And to his credit, the doctor gave Lenny the help he needed.

That day, I think I was a hero in Carla's eyes, but maybe not in Lenny's eyes. He never lets me forget that incident and still reminds me that I did not look after him that day. He says that I abandoned him because I was too busy with my girlfriend.

KITCHENER

St. Jerome's
Off to Boarding School

With Carla's help, the summer of 1953 flew by. But as much as I enjoyed being with her, and as reassuring as I found our relationship, my home environment—Mother—continued to be a source of pain.

Before I had met Carla, I'd told my father that I wanted to go away to boarding school that fall. With Carla going home to the States for school, there was nothing to keep me from that plan. The fact that both Jack and Doug had gone to St. Jerome's for part of their schooling (also to avoid our home situation) made a strong argument.

While Dad was reluctant to pay the boarding costs, and also wanted me at home to help look after Lenny, he finally realized I just had to get away from Mother. I was given the choice of three schools: De LaSalle in Toronto, Assumption in Windsor, or St. Jerome's in Kitchener. Without any particular reason, I chose St. Jerome's. And now I wonder if it was my destiny to choose St. Jerome's, so that I would meet my future wife.

Bill at St. Jerome's

Once the decision was made and arrangements complete, Dad drove me to St. Jerome's. Only about a hundred miles away, the trip took almost three hours on the Queen Elizabeth Highway. This was Canada's first four-lane highway, but with stoplights—and even a traffic circle. We had to travel all back streets to get through the City of Hamilton, and then continued on as a two-lane road through many smaller communities. Definitely, our "highway" was only a country cousin of the super highways of today.

During the three-hour journey, my dad and I did not talk as much as we could have, for I was caught up in my own thoughts about my new adventure and, at the same time, I knew I would miss Carla. Still, Dad was always good for a history lesson.

He explained that Kitchener, Ontario, was originally founded as the city of "Berlin," a German settlement. But when World War I broke out, there was a riot in the town, and a statue of Kaiser Wilhelm was dumped into the pond at Victoria Park.

The city was renamed "Kitchener," for Lord Kitchener, a highly decorated British Field Marshall. Lord Kitchener was not one of Dad's heroes. In my father's eyes, he was just as bloodthirsty as any of the Nazis who would come to power twenty years after Lord Kitchener's death.

My father often commented that during the Boer War, Lord Kitchener built one of the very first barbed-wire concentration camps, just outside of Cape Town, in South Africa. According to my dad, the Dutch Boers were fed up with British domination, which they had resisted with arms. Because of their resistance, Kitchener ordered that all the Boer woman and children be taken off their farms— and then he burned their homesteads hoping to starve the Boer army, which was proving inconveniently elusive.

At the camps, poor sanitation, lack of decent food, overcrowding, and hostile treatment by the British resulted in thousands of Boer deaths and even more women and children being affected with long-term illnesses.

With this sad, historical story battling in my mind along with Carla and excitement about being away from home, I was relieved when Dad pulled our car up the driveway at St. Jerome's. Once we arrived, he registered me, wrote a check for my tuition, and wished me good luck, before turning around and heading back to all that I had left behind.

School Daze

I met Father Bullbrook on my very first day at St. Jerome's. After having said good-bye to Dad, I climbed the stairs to the fourth floor and made my way down the hall to my assigned dormitory room.

As I opened the door, I was greeted by the sight of a huge priest slamming what looked like a fully grown adult man against the dorm wall. The priest had the man hoisted up off the floor and was yelling at him in a foreign language, which I later discovered was French.

When the priest saw me, he let the man go and walked right past me as though I did not exist. I introduced myself to the shaken person the priest had finished with. We clasped hands, and that is how I met my roommate, Reggie.

At twenty, Reggie was five years older than me, and as much an adult as he could be in the circumstances. His dad wanted Reggie to work in the family business, so he had sent him to St. Jerome's to become fluent in English.

As a new kid, it did not hurt to have a six-foot, 170-pound roommate, even if he was on the outs with "The Bull," as I soon discovered the angry priest was nicknamed. The other kids respected and admired Reggie, even if he made Father Bullbrook mad—or maybe because he made The Bull mad! All the kids, both boarders and day hops, were petrified of Father Bullbrook. He was not a person to mess with.

My first days in Kitchener were a whirlwind. I liked the city. The dayhops were friendly, and I met boarders from around Ontario, Quebec, and even South America. At our first assembly, I realized there were over thirty kids enrolled at St. Jerome's as boarders.

Thirty kids —and we were all in the same boat.

When lights-out rang for us juniors, at ten o'clock, I was surprised, as at home in Niagara going to bed that early was not thought of. But because everyone my age was doing the same thing, I rather liked it.

There was a schedule for everything. We were awakened at seven a.m. Chapel was at seven-thirty. Breakfast was at eight. Lunch was scheduled for noon, and then we continued with classes from one until four. From four to six in the afternoon was our free time. Then came supper at six, and, at seven, we studied until eight-thirty, attended night chapel, had a bit of time to talk, and then it was time for bed

Even though we had off-campus privileges on Tuesdays, Thursdays, Saturdays, and Sundays, for the first while, it felt like I had been sent to a minimum security prison! St. Jerome's was a huge change from my unstructured life in Niagara. But I got used to it, and I think the structure helped me in long run.

There was still room for "extra-curricular activities", even with the strict watch kept on us boys. For some reason, the South American kids seemed threatened by me, and on my very first day, I had to fight with two of them.

After school, nine of their countrymen jumped me at the bottom of the back stairway, by the door that led outside.

My early Niagara training came in handy right away, and with the help of two others—including John Cziraki who became a lifelong friend—we took care of the South Americans and did ourselves proud. (Of course, our adversaries were of small stature and weight.)

Maybe we did too well, because on my first day of school, I earned a reputation, one that all the priests eventually heard about. Still, I had learned my first big-city lesson: Always be sure you have someone to cover your back.

Always Hungry

Jake, one of my new friends, said, "Come with me after school. We will fill ourselves up."

I told him that on my meager allowance, I could not afford to.

"Just come with me," he replied. So off we went, down to King Street and into the A&P Grocery Store. Once we got inside, we looked around a little bit, and then Jake picked up some dates and handed me a few. We ate them as we proceeded down the grocery aisles. Next, Jake grabbed two packages of sliced ham from the meat counter. He ripped the packages open and stuffed the contents of the second one into the first one. "Two for one," he said.

He picked up two apples, gave me one, and said, "Enjoy."

I did—and we polished off both apples as we continued our store tour, during which we also opened up two bottles of pop and got a head start on drinking them. Then, Jake tore open a loaf of bread, stuck a wad into his coat pocket, and approached the cashier flirting with her and getting her to laugh.

As he made a date with the laughing cashier, we paid—but just for the pop and one package of ham. Safely out the door and down the street, we each slapped ham between two slices of bread and savored our illicit feast.

While this was before store surveillance systems, and there had been very few people in the store—which was how we got away with it—I was much too nervous to ever try that trick again. Instead, I found my own solution to the "always hungry, meagrely funded" problem.

Our favorite restaurant was called The Chicken Nest, about a block and a half from St. Jerome's. It was a large hang-out that could accommodate around seventy people. When some of us were hungry, we would head over to The Nest, sit down, and order a substantial feed. Then we would get our bill.

At that point, instead of just paying and leaving, we would go into another room at the other side of the restaurant, into a different waitress's section. There, we would order a very light snack which came with a correspondingly light second bill. It was only then that we would saunter up to the cashier's desk at the front entrance to pay—and what we paid was the small check, leaving the larger bill in the trash.

While this strategy worked well, and kept me fed, I finally ended up feeling guilty about my tactics, thinking that I would not want someone doing what I was doing at my dad's store.

I figured that what I needed, if I wasn't going to steal food, was money to pay for it. I still had a bank account from diving at the Cayuga and working at The Store, so I decided to put that to use. At St. Jerome's, there was always some kid who was short of cash mid-week. I became a loan shark, lending five dollars to whoever needed it, and getting six dollars back on the following Saturday when the borrower got his allowance.

Twenty percent interest earned on a three-day loan did wonders for my ability to keep myself fed. This, and playing cards, kept me in eating money for the next four years.

Love Letters

During my first week at St. Jerome's, Carla's letters came daily, and some days two at a time. Whenever my name was called for mail, I was teased about the pink, perfumed envelopes.

Shortly after my arrival, Carla wrote to let me know that she and her parents were coming to visit, just in time for our first school dance of the year, a "sock hop," so-called, because no street shoes were allowed on the gymnasium floor.

Since St. Jerome's was a boys-only school, very few of my classmates had a date, but there were girls there from neighboring St. Mary's.

Still, my new friends made a fuss over Carla and me, teasing us and about going steady. They also razzed us about Marty and Joyce being there. I tried to be on my best behavior. There was a saying about dancing close, "Leave room for the Holy Ghost." All I can say is that I hope the Holy Ghost didn't get hurt in our tight clenches!

I had to say goodnight at eleven o'clock to make curfew. I left reluctantly, especially since, as I was leaving, I saw Carla talking to some of the older boys. She had a way of attracting them wherever she went.

The next day, I was excused to go out with the Costas. Marty had learned about the cities of Kitchener and Waterloo and was proud to be our tour guide. Poor Marty, It's a good thing Joyce was there to keep him company. Otherwise, he would have been like a chauffeur for the two love birds necking in the back seat. After weeks of my seeing only boys, Carla felt warm and soft and cuddly, and she smelled luscious. I had really missed all the feminine attention I had had back home.

Under the circumstances, it's a wonder I heard anything Marty said at all, but I do remember him remarking what a clean, orderly area Kitchener was. Also, I remember that he was confused because King Street started as King East, switched to King West, then it became King South, finally ending up at the end of Waterloo as King North. East, West, South, North all in a reasonably straight line?

At the end of our drive, we returned to where they were staying, the Walper Hotel on King Street (West). The Hotel was very antiquated and housed the famous Walper House Restaurant. The meal was succulent compared to what I had gotten used to. Even better than the food, the Costas pampered me, making me feel very special.

All good things come to an end, though, and with one last kiss from Carla, I returned to the dorm, where Big Reggie teased me into the night. He wanted to know all the details. I just wanted to get to sleep.

After Carla's visit, her letters kept coming. The Bull would hand them out, as usual, but now he would always give me a stern, reprimanding look as I grabbed my letters and rushed off to read them. One Saturday, I went to his office to collect my five-dollar weekly allowance, and, when he pulled out the drawer to give me my money, I saw some pink envelopes that looked familiar.

When I asked him if they were mine, Father Bullbrook did not reply. He just gave me a challenging look while slapping a five-dollar bill onto his desk for me to pick up. I'm not sure what got into me, but I challenged him back.

I told him that those letters were sent via U.S. and Canadian postal services; that he was interfering with the federal postal laws of both countries; that in so doing, he was committing not one, but two, federal offenses.

True to his nickname, The Bull held his ground. I did not get the letters. I wrote to Carla asking her what she had written that might have been cause for the letters to be confiscated. She did not know which letters those were, but agreed to cool the steamy parts and to use a code to keep me out of trouble.

The next day I got a call from Dad. Father Bullbrook had phoned him after checking with the school lawyer. Dad told me that he had legally signed my guardianship over to the school. I needed to drop the issue because I did not have any recourse.

Then he gave a little chuckle. I had stood up for myself, and that increased my dad's respect for me in ways I could not have expected. As for The Bull, from then on he treated me with a stern, but kind, understanding. Even though I had stood my ground, what I did not understand at the time, was that he had also put up with my mother's pestering late night incoherent phone calls.

Years later, when he wrote me a letter of reference, it was even better than if I had written it myself.

Thanksgiving

For Thanksgiving that year, Carla came and stayed at my house. She arrived on Saturday, and during the afternoon, we hung around visiting with old friends. But that evening, we were going to Teen Town.

I walked into her room just as she was tugging on her stockings. She had her leg up on a chair, and her skirt was way pulled up way past her garter snaps to her panties. Instead of stopping, or pulling her skirt down when I entered the room, Carla looked directly into my eyes, and holding my gaze, slowly drew her stockings all the way up.

There was a devilish smirk on her face, as if she was daring me.

If it were not for everyone being in the house, I do believe that I would have given her my devil.

At that moment, I flashed back to being four years old and in Detroit with my Uncle on that service call. The young black woman that had been putting on her stockings—and putting on a show for me—had given me that identical look. I shuddered as Carla completed the snapping of her garters.

The scent of Teen Town that night was a mix of freshly showered sweetness, *Noxzema*, lily of the valley, and *Old Spice*. The tension came from a certain boldness coupled with a new strange shyness that we felt as our hot faces slipped on each other.

Carla and I held each other tight as we tried to renew the freshness of the affection that had fueled our summer together. But fall had arrived, and things were not quite the same. We started the evening with the hope of love, but by the end of the night, all that remained was the disappointment we felt as we understood how different we two were.

I brought Carla back to my house at eleven, explaining that I wanted to go see a couple of my buddies for a just a few minutes. I asked her if would she be okay with my parents, and she said that she would. She understood that these were my friends, and that I hadn't seen them since I'd been at St. Jerome's. But it was definitely my thing, not hers.

It was a cool, fall night, crisp and clear. I met up with Pat and Jack on King Street by Jack Green's Livery Stable. Jack had brought a gallon of his dad's homemade wine. Sweet and fizzy, it went down like pop, and in a very short period, the three of us had consumed the entire gallon as we made our way back towards my house.

We stood outside for a minute, laughing and pushing each other and just shooting the bull. Then I said I had to go in, as Carla was waiting for me. Not realizing anything was wrong, I pushed through the door. But once I hit the heat of the house, I was hit with a whirly-swirly buzz.

As Carla came over, I grabbed the railing at the foot of our stairs and held on to it trying to stand up. Carla shouted, "Oh my God. You are drunk."

The next thing I knew, my brother was carrying me up to bed. He undressed me and put a wastepaper basket beside the bed—and the hallucinations started.

They were worse than anything Jack Lemmon went through in *Days of Wine and Roses*: The wall curved. A huge crack opened up and devil rats came snarling out. Everything was spinning. Lights were flashing. Then there was darkness followed by bright lights. I was pulled up, only to be dropped back down. The night became an everlasting whirlpool of tossing nightmares.

My screams went unanswered; the basket was well used. The next morning I was hung over. I had caught my mom's "flu." My mom was cool, though. And Dad just laughed. But Carla was peeved that I had ruined the weekend.

Still, we all went to Mass. (It was so rare for mother to attend, that I think she was showing off.) All through the service, I worried that I was an alcoholic like Mother. As soon as we got back home, I phoned our family doctor telling him I needed something to settle my stomach so I could salvage what was left of the holiday.

The doctor, our family friend, was so helpful. I explained that I had had the DTs, and he asked me how old the wine was. I told him that Jack's dad had just made it in September. He laughed, then, saying, "Bill you were not drunk. You were poisoned."

It seems that when wine is fermenting, there are a lot of chemical reactions going on, most of them not good to humans. Unless you want to be poisoned, you have to wait until the wine is ready to drink, which takes a few months.

What a load off my mind. I checked with the other guys and found that they hadn't fared any better. At least I was able to offer some comfort by sharing the explanation that the doctor had given me.

I sort of made up with Carla.

But the poison-wine episode just really seemed to put a cap on a weekend that was already feeling like a wipe out. We agreed that we should date others.

After Carla's parents picked her up on Monday, my brother drove me to St. Catharines to get the bus back to Kitchener.

Carla and I continued to exchange letters that fall, but I also received letters from girls whom I had known back in Grade Eight in Niagara and also when I was working behind the soda fountain. Now I had letters coming from various towns and cities. My friends did not know what to make of it. Most of the guys did not even have one girlfriend yet.

I do believe I saw a smirk on The Bull's lips as he handed me my mail. I wonder if he was reading them.

Say Goodbye to Love

Christmas was just around the corner, and I did not know what to buy Carla. Since our disastrous Thanksgiving weekend, we were dating other people, but we were still close. I thought.

A well-known jeweler was going out of business, so I decided to buy her a ring that was on sale. It was in the price range I could afford on my meager allowance, and I thought the ring was pretty. It also had her birthstone in it.

We exchanged gifts when I got home, and while I do not recall what I received from Carla, I do very well remember that soon after Christmas her mother said to me, "Bill, you know the ring you gave Carla is not gold."

I replied that it was "Irish gold." She looked perplexed. I explained that in our Irish heritage if you got a copper ring at Christmas and it turned green by St. Patty's day, it was good luck for the rest of the year.

What bull! I sounded just like my Uncle Austin. However, like Austin, I got away with it. Joyce accepted what I said. I think.

Later that day, Carla and I went skating down at the slip where I was supposed to have drowned. Some of us started to play hockey. It was then that I became aware that I was no longer the star in Carla's eye.

I had always known she was a flirt, but that day, I could not miss the intensity that she was looking at one of the fellows knocking the puck around—while wearing my "Irish gold" ring!

Our relationship went downhill from there. By summer, it was done.

EXPELLED

Thank You, Pauline

The night the girls from Brantford Catholic School played basketball against the St. Mary's team, St. Jerome's hosted a sock hop. One of our chaperones for the evening was a teacher who knew all about my ups and downs with Carla.

So imagine my surprise when he called me over to introduce me to a striking, black-haired beauty from Brantford—and then left us alone!

Pauline was her name. She was a little bit older than I was, but this did not stop me from moving in close as we danced. However, she kindly—but firmly—controlled the situation, making room for a nice, fat Holy Ghost between us.

We jived and slow-danced, we talked and laughed easily, without any seriousness or tension.

Pauline was so attentive and understanding that, by the time the dance was over, I felt free of the past; it was time to move on. Just before she left, she gave me a reassuring hug and light kiss that lasted well into my pleasant dreams.

We exchanged letters for a few months, although she felt more like the big sister that I never had rather than a real girlfriend. Then, perhaps because she had found a real boyfriend, one her own age, her letters slowed, and finally stopped.

Although Pauline and I spent so little time getting to know one another, she had a true influence on me. While it would be a year before I met a girl as kind as Pauline, when I did, I made her my own. Thanks to Pauline, I knew what I needed in a way I hadn't before she and I danced that evening in the gym.

Scandalous

I was away at St. Jerome's when the first issue, hailed as an exclusive, one-time edition, of *Playboy* magazine, featuring Marilyn Monroe, hit the newsstands, so I don't know if The Store received that issue or not. If it did, it was probably returned, because the issue of banning public nudity was a hot topic of the day.

Father Weaver, along with other ministers had very strong (and strongly biased) views on the subject.

When I was working at The Store, a few years before the outrageous *Playboy* scandal, the news came hot off the press. Scandal sheets like *Flash* and *Hush* made public the private lives of many ordinary people, printing stories of their secrets and alleged crimes. Complete with tabloid type pictures they described the sickness of Ontario, giving the names, dates, and other details of perverted police investigations.

It was reputed that, in addition to sales and advertising revenue, these publications made their money from donations that were extorted to keep perpetrators names out of print.

For a bright kid, it didn't take much to figure out that you didn't have to strip naked and pose for a center-fold. If you had a dark secret, and it was exposed, the whole world would label you and your families without caring whose lives were destroyed.

With a muddy part of my life not long past, this awareness rocked the secrets of my mind.

Inspiration

Maw used to say, "Christ does not lend you a cross any heavier than you can carry." Once you seemed to understand that, she would follow up with, "He also gives you just the right weight of a cross so that you become stronger in order to carry the next cross."

I would reply, "The cross is okay, but those thorns are another story!"

From what I heard from Maw and from the pulpit, I used to wonder if life was anything but a series of crosses and thorns. It may not be a positive analogy, but it does have some merit. The road to sainthood might be paved with crosses and thorns.

I am not a saint, so I prefer grace to come more easily. For me, a moment of grace is an "Ah-ha!" moment. In a flash, an epiphany is revealed that I can choose to accept or deny, but the revelation has occurred no matter what I do with it.

This can happen when someone challenges me to be the best I can be at that very moment. Sometimes the way to accepting the offered grace is long and slow. At other times, Bam! I get it.

Most of the priests who helped raise me proved they were caring mentors. They helped me and others squirm through our teen years. And after I made it through those years, I had enough life experience to realize that we have choices, and, yes, things do happen for a reason.

Discussing Sex and Religion

I had learned a lot about sex in The Store. There were medical books there and the *Sunbathing for Health* nudist magazines. I could ask my dad most questions, and my brother Doug, everything else. I also got some less reliable information from my friends. And then there was my summer with Carla.

By the time I arrived at St. Jerome's, I thought I knew almost everything there was to know about sex—except the proper way to carry it out. I was street-wise, but I also wanted to be "good," not "evil." I knew I had a soul, and I wanted to make the most of it, so I had to find out how the rules of The Church applied to the rules of sex.

At boarding school, there was time to just "chew the fat." We were particularly comfortable with one priest. He was young enough for us boys to relate to.

One day, I was chatting with our proctor and the priest along with some of the others about a question I had regarding sperm and eggs. I knew girls had their periods because their eggs ripened, and if they were not used, they were rejected during the menses—and would come into The Store to buy *Kotex*!

"If girls reject their unused eggs," I asked, "is it like boys doing the same with their sperm?"

Father said it was the same. But he added that that was why we had nocturnal emissions. If we made the sperm come out on purpose, it became a sin of pleasure.

"Why is pleasure a sin?" was my reasonable follow-up question.

I was told that that particular pleasure is reserved for marriage, for creating children.

I wasn't done with my argument. I countered, "We make sperm with no sin. We get rid of excess sperm by pleasant nocturnal emissions, and that is not a sin. However, the sperm is continuously manufactured and does not know the time of day, but after a buildup, it demands release."

The discussion that followed had to do with our bodies being temples of God. Also, "That is considered 'spilt seed'."

"But," I said, "it is going to get spilled sooner or later."

Next came the reasoning that we should not be preoccupied with sex, "as we are a lot more than sexual beings. When people get diverted by sex, they forget who they are, and what they are meant to do. They focus on satisfaction rather than growth."

Although one of the married lay teachers actually told us that masturbation could lead to insanity and could grow hair on your palms, for the most part at St. Jerome's, questions I had regarding sexuality were met with reasoned responses.

As for masturbation, after much discussion, the topic was left for me to ponder. But, although I had once again challenged authority, I had been shown respect. I had not been shamed, had not been lectured to, had not been told I was going to Hell.

Later in my life, it was just this type of rational encounter that brought me to accept certain priests as spiritual individuals, rather than seeing them as instruments of a corrupt institution.

The same level of rationality was not present at the all-girls high school, St. Mary's High. The nuns there had very weird ideas that they passed on to the girls. For instance, the girls were taught that a person commits a sin if they touch their genitals, and that it was all right to use *Kotex*, but not tampons, because tampons are inserted.

The girls were also taught that French kissing was a mortal sin. Getting too close to a boy so that he got an erection was her fault—and heaven forbid the boy ejaculated! That was the girl's fault too. She got the blame, even though she did not even get any of the satisfaction. (I am sure the Nuns were trying to save souls, but their emphasis on sin left very little room for romance.)

In addition to the religious education we got as part of our regular curriculum, spiritual retreats were held at both St. Jerome's and St. Mary's. At these events, some of the visiting priests were advocates of a "You will go to hell" approach to spiritual encouragement. The way they talked about relationships with the opposite sex was so negative that they should have been called "anti-going steady retreats."

No matter their other differences, one thing that we were told by all the priests and all the nuns was that confession cleanses the soul. I hoped that this was true.

I went to confession at the end of one retreat at St. Jerome's and explained to the priest that I wanted to deal with a part of my past that kept haunting me. I was looking for spiritual understanding, but the only response I got was a directive for prayer.

My Father Confessor did not want to hear what I had to tell him. He did not want try to understand. What I had to share was too much for this man to deal with. All he wanted to do was to get me out of his confessional.

That experience left me struggling even deeper in my own personal quagmire. My spiritual mentors had all preached that confession would make me pure again, but instead of help, all I found in that booth was rejection. Once again, I was abandoned. Once again, I understood that I had to be very selective about whom I trusted.

Fun and Games

The fourth floor windows were the only form of air-conditioning. Outside them, a wide ledge circled the dorms. That ledge allowed us access to one another's rooms at night, without fear of being spotted. After lights out, we could crawl back and forth along the ledge to share food or whatever other good things—or good ideas—we might possess.

Fourth floor window in the background

One night, a couple of us filled some paper bags with water, tied them closed, then scampered along the ledge to the first open window we found and tossed the make-shift water balloons at an unsuspecting boy sleeping in his bed. We laughingly beetled back to our room and locked the windows.

From then on, it was risky to leave your window open. We put up some poles so that if an unwanted someone wanted to get in, or to throw something in, the poles would come crashing down. Luckily, when this happened the Prefect did not hear it.

(When I remember these hijinks, I realize how fortunate we were that no one careened down the four floors and splattered to his death on the cement sidewalk!)

The next year from our third floor window, we could peer over and watch the St. Mary's girls on their way to school. A couple of friends and I noticed that three girls in particular always passed beneath our window at the same time each day. We nicknamed them the Three Vestal Virgins, and, with our window swung wide open, we would call down to them.

One day, I arranged to meet them after school. They were so gullible that when I explained that my father was Catholic, but my mother was a Jehovah's Witness, and I had been sent to St. Jerome's to make up my mind as to what religion I would adopt, they believed me.

I told them that I did not know any Catholic girls, so I wondered if they would help me make up my mind.

They were such sweet girls, and wanted to help me, but I think this responsibility for my everlasting soul was too much for them to bear. (Actually, I know this for a fact, as these girls became friends with my wife and me when we were older, and they shared that I had really scared them with what they thought was my sincere request!)

A "Sheared" Doug

One of my classmates, Doug, slept so soundly that it was almost impossible to wake him. Capitalizing on this unusual attribute, eight of us made a plan. At three o'clock one morning, we tiptoed into Doug's room and grabbed his mattress, sharing the weight between us. With suppressed giggles, we carted him out into the hall and down the three flights of stairs, tilting him down, then leveling him, and then tilting him down again, as we headed for the ground floor.

Once there, we shouldered the back door open, only to almost drop Doug, who was, unbelievably, still sleeping. But we caught him just in time and made it safely into the back lot. From there, we carried him out to the middle of the football field, where we gently placed our classmate on the ground and made sure he was tucked in. Then we all went back to bed.

At six-thirty a.m., the bells of St. Mary's rang out the Angelus. Doug, being cold and hearing the bells, awoke and found himself far from the spot where he'd fallen asleep the night before. He was a real sport, though, and he just picked up his mattress and covers and made his way back to his room past the surprised stares of the priests.

Doug and I soon became good friends, which meant that we would find ways to challenge the boundaries together. One day he stated that for five dollars he would shave his head bald, like Yul Brunner's.

I was always quick to respond to a challenge. Within minutes I had collected the five dollars. We got a pair of electric shears and commenced. "Scoop", a student who wrote some articles for the *Kitchener-Waterloo Record*, was on hand to take pictures. One of them immortalizes me sporting my long, wavy locks, holding the shears, with Ed standing beside me. And then there was Doug, looking like a sheared sheep.

Doug unsheared and sheared
Photos courtesy of K-W Record

And he was sent home, expelled because of the haircut.

This incident hit the press. *The Globe and Mail* had a feature article about Doug's hair. Our story even made some of the international papers!

Gus Chambers, who was the proprietor of the store next to my dad's, came in waving a newspaper. Had Dad seen the article about his son?

Dad replied that he was proud that his son Doug had been made a Corporal in the Air Force.

"No, not that son," Gus said. "Billy, the one in Kitchener." And he handed the paper to my dad so he could see the picture.

Needless to say, I got a call from Dad. As usual he was not angry; he just wanted to know if I was all right. Was I going to be expelled also?

I was the instigator, as the article stated; I don't know why I wasn't expelled. Still, no one said anything to me.

Of course, I felt badly for Doug and told him so before he was packed off home. Years later when we reminisced about this incident, I apologized again. True to his good nature, Doug just laughed and said it probably had been for the better. I still suspect it was because Doug was not Catholic.

It is illogical and irrational, however, somewhere in my soul, I just know angels do exist. I wonder who had my back. Was it the "Bull" or Michael? Regardless, I cannot understand why on this occasion and others I was not expelled.

***

Authors Note: I felt very sad as I read the following. To me it is an Ode To Father Bullbrook.

***

The day after Christmas, 1969, Father Bullbrook took a group of eleven students to Quebec for a cultural weekend. Unfortunately a severe blizzard turned the trip into a thirty-hour ordeal. The following morning Bullbrook did not appear. Finally the students gained access to his room and found him dead, a heart attack having claimed him some hours before.

It was 27 December, his fifty-fifth birthday.

AWOL

Another one of my Kitchener roommates, Paul, was what was called a "local boarder." This meant that his family lived nearby, and he could go home on weekends if he wanted. He decided he was going home late one night and asked me to join him for a big celebration for his football-hero brother, Bobby.

After everyone in the dorm was sound asleep, we crept down the stairs and out the back door. Then we ran the couple of miles to his house on Pandora Avenue.

There were so many people crowded into the house that no one seemed to notice our presence—except for Paul's brother Bobby, who told us to get back to the dorms. He was concerned that we would be expelled if we got caught.

We took his advice and ran all the way back to St. Jerome's. So much time had slipped away that only a couple of hours remained before the priests would be getting up. Shushing each other, we pulled on the handle to the back door.

It was locked.

We could not go through the front door, as it led to the front office and into the priests' residence.

Panic set in. Then, one of us thought of the fire escape that ran up near our room. Slipping around the building, we stealthily pulled down the fire escape, and then hiked ourselves up to the first floor landing and made our way very quietly to the second floor landing.

Then, despite our caution, the iron steps clanged loudly. We paused, holding our breath. We were at the priests' floor.

Flash! A light had been turned on. We hugged the wall. The drapes parted, and old Father Winters appeared at the window staring right past us. Then the drapes closed. The light was extinguished.

Whew. Now we could breathe. It was onward, upward to the third floor. The window was shut. Damn! Was it locked? We had nothing to lose at this point, so we just shoved as hard as we could, and it flew open.

Silently, we slipped back to our beds as though we had never left.

I thought this brief night prayer: *Oh, Guardian Angel, Who art Thou? If I knew You better, perhaps we could collaborate. Do I need all these tests? Why do I keep getting into these situations? Is it because I am so dumb, or is it so You can keep your job?*

MY FIRST REAL LOVE

Joan Tank

Paul did not get me expelled. And, also, he told me about a great girl he had gone to grade school with. He said he had really liked her, but her dad was strict. He made sure that she did not get involved with boys.

The thought of her strict father didn't scare me off. When Paul finished extolling this girl's virtues, I told him I had to meet her.

He said, "Her name is Joan Tank. I bet you can't get her to go out."

Well, that was all the challenge I needed. I was going to get a date with this girl.

On a February Sunday afternoon my friend Denny and I went skating at Victoria Park, just a few blocks from the school. The park had a large pond. In warm weather, we would rent a canoe and chase the ducks and swans. In winter, the pond froze over and created a skating rink, with piped in waltz music to complete the atmosphere.

That cold day, crowds of naive young girls were standing around hoping for a skate. Denny and I made a game out of seeing how many girls we could skate with.

We weren't serious about the girls; we were just having fun and acting with bravado.

After some good skating, I realized it was getting close to four; we had to leave soon to be back to the school on time. Suddenly, we spotted two gorgeous creatures standing on the ice. One of the pretty girls had long blond hair and blue eyes. The other, a brunette, had eyes and a smile that made the air seem like it was ten degrees warmer.

Denny and I quickly made a deal: We would race, and the faster skater got his pick of the two girls.

I beat Denny by five strides.

The girls watched us as we approached them, and, immediately, I knew which one I was asking. It was the girl with the smile.

"Hi, my name is Bill. What's yours?"

"Joan," she said.

"Would you like to skate with me?"

"I guess. Maybe."

I took her hand, concluding that meant, "Yes."

We skated, but she was shy, and I could not press a phone number out of her. Oh, well. "Nice try," I told myself, and I put her out of my mind.

A week later, at a sock hop, I went over to join a friend who was talking to two girls. I asked one of the girls to dance. Out on the dance floor, I asked her name.

She looked me in the eye and started laughing. She said, "You do not remember? We met at the park. I am Joan Tank."

I reddened and replied, "Way to go, Bill!" But later, when I asked her for a date, she agreed. I just knew this was a special girl. I don't know if it was a pure coincidence or whether by destination, but somehow, I had gotten to meet the elusive Joan Tank. And we had a date!

Back in the room, I told Paul she had agreed to go out. He said he doubted that her parents would allow it. And sure enough, Saturday morning I got a phone call. It was Joan shyly saying she wouldn't be able to meet me as she had the flu.

Damn. Paul was right. Her father must have put his foot down.

I reported what had happened to Paul, who was going home for the weekend. When he got back to school on Sunday evening, he told me that he had dropped by to see how Joan was doing; she had answered the doorbell in her pajamas and robe.

Paul's comment? "Oh. You really are sick."

And she was.

Once I got the word, I phoned Joan. We had our first real date at the Lyric Theatre, the next Saturday.

Joan and me

Joan as Queen of Mardi Gras,
with my roommate Paul

Joan as Queen of Mardi Gras

School Food

We had nicknames for the food at St. Jerome's. The sausages we saw on the table so often we called "donkey dicks." The tea was "panther piss." The porridge, a far cry from the delectable dish Maw prepared, was "mush" whether it was Cream of Wheat or just plain oatmeal.

On Sunday or holy days of obligation, if we were lucky, we would get creamed chicken with biscuits. We called this dish "Chicken ala King." Sometimes we would get actual sliced turkey or chicken or, our favorites, meat loaf or shepherd's pie.

Otherwise, it was sausages, pork chops, grilled pork liver—which I learned to enjoy—cold cuts, or ham. There was so much pork, in various forms, that I suffered from boils and would have to have the doctor lance them so they would drain. We did have a reasonable lettuce salad, a variety of canned vegetables, and a glass of powdered milk with every meal.

(I griped with everyone else about the food. However, I realized that our school food was much better than what Dad and I threw together when we were left to our own devices.)

In addition to serving Mass, I would sometimes wait on the priests' table, as one of my roommates, John, had clued me in that this was a way to eat the same food as the priests. Hey! I wasn't proud. I was a growing sixteen-year old who was always hungry and was happy for the priests' leftovers.

To make sure leftovers were available for the servers, Harry Pringle, the cook, ex-army, would always make more bacon and eggs than the priests could eat. He was one of the good guys. He knew that for us, cold bacon and eggs were better than none at all.

Harry was also wise to everything that went on at the school. When he heard about some of my antics, he would call me aside and caution me with a friendly, stern laugh. I think he actually liked me, as he always let me check to see if there were any leftovers.

We had heard rumors that the army used to put saltpeter in the soldiers' beverages during the war to keep the men from getting "horny." Some boys swore that the priests did the same with us. But if they really did put saltpeter into our tea and water at St. Jerome's, it did not work on me. And I know I was not alone in this department.

Father Feeney's Vendetta

Father Feeney replaced The Bull as our new Disciplinarian. He was a short, rough, huffing, puffing, pipe-smoking Irishman who always seemed out of breath. Father Feeney was aware of Mother's problem and of my recent relationship with Carla and tolerated me—barely. For sure, I was not his favorite Mass server.

One day, I was down the hall when Feeney rushed over and, crimson-faced and huffing, grabbed my throat with his two hands. God knows what I had done to tee him off, but as I looked down into his blurry eyes (he was shorter than I) I realized that the crazy bastard was trying to strangle me.

I shot my hands up sharply, breaking his grip, and then started to slash downward in a karate chop. I checked myself just before I slammed my hand into his Adam's apple. Shaking, I dropped my hand and pushed him away.

"Don't you ever dare to try that again," I hissed, and continued to my room.

Nothing else was said at the time, but the next day at lunch, I was sitting at my table with my back to the priests' and lay-teachers' table, when, Wham! Bam! I was yanked backwards out of my chair, thrown across the room, and pummeled by the gym teacher.

I had no choice but to take it. I did not want to risk being expelled for hitting back. Besides, it happened so fast that I was stunned. I just curled into a ball on the dining hall floor.

After he had tired himself out on me, I picked up my chair and, red-faced, returned to the table. In my mind, I wanted to sue the bastard. I dreamt about ways of getting even. However, in reality, I had to accept that I was trapped once again. I could not leave, as home was no better an option.

After that, I had very little to do with him, but I still took regular punishments from Father Feeney. He would cut my privileges or make me kneel for long periods of time on the hardwood floor.

I suspect that finally the other priests noticed what was happening, and that one of them intervened, because at some point, both Feeney and the gym teacher began to give me a wide—and sneering—berth. One day, not long after the incident in the dining hall, I decided to test the boundaries. I walked right up to the teacher and looked him straight in the eye. He would not hold my gaze, and, to my amazement, he sheepishly walked away.

The mystery of Father Feeney's dislike of me was solved when I found out that he was a frequent visitor at Joan Tank's house—no doubt taking ample advantage of the food and drink. (By the crimson shade of his face, I'd have to say, mainly the drink.) And somehow he had elected himself to be Joan's protector.

At St. Jerome's, Joan, along with my boarder friends, was one of my few bright lights. She was my new girlfriend. We were going out regularly, and I was just getting to know her.

When Joan's dad asked her if she knew about my mother's problems and my past relationships, relating that Father Feeney was not one bit impressed with me, she simply replied that she knew all about me.

She knew, because, although I seldom told anyone about my home life or past girlfriends, I had shared this with Joan. There was just something about her that made it comfortable for us to talk about our respective pasts.

By acknowledging what she knew about me to her father, she ended Father's Feeney's vendetta against me.

But no matter how special Joan was, and how comfortable I was with her, I was still holding onto one secret. It would take some time before I could share, even with Joan, all that had happened to me.

What appeared to be unforgivable at the time changed as an adult when I read his obituary in the Resurrectionist Congregation bulletin. Believe it or not, I actually said a prayer for him.

In 1962, Harry Feeney became the resident chaplain at St. Mary's Hospital. But these were difficult years as he struggled with alcohol and, in 1965, he entered a rehabilitation program. This proved to be a defining moment in his life as he was re-energized spiritually and devoted himself to Alcoholics Anonymous (AA)

In 1974 he was transferred to Bermuda as pastor of St. Anthony's parish, arriving there just prior to the death of Fr. Joe Lehman. Humorous and loved by his parishioners Harry also continued his involvement in the AA fellowship becoming a founding member of the AA program in Bermuda.

In 1976, Harry wrote: "I cannot take credit for my sobriety or for any of God's gifts to me. Therefore I have to be daily and everlastingly grateful to God, not just in words, but in my way of life." He actively continued this way of life until November, 1978. On the morning of 29 November, he was discovered lying on the kitchen floor by a parishioner, dead of a heart attack. So outstanding was his work that, after his death, the bishop was asked to please send another alcoholic priest.

EXPLORING THE GRAVEYARD

My Secret
The Secret is the Cornerstone

During the late spring of 1956, towards the end of my second year at St. Jerome's, I had a lingering infection in the middle finger of my left hand. Even after months of soaking it in Epsom salts and treating it with salves, the infection got persistently worse. The only recourse, it seemed, was to remove the nail so the nail bed could heal.

I went to St. Mary's Hospital for the minor operation. The doctor told me that he would have to anesthetize me and that I would stay in the hospital for a few days. By rights, he should have put me on the men's ward, but he said he was putting me on the children's ward instead.

"I would rather you share a room with a child, than with an old goat," he said. "Besides, on the children's floor, the nurses are new trainees. They are your age, so probably you will be able to relate with them. Is that okay with you?"

I replied, "Sounds good to me."

It turns out I was given a private room that came complete with teenage nurses. Only a couple of years older than me, they wanted to wash and rub my back and give me lots of other special attention. Who was I to complain? (When Joan came to visit, this "special treatment" caught her eye. It did not do any harm to our budding relationship.)

The operation went smoothly, leaving only a bandaged, throbbing, and nail-less finger to heal. After the anaesthetic wore off, and I was lying in my hospital bed dozing, two of my "special treatment" nurses came in, saying they had attended the operation.

Then they dropped the bomb: "What are the secrets of Niagara-on-the-Lake?" they wanted to know.

I played dumb. "Why would you ask such a question?"

They said, "All during the operation you kept mumbling about the great secrets of Niagara-on-the-Lake."

My immediate thought was, Oh my God! I was given a truth serum and have spilled the beans. All the interrogation scenes in Nazi movies came rushing into my mind. I wanted to run to lock the doors and bar the windows on the secret compartment of my mind.

One of the nurses leaned close and looked into my eyes. As I returned her mesmerizing gaze, I saw a sparkle of conniving coyness. She purred, "You can trust me."

Exercising my masculine willpower in the face of her feminine wiles, I replied, "Niagara is a mysterious place. It is full of history and intrigue. That's all."

Whether or not that convinced her, I don't know. She did back off, but for the rest of my stay, my young nurses mothered me in a way that made me apprehensive. It made me wonder, did I surrender my secret during the operation? Would this be my unraveling?

While I believed that they heard much more than they were letting on, I had learned over the years, as part of British Niagara's influence, to keep a stiff upper lip and betray no confidences. This philosophy came in useful for me, a person who was, even at such an early age, hyper-vigilant when it came to holding my secrets close.

But now, so many years later, as I look into my soul, I realize that I have to unbolt the doors, unbar the windows, and enter into the cemetery of my own mind so that I can discover for myself exactly where all my buried demons are.

Evil Enters Like a Needle and Spreads Like an Oak Tree
—Ethiopian proverb

When he arrived in Niagara-on-the-Lake in October of 1949, Father Major Eugene Weaver, honored by the King of England, was a hero. He capitalized on his military reputation by encouraging the Catholic townsmen to become more active in the Church and soliciting commitments to re-energize the Holy Name Society.

My dad admired Father Weaver for his accomplishments and for his intelligence. As they were both well-read, they soon found they had many common topics of interest to discuss and became friends. Weaver impressed my father with the religious caring he displayed as our parish priest. He sympathized with Dad about Mother. But, too, he needed my dad's help with the stiffness and pain his arthritis caused him and the aching of his war wounds. And then he enrolled my older brothers, Jack and Doug, as altar boys.

The upshot? Very quickly, Father Major Weaver had enmeshed himself not only in my town and my religious community, but in my family as well.

At the time, I was just ten years old. I was also a Cub Scout. Another British hero, Baron Robert Baden-Powell had founded the Scouts, and given us the Cub Scout Promise which asked me to do the following:

1. On my honor to do my best.
2. To do my duty to God and the King.
3. To help other people at all times.
4. To obey the Scout Law.

(This was the British way. Rule Britannia!)

In all of that, the key was the word "obey." I was to obey my parents—even if one of them was an alcoholic. I was to obey teachers, political rulers, and other authorities.

But most of all, I was to obey God. And here is where the trouble began.

For Catholics, the priest is a direct representative of God. The priest has the mystical power to change bread and wine into the Body and Blood of Jesus Christ. He has the power to hear confessions and forgive sins. To not obey a priest is a venial sin.

Although I was a bit of a wild kid, I took the rules of Catholicism and the principles of the Scouts to heart. I did not want to jeopardize my immortal soul. I was so influenced by my religious training that I even scrutinized the labels on all cans so I wouldn't eat a particle of meat on Fridays. Even though it may not have seemed like I cared for rules, I obeyed what I deemed essential to the very best of my boyish ability.

On August 31, 1950, I, among others, was mentioned in an article in the *Niagara Advance*. We participated in Father Weaver's Silver Jubilee. I had the honor of reading an address, and Weaver managed to also involve my brother Jack as the Master of Ceremonies, my cousin Donna as the presenter of the illuminated bouquet, and Jim Marino, Rudy DalBianco, and Bruce Sherlock as acolytes.

All in all, the only person in my close circle that Father Weaver left out was my main protector, my brother Doug. In fact, he seemed to have deliberately gotten Doug out of his way.

At a catechism lesson, Weaver had challenged us, saying he would give fifty cents to anyone who could write out the Lord's Prayer from memory. At the next class, Doug was the only one to take up the challenge. He wrote out the prayer word for word, but Father Weaver refused to pay Doug because he did not include the punctuation. That was the last class Doug attended.

With Doug gone, Weaver was able to focus his attention on me. He taught both Pat and me how to serve at Mass, but then he told me that because Pat was adopted, he was a bastard, and a bastard could never become a priest. Somehow, this designation created a schism between my childhood friend and me, and had the effect of taking me further from the safety of friends and family, and closer to the viper's nest.

From that point, I was asked to serve at most of the weddings and funerals that were performed in our parish church. For my duties, I received envelopes of money from the families of the deceased or of the bride and groom. The dollars I was handed ensured that I would return to serve again the next time Father Weaver asked me.

In addition to services, Weaver always had other special duties for me. I helped count the collections, because, as he said, I had experience counting money at The Store. Father did not pay me for my help directly, but he made sure that the U.S. money was not recorded. It was kept back for personal spending in the States. That was a secret between us, of course.

In the U.S., he took me to shows. He took me shopping. He would buy me anything I wanted. He took me to a magic shop in Buffalo and bought me magic tricks. He bought me a pellet pistol for my very own that not only shot pellets, but darts, as well—and the good Father made sure I had a large supply of ammo to go with it.

Father Weaver bought me the first commercial *Wham-O* slingshot in Niagara; a set of throwing knives; a stiletto knife and a spring release switchblade; a hunting bow and arrow set. To add to this arsenal he gave me his under-and-over 22 plus 410 shotgun combination, a World War II paratroopers' survival gun that he brought back.

I shot a lot of game with that gun. I would go out by myself on my bike, with the gun hidden in a shoulder holster under my coat and shoot whatever I could find.

How did we get most of this weaponry back across the border? He wore his collar and, because he was always importing religious articles, it was routine for us to hear, "Go ahead, Father," as we crossed. The one time when that wasn't the case, he used attack as his defense: "Hey, Mr. Custom's man, I have not seen you at Mass. Is everything all right?" The man sheepishly waved us through, mumbling something under his breath.

The Secret is Always Wrapped in Fear

The hook was set. Father Weaver had made himself the source of my personal treasure. Slyly, he had also made sure that we shared secrets, like my possession of the extraordinary weapons.

He also had two pistols, one being a *Colt 45*. He offered to let me shoot it. I declined, for I could hardly hold it straight. It was heavy, and he confirmed it had quite a kick.

Another secret was how we spent the U.S. currency that was donated to the Church. He shared that he could say a Black Mass and damn the persons that he did not like. His curse would make bad things happen to them. He had even "taken my measurements," stating he wanted to be sure that I was healthy. Of course, for accuracy, I had to be nude.

How did things get this far?

It started with Father Weaver's "concern" about his friend, John Bates' younger boy. He offered to help me with my grades. Also he groomed me to become his favorite altar boy.

For my dad, who was working sixty hours a week at The Store, forming the first Niagara-on-the-Lake Chamber of Commerce, and trying to cope with Mother, the offer of help from a man he trusted and admired was welcomed. It allowed Dad to relinquish a situation with which he could no longer cope.

Father Weaver used the cunning of a wolf, cultivated trust and secrets to ensnare the naive. This priest knew what he was about. He took time with me, listened to me, taught me about life, and shared the gossip of the parish with me. He confided in me and made me feel special.

If only I had known then what I know now: I was being entrapped, first with family friendship and religion; then with illicit gifts and shared secrets; finally, with the biggest invasion of all.

Bluebird Freel had built Father Weaver a boat. Weaver often asked me to join him on a fishing expedition or just putt-putting along the river. Finally, he convinced me to sun bathe nude. I had often swum nude before. Sometimes we kids would even lie on the warm, secluded break wall. However I had never sunbathed nude on a boat, and I had to be convinced no one would see me.

While I was lying on the deck, face down and feeling self-conscious of my naked state, the boat suddenly shifted, and caught my tiny penis in a crack. Modesty forgotten, I jumped up, screaming, and tore at what was left of my foreskin in the process.

This must have been the moment the fox had been hoping for. He immediately came to my rescue and graciously rubbed salve on my penis until it stopped hurting.

After that, he took me to Toronto to ball games and wrestling matches. We went to see Bob Hope and to a wrestling match where I got to meet professional wrestler Whipper Willie Watson. Somehow, I had become Father Weaver's traveling companion. I still worked in The Store and spent time with my friends, but routinely I saw Weaver at least once or twice a week, except when he went away in the winter.

One day, Father Major Weaver explained, quite solemnly, that he was a wounded veteran, and that the "flak" he'd been shot with had stored up poison in his body. He needed help to purge himself of the build-up. Would I be willing to help him get rid of it?

I had been indoctrinated by Church and Cub Scouts "To do my duty to God and the King" and "To help other people at all times." How could I refuse to help a wounded priest? My mentor? My friend?

I'll leave the poison and the manner of its release to your imagination.

Double Barrel

From the time I was eleven years old, I was living what was, for all practical purposes, a double life. On the outside, I looked every inch a kid living life to the fullest, making much mischief but doing no irreparable harm. I was committing only venial sins, not mortal sins.

But that was out where everyone could see. Behind closed doors my life was dark and frightening. With Father Weaver's first sexual contact, I heard the gates of Hell slam shut behind me. And no one could hear me screaming because I kept all the terrors locked inside.

There were so many reasons I could not reach out for help. First, the abuse I was being subjected to was homosexual, and on the street, the label "queer" was a point of no return. Then, there was the question of how I could ever point the finger at a war hero. Who would believe me? I most certainly dared not share this with the anti-Catholic Masonic teachers.

Finally, if my shameful secret were to be discovered, I thought it would destroy Dad's reputation in town. Then what would happen if the tabloids got wind of it.

In all my confusion, I looked up to, respected, and admired this person. I later learned that this was the typical Stockholm Syndrome that develops with many victims who are in some way held captive by their abuser. Instinctively, the abuser counts on this response. Also, my fear paralyzed all reasoning.

For all of these reasons, I kept my mouth shut and, yes, obeyed

After Neil, Pat, and I broke into the boat, causing the town to drag for our bodies, this Father Weaver, our family friend, thoughtfully offered to take me away from the bad influence of my Niagara friends.

We headed to Florida. It was hot, and I got carsick and slept most of the way. Although I did enjoy *Sea World*—and when I swam in the ocean at night, I was impressed by the phosphorescent bubbles that lit up like millions of fireflies—I hated Florida, generally. Father Weaver must have wanted to keep me happy, because he just turned around and drove straight to Sault St. Marie, where we stayed at one of his friend's houses.

At the friend's house, I met a girl of about fourteen. She and I were playing in private, and she came on to me. I responded by kissing her, and she manipulated me into feeling her breasts—then hurriedly said she had to go.

Was she checking out my sexual preference? Did she know about Weaver's predilections?

We traveled on to the Bishop's house. I found the Bishop to be open and friendly. That is why when we were alone I cautiously broached the subject of my situation, hoping for help. I was quickly rebuked.

I was trapped. I wanted to believe what Father Weaver told me: It was okay because I was special. Also, some of what I was getting I liked: I liked my toys. I liked the attention I received.

I believed that I was the only one that he ever did this with. In my naivety I interpreted this sickness as a form of love.

But none of that was a true reward for what I was going through. There were times when I thought I was losing my mind. I experienced a deep-seated anger that bordered on hopeless hate. Worse, I believed that I was part of the problem, that somehow I deserved what I was getting.

I was as bad as my mother had always told me I was. Therefore, the abuse was my fault. The sexual contact occurred again and again, but I could tell no one. I tried to hide the secret in the recesses of my mind, but I was always afraid it would spill out of my mouth.

But when I had my dark night of the soul, on the night that the only light available to me was the pulse of the lighthouse across the river, I was given the gift I needed, the gift of determination. That gift gave me the courage I needed to walk up to the door of a decorated hero and a sexual abuser, carrying all that I could find that he had bought for me.

I wanted him out of my life. I wanted to be rid of the past. To be free. When I told him I did not want to see him anymore, his only response was, "At least you know you are not queer."

No. Weaver was right; I wasn't homosexual. But I was damaged. I carried the burden of having lived that double life. This continued for many years after the abuse was no longer a part of my existence.

***

Later in life, when the tension of keeping everything inside made me physically ill, I went to see the doctor but was unable to tell him about my secret—and he never asked. Instead, he just prescribed medicine for my bleeding ulcer, which stopped the bleeding, but nothing else.

By adulthood, the secret had become a deeply embedded part of me, and I was angry. To keep my anger under control, I worked compulsively, smoked, and drank too much. It wasn't until my children were growing up that Joan was able to convince me to get the help I needed, the help I had been refused first by a Bishop and then by a retreat priest in confession.

Unless you have experienced something similar, it is difficult to understand how such a thing can affect one's rational behavior. But people like me live with a sense that they have to be in control. I had to be extremely vigilant. Trust did not come easily. I had to put on an armored front to protect me. I had to become a survivor.

I wish I could say that after getting help and support, I lived happily ever after. But if that were true, I would not be writing this book, would I?

BACK TO THE OLD TOWN

Premonition or Faith?

In the summer of 1956, the Niagara District High School was being built. I worked on the building as an employee of Smith Brothers Contractors. They were implementing a relatively new construction technique, developed by Canadian Lift Slab, in which each floor was poured on top of the one below it and was then raised up to its final position. This meant that the last level to be poured was the roof.

I was making more money than I had ever made before. My job was much easier than it had sounded at first. I worked at night and was supposed to be keeping the freshly laid concrete wet. That meant walking around every hour hosing down the concrete to keep it cool. Of course, I developed a better method.

After everyone left each evening, I put up a straw berm all along the periphery of the new concrete. Then I flooded the slabs with about an inch of water. That task done, I could sleep in the straw, write letters, or listen to the radio. Dad even let me take his car sometimes so I would have a comfortable place to rest. At dawn, I would sweep up the straw and sign out before the day crew arrived at seven.

Towards the end of July, I was on the day shift, working on the main floor. The top floor had just been raised, and part of my job was to clean out the supporting posts so the next floor could follow along the girder. I was on the ground floor chipping out loose concrete, when, suddenly, something happened which I cannot explain. It was like a bright flash. Then a megaphone-loud inner voice caused me to roll over onto my side and look up. I did so, and watched, frozen and stunned as I saw a two-by-four bulleting towards me from four floors up. As if I were being instructed, I pushed away with all my might and that cannoning missile, which would have splattered my brains all over the floor, instead, only hammered my index finger to a pulp.

I screamed, clutching my finger in pain and panic. The foreman was there in seconds. He tried to pry my hand open, but I wouldn't let him even look at it.

I was in shock, but I still managed to mumble that our doctor's office was close by. They rushed me to the doctor, who froze the finger and sewed me up. The X-ray showed that my finger was smashed, broken in seventeen places below the last knuckle.

The doctor continued to treat my finger weekly, making sure it was not infected. Finally, in September, two months after the accident, he told me to look at the wall. I did so, but out of the corner of my eye, I could see the needle he was going to stick into the end of my finger. I jerked as I saw him pricking it, but I felt nothing. My reaction saved me from amputation.

"Great," he said, "Now I won't have to remove it."

It took years before I got most of the feeling back in my claw, but some of the inconvenience was tempered by the worker's comp payments I continued to collect into November.

Still, when my dad had inquired, the foreman denied that there had been any two-by-four at all. I guess they wanted to avoid a law suit.

***

For some time, Niagara District High School, the building which almost claimed my life, was in its own life-or-death struggle—to keep its doors open. Unfortunately, its death knell has been rung. Still, whenever I pass the corner of East/West Line and Highway 55, I am reminded of how I literally put my blood, sweat, and tears into the education of generations of high school students in Niagara-on-the-Lake.

But even deeper, is another association I make with that school building. Seeing it always reminds me that I cannot count the number of times that, out of the blue, someone or something has come to my aid. Although I have tried to deny it, after a lifetime of such help, I am resolved: I just have to believe in angels. As I write this, I know that the little boy I was, the one examining the prayer card Maw gave me all those years ago, has been proved right. Michael, or one of his agents, has always had my back.

World Scout Jamboree

The World Scout Jamboree has been held in a different international location approximately once every four years since 1920. When a Jamboree location is named by The World Organization of the Scout Movement, that town begins to make plans to have tens of thousands of Scouts—mainly fourteen- to seventeen-year-old boys—and other Jamboree visitors arrive for the Scouting events and exhibitions and to engage with the local culture. Like having a small-scale Olympic Games arrive on your doorstep, hosting a World Scout Jamboree takes years of coordination and planning—and can put a town on the world map.

This was the case when Niagara-on-the-Lake was invited to host the 1955 World Scout Jamboree. Our Jamboree was the first one to be held outside of Europe, and much preparation was required. Thanks to the effort of various government agencies and, notably, Fred Curtis and the Niagara-on-the-Lake Chamber of Commerce, the Herculean tasks facing Niagara were completed in time for the opening of the Jamboree.

One of the biggest tasks to be undertaken, the widening of the Niagara Stone Road, had to be completed to allow the traffic to funnel from the Queen Elizabeth Highway to the Jamboree site at the Commons. In addition, the roads and bridges from Toronto to Niagara all needed to be upgraded with the cooperation of the Town, the Province, and the Federal Government.

Of course, advertising was in full swing. Although, initially, many thought the Jamboree was being held in the more famous city of Niagara Falls, the international press soon corrected that misperception, and the television and print exposure given to this international event—including the world-wide televising of the ten-day event itself—gave Niagara-on-the-Lake the sort of publicity that comes along only once in a lifetime.

In fact, long after the Scouts and other Jamboree visitors had gone, the fame that Niagara-on-the-Lake earned from the Jamboree continued to draw entrepreneurial-minded businessmen to the town. They came with a variety of ideas, all hoping to build upon the success of the Jamboree. With its new, high profile and the modernized roads and bridges, which made for easier access, Niagara-on-the-Lake had become Canada's new in spot.

But before our great success, we had to deal with one last, completely unexpected, challenge! Three days before the opening, the tail end of Hurricane Connie whipped in and slapped at the Jamboree camp grounds for almost 24 hours. Connie's last breaths were enough to flatten what had taken six weeks to set up.

In a heartening, community-wide response to the almost-disaster, volunteers arrived on the scene—including employees from the Coca-Cola Company, which sent many workers to aid in the effort—and restored the camp to its original state in time for the opening ceremonies.

On Saturday, August 20th, 1955, the World Scout Jamboree was officially opened by His Excellency, the Right Honorable Vincent Massey, Governor-General of Canada and Chief Scout for Canada. Among other dignitaries also in attendance were Jackson Dodds, the Jamboree Camp Chief; Lady Baden Powell; and Lord Rowallan, Chief Scout for the British Commonwealth.

All told, over 11,000 Scouts from 71 countries and colonies attended. Counting the support crew, the Scouts' friends and relatives, and the general spectators, some speculate that during that famous ten days in her history, Niagara-on-the-Lake at times played host to more than 100,000 people.

The Store, as a central location for visitors, had its role to play in all of this. I was front and center, helping my dad during the Jamboree. We were so busy, we had to let people inside, lock the door, wait on them, escort them out, and then let the next group in. To aid efficiency, Dad set up a booth outside to handle the most popular items: pop and ice-cream rolls. Inside, the biggest seller was the diarrhea treatment, extract of wild strawberry.

Whether we were inside or out, we were so busy that we were continuously sending out for new supplies. There were times when I was so busy, I was just guessing at prices, as I didn't have even a minute to look anything up, and all the other store helpers were busy with their own customers.

Traffic was another challenge—and parking was in short supply. To help, Dad opened up his open lots on King Street and had Doug and me place boards across the ditch so drivers had easy access to the grassy areas he was offering for public parking.

Working behind the counter, I made many short-term friendships with kids my age—and even with many of the older Scouts, who were only too happy to have someone to practice their English on. From them, I learned that, while the Scouts originated in Great Britain, other countries had different pledges and salutes. For instance, the U.S. salute, which did not acknowledge the British King, raised only two fingers, while our Canadian salute comprised three raised fingers.

No matter their language or salute style, though, what all the Scouts had in common was their fierce loyalty and their commitment to service and giving.

But even when they were familiar with the generosity of the Scouting community, I could tell that some the parents of the visiting Scouts were very impressed by the efforts put forth by the citizens of Niagara for the Jamboree. When they got home, these parents spread the word: Until then, my quaint little town had not been well-known, but once the Scouting families told about their experiences in Niagara-on-the-Lake, many Americans put us on their must-see lists.

With all of this excitement, the summer was passing quickly, but a part of me was still in Kitchener. I missed Joan. We had known we would be separated during the summer, and the sadness we felt twined around us. Our hearts were linked by our adopted song, the Righteous Brothers *Unchained Melody*.

Little did either of us know then that this song would wind its way through our lifetime together, its popularity revived by its use in the 1990 movie *Ghost*. Thinking about it now, I cannot fathom how I would have reacted to seeing *Ghost* if Joan had not married me.

Still, although we were sad, Joan, strongly influenced by the Church, had made it clear to me that she could not go steady. While I was disappointed, I understood—but her lack of commitment left me free to "explore" that summer—and "explore," I did.

One opportunity occurred when I learned about a group of girls who were having a slumber party. "What is a party without guys?" I asked myself. No sort of party at all! And I made it known that three of us were available: myself, a Scout friend from Europe, and one from eastern Ontario.

We were welcomed and enjoyed a relatively harmless evening, experimenting with our make-out techniques.

Eventually, I had to travel back to what felt like the completely different world of Kitchener and St. Jerome's and left the events of summer far behind me. Almost.

When I came home at Thanksgiving, Dad said there was a letter for me from Europe. The envelope, which turned out to be from my European Scout friend, had an official crest on it. In his note, he graciously thanked me for his first introduction to real teen life, for generally, his life was and had been closely protected. I was surprised, as I had always envisioned that the Europeans were far more sexually advanced to us. I guess that might be true—unless you are royalty.

I was too involved in my own life to reply to this royal missive, a fact I regret to this day. But almost fifty years later, when I visited Europe in 2002, I did try to find the man—that boy who had been my friend for those short few weeks, and I managed to narrow his identity down to one likely prospect—a man who appeared to be a king! Not surprisingly, all my attempts at contacting this man, who might or might not have been my boyhood friend, were protectively blocked; I was not even allowed to leave him a message. Oh, well. That is one opportunity I missed, and not the only regret I have about moving through life and leaving friends behind.

The Cayuga's Last Days

The Cayuga was in dire financial trouble. The union was demanding salary rates commensurate with those for freighter workers, but the Cayuga, which was a passenger vessel, whose revenue fluctuated with the tourist trade, could not sustain those pay rates for her crew. And after 75 years of service, the Cayuga stopped running.

In 1954, just before the Jamboree arrived in Niagara, the townspeople, aided by Canadian Crown Corporations rallied to buy the Cayuga. They struck a $100,000 deal with Canada Steam Ship Lines, enough to get the ship back in the water starting June 1, 1954. The deal included the Toronto slip, the Niagara dock, and the Queenston wharf. Soon moonlight cruises were offered: "Board the Cayuga, and Dance to the Enchanting Moonlight Music of Tex Armstrong," the advertisements read. "Return ticket $9.75."

At 16, I was too old to dive beside the old girl, but I was exactly the right age to stroll up the gangplank and enjoy her new, romantic possibilities. Even if we could not go to Toronto, we former river rats and local girls were able to ride our old friend in style, dancing all the way to Queenston and back.

That grand old lady survived to transport tens of thousands of Scouts and visitors in 1955, and soldiered on until 1957, when the fight to keep her alive finally gave up the ghost, due to the union's demands, new government regulations, and the final nail in her coffin, the refusal of the Province to grant her a liquor license.

If the union's greed put this Niagara stateswoman into a death struggle, the Ontario government's refusal to grant her a liquor license put her out of her misery, and a huge chunk of Niagara-on-the-Lake's history died with "Her Majesty, the Cayuga."

The last photo I saw of this once-majestic icon ship was of her listing in ruin at Toronto Harbor, waiting to be dismantled for scrap.

Thanks to Jim Smith's newspaper articles and photographs, and his model, which is proudly displayed in the Museum, many memories return to those who dove alongside her, witnessed her proud bulk manoeuvring the waterways, or traveled aboard her, and we proudly declare, "I remember when."

If it is not possible to mourn a ship, it is at least, possible to mourn the passing of memories which included her.

Homecoming

I had had enough of boarding school and was returning to Niagara for Grade Thirteen. I'd spent the summer working at J.M. Schneider's meat packers in order to be with Joan. The night before school started, she and I were making a late and prolonged farewell. I finally left Kitchener at six in the morning, with only a few hours' sleep under my belt.

I was not paying much attention, and suddenly I saw a stop sign looming and a transport truck just entering the intersection. I slammed on the brakes, but my 1956 Volkswagen hit first a pothole, then the stop sign, and then rolled over into the intersection.

A schoolteacher, who lived nearby and had seen the accident, came running from her house and helped me escape the car through the smashed windshield.

My head was bleeding profusely. I should have been dead (again), but I was so strong from shoveling tons of sausage each morning and lugging carcasses each afternoon at my Schneider's summer job, that during the accident, I had managed to hold on to the steering wheel. In fact, I held that wheel so hard that I bent it in half trying to keep from hitting the roof. And I did not hit the roof— the roof hit me. It caved in on top of my head. Seat belts and air bags were not installed in cars.

The teacher kindly drove me the few miles into Dundas to see a doctor. Once my lacerations were cleaned out, my dad, who had been called, arrived to take me home. Back at the house, I had a blinding headache and took two 222s. After sleeping for about a half-an-hour, I woke up to such blinding pain behind my eyes that I could not see or think.

Dad took me to our doctor. Finding that I not only had a whiplash and a contusion, but also had multiple splinters of glass embedded deep into my skull, the doctor closed the doors to his practice, so that he could operate immediately.

Ultimately, he sewed me up with twenty-seven stitches, but reassured me by saying that I would hardly see the scar when I went bald like my dad. (He was right. Now I am bald, and you can only faintly see the scar.)

Because of the accident, I ended up a week late for school and just did not have the wherewithal to catch up. I was more interested in helping Fred Sentinel repair my totalled, uninsured Volkswagen. Fred was indebted to Dad for all the financial support he had given Fred in the past. Dad, of course, had refused to acknowledge any obligation on Fred's part; that was just Dad's way. But Fred's way was to pay back—which he did, by rescuing my VW and more importantly, teaching me something about auto bodywork.

I only passed two subjects that year and probably would not have passed even those if it were not for the help of Bob Kirkby. But knowing that my dad hoped one of us boys would take over the store, I returned to school the following year, and this time, with the help of two kind teachers, passed another two subjects.

With so few academic achievements, I could have considered these two years a total write-off. But actually, I learned two important life skills: acceptance and appreciation.

The acceptance, I applied to my mother. I finally understood that I was responsible neither to hold her accountable for her actions, nor to try to change her.

The appreciation, I applied to my father. I finally understood that his spirit connected with mine. I could both see and take pride in his honesty. Someone I had considered somewhat "wimpy", I now saw as a genuine, kind, humble, and intelligent man. Even though he never outwardly expressed it, I knew he cared about me and loved me very much. Before, I had respected my dad, but had wanted him to be different from how I saw him. From that time on, though, I was able to love him very much, just the way he was.

Unfortunately, I still gave him a hard time. Back then, I did not know why. Once I had my own boys, though, I realized how natural it is for a son to push against his dad, as he struggles to become his own man.

PART TWO
- LIFE AFTER NIAGARA -

I can enhance the pleasure of life by meeting and experiencing the pain first and then I have to get it over with.

Adapted from M. Scott Peck, *Road Less Travelled*, p. 19.

LOVE DETERMINATION, LIFE EXPERIENCES

The Greater the Challenge, the Greater the Reward

Joan and I went together for over four years, but finally, our bumpy relationship ended. There were several issues that contributed to our break-up. For one, we lived almost a hundred miles from one another, which was a difficulty in itself.

And then, our personalities were so different: Joan was preparing to become a teacher. Teachers are rule-makers and rule-followers. I, on the other hand, was a rule-breaker. So, while Joan had a career planned out, I had no clue what I was going to do in life. I only knew that school was defeating me.

We also had different ideas about what it meant to "go steady." Joan relied on the Baltimore Catechism for guidance, while I relied on a logic that migrated back and forth from heaven to purgatory. We even explained ourselves to each other in diametrically opposed ways, Joan speaking in concrete terms and perfectly structured sentences, me, in the abstract.

Add to this the issues I had to deal with, both from my mother's alcoholism and Father Weaver's sexual abuse—which I had yet to realize I would need to deal with. Joan found it difficult to understand some of my dysfunction. It is understandable that Joan would ask respectfully, but firmly, to end our commitment.

Rather than just making a phone call or sending me a letter, Joan drove all the way to Niagara to explain why it was over: She told me how much she cared, but that our long distant relationship was too confining. It was too stressful.

We cried and said goodbye. But after she left, I had such serious regrets, that I hopped into my dad's car and raced up Highway 55 until I caught up to her, intending to get her to pull over and reconsider.

As I passed her, though, I saw that her face was focused, she was staring straight ahead. She did not even recognize me. I truly loved Joan and always wanted what was best for her, so, reluctantly, sadly, I accepted our fate. I pulled off at the next road and returned to Niagara with my heart between my knees.

Now single, on June 24, 1959, my 21st birthday, I found myself alone. I had two choices: I could go out and get drunk with my old drinking buddies, or I could meet up with a non-drinking friend. I opted to go to a movie with my non-drinking friend.

This meant that the next day, when I found myself standing in our small, dirty, cluttered kitchen, in my father's house in Niagara-on-the-Lake, I was not only absolutely alone, I was also absolutely sober. In this state, I could see things very clearly.

First, I could see that my parents appeared to have forgotten a very important milestone in my life. Second, I could see that Joan was the girl for me. Though it had been a while since we had separated, I still missed her deeply. I wanted to marry her. I wanted her to be the mother of my children.

Yes, life was unfair, I thought. Sure, it sucked big time. But I did not have to take it anymore. I mustered my determination, and, the next thing I knew, without saying goodbye to any of my family, I had thrown my clothes into the back of my only partially repaired Volkswagen and, with little money, no job, and no place to stay, I was on my way to Kitchener. I was on my way to Joan.

The Marines say, "The greater the challenge, the greater the reward." And Joan, who proved to be quite a challenge, also proved a great reward.

The first piece of this particular challenge was to find a source of income. I went to J.M. Schneider's only to be told that they were not aware that I was coming back, and did not have any openings for me. Fortunately, John Schneider went to bat for me. He called my old foreman, Ed, who was overjoyed to hear that I'd returned. His new rookie was proving difficult to train.

I was told to report at seven the next morning.

The people at Schneider's treated me like family, even keeping me on when the summer help went back to school. I became a floater, working in different parts of the operation. Some jobs I immensely disliked, like shackling the pigs, hooking them onto a conveyor belt, and sending them to be stuck in the jugular vein to bleed to death. (Even now, if I hear a baby scream, I flash back to the sounds of the "kill.") Another unpleasant job was pulling apart the intestines, washing out the fecal matter—including very large worms. These intestines would then be brined and sent to be filled with the meat I had prepared in the morning.

But whether I liked the task or despised it, I did whatever was asked; I needed the money to pursue my dream. And my determination finally wore her down. Joan and I were together again.

My various bosses were pleased to show me how their departments were run. They found work for me into November, when I was invited to train as a full-time foreman. This was a great honor, but I could not see myself cooped up in a factory for the rest of my life. By then, I knew I wanted to learn sales. Unfortunately there were no sales openings at Schneider's.

(To add an interesting and probably controversial note, some years after this, Joan and I went to Bingaman Park Lodge, a place famous for German food and good beer. As we were looking for a seat, John Schneider of J.M. Schneider's spotted us and invited us to join him. It was a bit of a reunion, and John told us they were celebrating the first, unofficial Oktoberfest and gave me a blue paper Bier Doktor souvenir that I still have to this day. As I watched John Schneider seated in his wheel chair and raising his glass in a toast to making Oktoberfest an annual event, little did I realize that what we were attending was the first of what would ultimately be billed as the largest Oktoberfest celebration in the world, outside of Munich.)

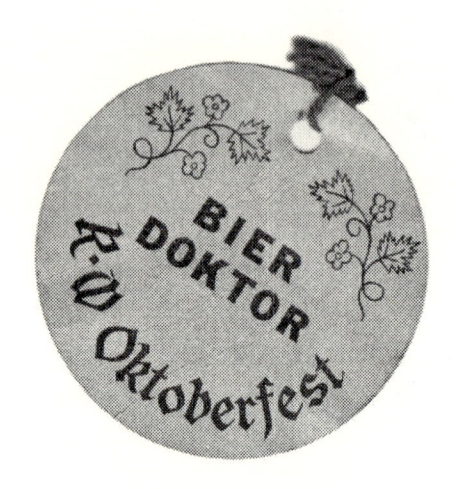

Bier Doktor souvenir

Reluctantly leaving the "family" at Schneider's, I found a sales job at a sporting goods store, which took me through Christmas. Then, taking a cue from my friend Bernie, a door-to-door Bible salesman, who always seemed to have lots of money, I decided to give that a try.

Since I arrived on the Bible-sales scene armed with a glowing letter of introduction from the famous Father Bullbrook, the local priests endorsed me and sent me all the leads I could handle.

Noticing that, in my travels, I was passing by a lot of non-Catholic homes. I quickly requested copies of the King James Version, which I kept in separate compartments of my case. When I was at a Catholic home, I asked who in the neighborhood was non-Catholic, and, because, during the late 1950s and early 1960s, everyone in smaller cities knew their neighbors, I would get directed to houses where I could pitch my non-Catholic Bibles, too.

From this experience, I learned I was a natural, an easily successful salesman. I had never made so much money, and from my customers, I heard a tremendous number of first-hand stories about real life. However, going door to door was not a profession for a family man, and I was determined to be a family man!

I applied to Traders Acceptance Corporation. Here I learned about contracts, money-lending, and repossessions. My friend John Cziraki, who had covered my back during that first fight at St. Jerome's, joined me. The two of us, now repo-men, considered ourselves a detective duo. No delinquent was going to get away with not paying, we decided, and went out of our way to "get our man", using tactics that would not be quite as acceptable today!

For example, a car-dealership owner pleaded for us to repo a car on which the payments were many months overdue. John and I learned where the defaulting vehicle owner lived but never found him at home. Finally, around two o'clock one Sunday morning, we decided to stake out our fugitive. His house was dark, but we could see the car in the shadows.

Quite handy with the tools of our trade, we prepared to hot wire the car and get it started. I popped the hood and removed the air filter, spraying ether into the manifold. John crossed the wires. Bam! The carburetor erupted into flames. I doused the fire with gravel, threw the filter into the back seat, and hopped in beside John, who revved the car and made the tires squeal, breaking the Sunday night silence.

The door of the house flew open to reveal a madman, shouting, swearing, and waving a pistol. But before he could take aim, we were gone.

John raced back to my car so I could follow him back to the dealership. There, we locked the repossessed car and went in search of a pay phone to call the police, as we'd been trained to do. When we told the desk sergeant all the details, he suggested we get back to our homes as quickly as possible, before the Italian brotherhood found out who we were.

Now I was gainfully employed, and Joan and I were together again. While I was happy in my relationship with Joan, I wasn't moving toward anything further, not yet. However, Joan had different plans. If we were going to be together, she told me, it was time to take things to the next step. She wasn't going to wait forever.

So, having just paid my dad the money I'd borrowed for a car to replace the VW, which quite pleased him, I had to ask him for another loan. This time, to buy a ring. He obliged, and with a few dollars to my name and a good job, I proposed to Joan, and we set a date: The happy day was scheduled for July 15th 1961.

***

Nothing in my life has been simple, so why would I expect this day to be any different?

Catholic weddings of that era followed a formula: a Mass, always held on a Saturday morning, followed by a lunch reception for close friends and relatives, then a party, complete with dinner and dancing in the evening. All very proper.

That is, until my loving mother showed up before the service with her hat on cockeyed, her stockings twisted, and her speech slurred. She practically needed to be carried down the aisle to her seat.

Joan's mother, Olive, and her father, Orland, were aghast. My about-to-be bride was in tears.

My mother's behavior was so outrageous that even Father Jack, Joan's mother's cousin, who was officiating, was a nervous wreck. He ended up marrying Joan Tank to "William Tank," not to William Bates, the man standing at the altar!

To make matters worse (if that's possible), Joan had given her mother her engagement ring for safe-keeping before going to the church. After the ceremony, Joan asked her mother for the ring, only to be told that someone had gone back to the house to retrieve it.

After the luncheon, when the ring had yet to be produced, Joan repeated her request, which was met with more stalling.

Finally, we returned to her parent's house to be told that the ring had been lost—the very same ring for which I still owed money to dad. Fortunately, I had been smart enough to buy an insurance policy on our belongings. So what could go wrong—right?

Still, despite all the awkward blunders of the day, those vows stuck. When Father Jack was completing his blessing at the altar, he said, "Now the two of you are one." Back then, how could we ever have envisioned that, after fifty years of marriage, being "one" would mean it would take the two of us to do one thing?

I Never Walked Alone

Joan and I honeymooned in South Florida. Joan's aunt and uncle lent us their older model car for the trip, but warned us to be careful, as the gas gauge did not work properly. I should have listened more carefully, as the country we would be traveling through was a very different world from Ontario, Canada.

While there was still segregation throughout the United States at this time—separate drinking fountains and washrooms for whites and for blacks was common—in the southern states, including Florida, segregation was more pervasive, meaner, and more stringently enforced.

People of color had to sit at the back of buses; they were not allowed to enter through the front door of a "white" store. When Joan and I crossed the Mason-Dixon Line, we had entered the domain of the hooded, white-robed, Ku Klux Klan, a world where crosses were burned on lawns, and Negroes were hung from trees.

This was also an era during which very few four-lane highways had been constructed. The Tamiami Trail, which sliced right across South Florida, was one of the first—although it wasn't four lanes for its entirety. Still, it was a novelty for its time, and we were traveling the historic road on our way from Miami to Tampa, just as it was getting dark.

Joan, who was driving, looked at the gas gauge and said, "I think we should get gas. I do not trust the gauge."

I glanced over. "It says the tank is over a quarter full," I said. "Traffic is too heavy to cut across, so let's just get to the next station on the right. Just keep going."

Joan listened to me, and soon the wide, modern, four-lane Trail narrowed to two lanes—two very dark lanes. As we traveled a few miles without any sign of civilization, through the open windows, we could hear the eerie, swampy noises of the Everglades calling from either side.

Finally, we saw a lane that led to a gas station. Joan pulled into the station, but it was closed. The car coughed as we coasted up to the locked pumps, and then it died. The tank was empty. I tried to siphon a few drops from each of the hose nozzles, but to no avail. We were stuck. It was pitch black. It had to have been ninety-five degrees. And the dive-bomber mosquitoes were shrieking straight out of the swamp, aiming for our flesh.

I walked back to the road and tried to flag down a passing car, but no one would come to our aid. They just sped by. Thinking that they might be afraid of me, I told Joan to give it a try, hoping they would stop for a woman. Joan did as I asked, and stood at the side of the road waving her hands in distress, as I flashed the headlights to draw attention.

No luck.

The later it got, the fewer cars passed. We huddled together in the safety of the car wondering what to do. At first we'd rolled up the windows to keep the mosquitoes out, but as the interior of the car became a steam bath, I took a pair of my wife's pantyhose and stretched them over an open window as an ineffective screen.

The pine-like scent from the dark, damp, cypress swamp crept through the pantyhose, irritating our sinuses until we felt like we were suffocating.

We had just about decided that we would have to camp out in the car until the gas station opened in the morning, but I wanted to give it one more try. I went back to the road, where I could see lights in the distance. This time, I stood way out in the middle of the pavement where whoever was driving would be sure to see me, and Joan flashed our car lights.

I jumped back to the side of the road as the oncoming vehicle flashed its headlights back at us, blinding me momentarily. Then I heard a great squeal of brakes skidding past. It was a huge transport truck—and the driver had stopped.

I hopped into the passenger's side and explained what had happened. The driver, a black man, agreed to take us for gasoline. I called for Joan to jump in beside me.

My wife of less than a week had her doubts. Because I was in the middle, closest to the driver, she leaned over and whispered, "Give me your wallet."

I pushed her hand away. I couldn't imagine how she would protect my wallet, if I could not. Besides, I had more confidence in this enterprise than Joan did. From my days of hitchhiking from St. Jerome's to Niagara, I knew something about truck drivers. They might be tough, but they also tended to be generous and caring.

As for the man's skin color? That was a fact that did not concern me.

The driver turned his fourteen-wheeler back in the direction from which he had just come, taking us about ten miles up the road to a gas station that featured a dilapidated general store, with Spanish moss drifting from the oak trees to complete the spooky, dimly back-lit southern-swamp scene.

I asked our truck-driving savior if I could buy him a pop. Then I held the door to the general store open so he could enter before me. He hadn't even stepped over that threshold when a gruff voice boomed out, "BOY! KNOW YOUR PLACE. YOU STAY OUTSIDE."

The driver looked at me and mouthed, "It's all right," and stepped back towards his truck. I went on in and found the gruff man, none too friendly, but after I gave him a twenty-dollar deposit, he allowed me to have a gas can and two gallons of gas.

I didn't have very much cash, mostly traveler's checks, which the store would not take, but I paid for the gas, and three pops, and climbed back into the fourteen-wheeler.

As we made our way back down the road, we told our driver that we were on our honeymoon and learned that he was from Washington State and was carrying a load of watermelons from Florida to take back west.

A well-educated man, he understood he was in Ku Klux Klan territory. He had to deal with it, and stay out of trouble as best he could, as he had his job to do.

Back at our car, he graciously helped put the precious gas into our tank. Thanking him, I folded the only cash I had left, two dollars, and put it into his shirt pocket. He protested, but I told him to please keep it. We shook hands, and he headed to his truck.

As I revved the motor in the pitch-black darkness, I saw a silhouette. It was the truck driver coming back to the car. My bride asked me what I had put in his pocket. I told her it was our last two dollars.

Joan moaned, "Oh, no!" and I mentally finished her thought, "Oh, no, you cheap skate!"

A loud rap at Joan's window startled her, and reluctantly, she rolled it down. Through the window, our driver, our rescuer, handed my wife a huge, ripe watermelon and added a wish that we share it with prayerful love.

Back to the Ring

When we returned home at the end of two weeks, I phoned the insurance company to find out that my belongings were insured from twelve o'clock noon, not from eleven a.m., the time we made our vows.

Okay. No problem, for it was Joan's mom who lost the ring, not me. Therefore, their household policy would surely cover it.

And it would have if Joan's father would only have made the claim, but he would not.

He had spent a lot of money on the wedding which he had promised to do. And we certainly appreciated it. But he would not set in motion the process by which we could recover the amount needed to replace his daughter's engagement ring, his daughter who had always been attentive and there for her mother and father.

Sure, I could understand that my mother had upset them. And I wasn't kidding myself that I was their ideal son-in-law. In their eyes, I was a high-school dropout, a sausage maker, and a bible thumper, who had become a repo man. But I also knew that my father-in-law's own marriage had not been sanctioned by his parents, so I thought he would be able to relate. No such luck.

But, blessed with the gift of determination, I sloughed off my feelings and did what needed to be done. Going to our Traders Acceptance lawyer, I told him my predicament. I made a case that the ring could not be considered lost until I knew it was lost, which wasn't until two p.m.

The lawyer thought I had a point. Besides, Traders Acceptance and Travelers Insurance, my insurance company, were sister corporations.

He made a call. I settled for seventy-five percent.

***

When I was originally looking for an engagement ring for Joan, I had spoken with a German diamond dealer whose English was poor. Not feeling comfortable with his interpreter, I left his shop and sought out a popular store to purchase that first, ill-fated ring. With my recovered seventy-five percent in my pocket, I returned to that popular store and told the owner what had happened, thinking surely he would give me a price-break for a replacement.

Instead, he demanded full price. So back I went back to the German fellow, who proved very sympathetic. In the intervening months, his English had improved, which made our communications easier and helped as he taught me some of the subtleties of the different grades of diamonds.

Both a certified gemologist as well as a goldsmith, this man was able to give me a quick, deep education. While I'd done research on this topic before purchasing Joan's original ring, what I learned from this dealer was nothing like what I'd found in the books.

Then he offered me a deal: If I would be his friend and would recommend him to others, he was more than willing to replace the lost ring with a larger, brighter diamond. I agreed, and Joan got her ring.

A couple of years later, the German goldsmith designed and crafted a piece of jewelry for the Canadian Government to give to the Queen of England. He offered to create a copy for Joan, which pleased her, as she said a woman can never have too many baubles.

It was exciting to be friends with an internationally famous jeweler, and we remained in touch occasionally until his death in a traffic accident some years later. But while I wish I could say that he had a happy life, this was not the case. His evil dog had gotten a hold of him. He had finished rehab and was a changed person. I was told that the accident was from his crossing a main street in Europe, when he got hit by a bus. I learned by observing his transformation that the gift of too much success that comes too quickly is not a kind gift at all.

Follow Me

Two summers after our honeymoon adventure, Joan and I traveled to Florida again. Our route took us down I-95 past Washington, D.C.

Or, it should have taken us past Washington.

But it was evening, and somehow I ended driving directly into the city. And not just into the city, but into a poverty-stricken, black area. Joan was rightfully, quite concerned. Finally finding a gas station, I pulled in and got out of the car to ask directions back to the highway.

But before I could open my mouth, the black man in the station greeted me with a sharp, "What are you doing here?"

I explained I was lost.

"You must be," he said. "This is not your area. Your lives are in danger. I have to get you out of here."

Later, I learned there had been violent race riots in many large, U.S. cities that summer. No one could tell where the next disastrous riot would occur. Washington was a tinder box. Truly, it was not a safe place for us at that time.

The gas station attendant went over to a taxi driver who was waiting at the station, hoping to pick up a fare.

The cabbie, also a black man, understood our predicament immediately. "Follow me," he said. "And stick so close to my bumper you feel like you're attached."

I did as instructed, following right on his bumper racing for miles, until finally we reached the sign for I-95. When we stopped, the driver jumped out of his cab and came over to ask if we were okay now.

I said we were fine, and asked how much I owed him.

"Nothing," he said. "But you owe someone else when you have the chance to save their life."

I persisted in trying to pay him, but he refused. "If you want to give me something, say a prayer for me," he told me, and drove off into the dangerous Washington night.

***

Joan and I have reminisced about the two late-night incidents when we, traveling in the States, found ourselves dependent on the help of strangers. Each time, I say a silent prayer of thanks for the kindness of the long-distance trucker, the gas-station attendant, and the cab driver, all of whom were willing to put our safety before their own. And then there's the mystery: Is there some meaning to the fact that each of these was a black man? And why did two of them include the word "prayer" as part of their goodbyes?

But whatever the answers to these questions, as I consider how they helped us, I am reminded that no matter how many times I have felt alone and abandoned, the truth has been that helpers and mentors have always arrived just when I needed them most.

Business "Plan"

After the honeymoon, it was financial-planning time. Joan was making more money than me. We invested her salary and lived on mine, starting our life together in a basement apartment costing sixty-five dollars a month.

Once I left the finance company and started to work with Boehringer Ingelheim, a pharmaceutical company, I was making a decent living, and we soon moved into a two-bedroom triplex, and, for five years, tried everything but could not have a baby.

I changed jobs, taking a position at Standard Chemical, and we finally had a down payment for a brand-new home. We could afford for Joan to stay at home, as we put our name in to adopt, and on December 8th 1967, picked up Kelly Jo, our daughter. (Two years later Michael was born. And although we thought we were done, a few years later, Andrew was born to complete our family.)

But for now, responsible for a daughter, I decided to better myself by going to University part-time. It was hard work. I was always buried in the books—so it was off to new adventures, one of which involved wine-making.

A group of us had been making homemade wine to offset the very high cost at the Government Liquor Store. When traveling on business to Niagara, I came across Younie Watson and found myself intrigued by the business that he had started. Working with research grapes from Vineland Research Station, which was investigating the viability of hybrid wine grapes replacing our old, rough Niagara varieties, Younie de-stemmed and crushed them and immediately put the juice through a milk chiller. The ice-cold juice could then be frozen in plastic pails which were labeled with numbers that corresponded to each different variety—numbers only, no variety names, mind you. This way they could be used for experiments at the researcher's leisure.

I asked if there was any chance of me getting a few gallons for our own wine-making enterprises. As there was a lot more juice than Vineland Research wanted, Younie said yes, and a friendship was born.

To turn grape juice into wine, though, I had to find a source of wine yeast, yeast which had to correlate with the various grapes from which the juice had been extracted. With Younie's help we guessed at comparable European types, and then Dad found an entrepreneur who was selling yeast to the wineries and was willing to supply us.

We were in business.

The word spread around Kitchener that I had juice of better quality than that from California and, additionally, my juice was fresh and did not need to be crushed. Before long, I had to turn down customers who called from all parts of the Golden Triangle (the four cities surrounding Kitchener).

Since the Niagara Peninsula was part of my territory, it was easy to arrange to be near Vineland two or three times a week. I could squeeze fifteen pails into the car, but even with that, I could not keep up with the demand.

But a solution was at hand. My father-in-law owned a dry cleaning plant, complete with a fleet of delivery trucks—and he was also interested in wine-making.

I offered him a deal: "Lend me your truck, and I will get juice for you." I'd done the calculations: One of his trucks could hold thirty to forty pails. Kitchener to Vineland was approximately sixty-five miles. If I double stacked the cans by bungee-cording them in place, I would be able to carry close to six hundred gallons. (Sure, I would probably be overweight, but that did not bother me.) This way, for a couple of years, I earned some extra income for my small family.

And for those two years, on Saturday mornings in autumn/early winter, in our quiet neighborhood, people would line up outside our door waiting to get their thawed juice. Now, I appreciate how tolerant my neighbors were. And it sure helped that some of them were also into making wine.

It seems my salesman mind was always alert, and not just when there was grape juice around. For instance, when Kelly Jo started swimming lessons at the YMCA, I noticed some of the kids were wearing something called "water wings." I wanted a pair for her but learned they were new on the market and relatively hard to get. Apparently, a company in Toronto was importing them from Germany.

When Kelly Jo's swim instructor asked if I could contact the company on behalf of the YMCA, I found out that the Toronto Company was really just a clothing business and only took the water wings to help a friend in Germany.

Needless to say, this led me to another successful sideline. I was able to get Royal Life, which is the equivalent of the Red Cross, to endorse the water wings as a teaching aide, and very soon Joan was shipping orders to most of the YMCAs in Ontario. Once word of mouth reached the U.S., our sales increased so much that I was forced to register a company. Finally, I had to choose between being a chemical salesman or becoming Mr. Water Wings.

We moved to St. Catharines, and I was working as a chemical consultant for a Buffalo firm. Sadly, the water wings had to go. However this was not the end of my sidelines. I began exporting chemicals from Canada to the U.S. And then, with the support of George Lodick, decided to build my own distillation company. This proved more difficult than I had thought because I had to procure four stills and then import them into the U.S.

I remember being very nervous when I pulled up to the border and had to declare I was bringing stills across. Fortunately, the stills were made in the U.S., so the paperwork was easy. Then, all that was left was for me, "Sloppy Willie", to install them.

More good fortune—and good help—arrived when the word got out about this greenhorn. Suddenly, out of nowhere, experienced helpers showed up to teach me what was what in my new business.

Nonetheless, owning my own business was very challenging. But I had Joan at my side, which made such a difference. As I remember them, these times were an economic roller-coaster ride, with expansions, recessions and even a full-blown depression thrown in for good measure. I remember doubting my ability to stay solvent. We had money put aside, but it was being depleted quickly. Somehow, though, we held on. Our business grew, and we learned how to survive.

Ironically, Joan's Dad did not envision having his daughter involved in his business. His loss was my gain, and the caveat was she handled accounting and the details of the business, and I handled the marketing, sales and the contracts part. We did it our way, without family help.

Our survival, however, was not something we accomplished on our own. Both our associates and our competitors gave us support. This assistance came from many sources: from Arkansas, Florida, Illinois, Indiana, Kentucky, Louisiana, Michigan, Mississippi, New York, Ohio, Ontario, and Pennsylvania.

Included in the list of those who helped me at this time are one chief research director and an international patent attorney, both of whom mentored me, treating me like an adopted son. Then there were the chemical-plant owners, who, on just the guarantee of a handshake, allowed me the use of their facilities, which, in turn, allowed me to be a major company in the U.S.—even though, in truth, we were mainly just myself, Joan, and a secretary, operating from a small office in St. Catharines.

During this period in my business life, I learned the hard way not to count my chickens until the eggs are hatched. I was dealing with a major cement company and realized their waste dust, which was being dumped into their quarry, had the potential to be a valuable fertilizer. I convinced them to put in a pilot plant and, for three years, worked in my spare time to build this plant.

I was successful in extracting the desired product and received an endorsement from a major U.S. university as well as certification from a large fertilizer manufacturer, and even had an intent-to-purchase agreement from some major Ontario wineries. A Quebec company that I consulted for even lent me their drying equipment so I could produce tons of finished product for field trials.

I used the fertilizer to grow my own tomatoes, which were bigger than baseballs, the plants exceeding ten feet in height. These tomato vines were so huge, cars would stop and the occupants stare at my plants in amazement. With my fertilizer, I even grew the sapling which was in front of our house, to death. It literally popped its bark because it had grown too fast.

Of course, I was prepared for fame and glory. Until, that is, the CEO of the cement company decided they were in the cement business, not the fertilizer business and shut down our plant. I was dejected and a bit deflated, but I learned a valuable lesson: Never make a deal unless it is endorsed in writing by a qualified decision maker.

Who Has The Keys?

1963 brought tragedies. It was the year President Kennedy was assassinated, and it was a year that marked a milestone in my personal education.

I had been lucky enough to obtain employment with the pharmaceutical company Boehringer Ingelheim (BI), which was an accomplishment in itself. While at Traders Acceptance, I knew I had to improve myself. I saw an ad in the *Globe and Mail* and applied, ignoring the fact that they were looking for university graduates.

My application was well-received, and I was invited to write a qualifying test. Thanks to my experience in my dad's pharmacy, I passed the test and was hired. Weeks later, when my lack of a degree came to light, the company decided to keep me on if I would continue my pharmaceutical education via the company's home study program.

My job was to call on drug stores in the morning, then meet with four to six doctors a day so I could tell them about our pharmaceutical products. With doctors' busy afternoon schedules, that was not as easy as it sounds. One solution was to visit doctors in a tourist area during the off-season. That would guarantee that the patient-doctor ratio was low, allowing doctors more leisure and, thus, see "detail men", as the pharmaceutical reps were known at the time.

Owen Sound, a small, northern Ontario city, was just the place to rack up a goodly number of calls in the off-season. To those doctors, we provided relief from boredom. When a few of us detail men descended on a town like that, it was like camping. We would try to get in to see the doctors during the day, then, at night, we would always find a place to play cards, smoke, and drink beer.

We would also call on hospitals and institutions—especially governmental institutions—and catch the doctors there. Sometimes, all of the doctors would gather so as to meet with a detail man at one time.

One cold, snowy December afternoon in 1963, four of us headed off to the mental institution just outside Owen Sound. There was a lot of snow on the ground that day. The snow had been blown up so high by the plough that it covered the telephone lines. The sides of the road were such that we felt like we were driving through a snow tunnel.

We arrived at the asylum—a stand-alone, stone building dedicated to the hundreds of mentally ill, non-violent inmates it served—at two o'clock. We took turns seeing the doctors and had planned that when we were all finished we would go back to the motel and get ready for supper. But at three-thirty, one of the doctors told us a blizzard had blown in, and that we would have to wait to leave, for they were having difficulty plowing out the parking lot. At five, the doctor came back and told us that the plow was socked in, but that a bigger plow had been ordered and would be coming along soon. Then he invited us to the cafeteria for coffee.

As we walked down the wide, dimly lit corridor, I noticed the peeling beige paint on the walls and the stale smell of decades of smoke and institutional food. A man approached us with a cigarette tucked behind each ear and a package in his shirt pocket. He was patting himself down as though searching for something, perhaps matches. Then, in a highly-stressed tone of voice, he asked if we could spare a cigarette. The doctor laughed and handed him a cigarette, which the man immediately squeezed into his shirt pocket.

Next, a well-dressed man interrupted us, explaining he was an intern. He inquired if we had any drug samples, for he would help us to evaluate them. The doctor replied for us, telling the man that he would give the samples to him at bedtime. That well-dressed man was an inmate, not an intern.

When we reached the cafeteria, I observed that the inmates dressed in similar attire to the doctors, custodians, and supervisors.

"How do you distinguish the sane from the insane?" I asked.

It was that psychiatrist's response to my question which was the milestone in my personal education: He replied, "Bill do not try to figure it out. Just find out who has the keys."

This lesson has stood me in good stead. Whoever has the keys, be they sane or insane, is in charge.

Michael, The Archangel

My "arm's length" partner, George, the mentor who helped me install the stills, one day asked if I would accompany him to a high-level meeting. While I was usually reluctant to go to such meetings with George, for I was apprehensive that he would want me to get more involved than I was comfortable doing, I agreed on this occasion, as long as he understood that I was just going to support him and would be taking no active part in the negotiations.

I owed a great deal of my entrepreneurial development to George. He had shown me how to take risks, and although I had some losses under his guidance, mostly, I had made good returns. We had opposite approaches to life, however, and could get into heated disagreements. But essentially, George had a kind, giving spirit, and after a cooling-off period, we would return to being the best of friends.

In business, George's main weakness was that he spent money before it was deposited in the bank. This meant he was continually looking for more financing, which I suspected was the purpose of the meeting I had agreed to attend.

To get to this particular meeting, we had to fly to the outskirts of a large city, where George rented a car and drove us for some distance. Finally, he parked the car and led me up a long marble pathway, bordered by magnificent gardens that were prepared for the burst of spring. At the end of the path, a tall, pillared home awaited us. To reach the front doors, we had to march up a set of marble steps that would have made an appropriate entrance to any Roman museum, then cross an expanse of more exquisite marble. The doors themselves were massive, highly polished, and ornate.

George rang the doorbell, and a smartly dressed older gentleman opened the door and invited us in. Stating that the meeting was to be informal, he (firmly) requested we remove our jackets and ties. As he "helped me" with my coat, I felt his hand lightly graze all of my pockets. George, who had taken off his tie first, was about to take off his jacket, but, as if he were quicksilver, the butler slipped to George's side, saying, "Here let me help you."

I looked to George for reassurance, and he gave me one of his best Ronald Reagan smiles. This was his signal that everything was all right.

We followed the butler down a long hallway, past many closed doors. At its conclusion, the corridor opened into a medieval, European-style banquet hall, complete with tapestries, huge chandeliers, and a patterned marble floor. The men who were gathered there warmly introduced themselves, greeting us by shaking one hand and putting the other hand on our shoulders in a partial hug.

George and I had no choice but to do likewise. Still, despite their apparent friendliness, the men's dark, piercing eyes told me to stay alert.

George and I sat at the end of one of the many long tables, while the men explained a bit about who they were, and we told them a bit about ourselves. But when the chitchat finished and the serious business started, my gut told me the way this meeting was going. I excused myself and went to the lavatory.

On my way back to the hall, I noticed an older man sitting by himself. He said, "Please sit down a moment." I sat across from him on the carved wooden bench with a small hand carved wooden table, my back to the distant meeting. I was shocked to hear him say next, "You must be Bill Bates."

I acknowledged that I was.

"I am Sal," he said, "Michael's father."

Ah. Michael was the man who had coordinated the meeting with George. Sal was different from the men in the meeting. He seemed like a grandfather—a smiling grandfather dressed in a brown shirt with a red cardigan. In contrast to the piercing eyes of the businessmen, Sal's brown eyes looked deeply troubled, but not at all frightening. While he had the air of someone who was used to being in control, he was also obviously a family man, as he told me about each of his family members, including their full names. Then he asked me about my family.

As he had, I gave him the full names of my wife, each of our children in order of age, and my own: Joan Elizabeth, Kelly Joan Andrea, Michael William John, Andrew John William, and myself, William Michael Byron.

Sal noted that Joan only had two names; therefore, she was not Irish. He was correct, I said, explaining that Joan was of German descent. And then I asked, "Why did you say 'Irish'?"

He replied that "Anyone with a name like Michael Byron had to be Irish."

I explained I was only Irish because of my grandmother.

"Ah, she was the Kelly," he said.

It seemed that grandfatherly Sal knew far more about me then he was revealing. But all he said next was that he felt like some wine. Did I like wine, he wanted to know.

When I told him that I had grown up in the Niagara wine country, I had the feeling that I wasn't telling him something he didn't already know.

He invited me down to the wine cellar, and then led me to a door, beside which was a button. Sal pushed the button and the door slid open, revealing an elevator. We stepped inside and descended three floors to the "wine cellar", which proved to be more like a huge "wine cave." I could not even estimate how many barrels that cellar held. A couple of the barrels were at least eight feet tall, and there were racks and racks of sixty-gallon barrels stacked three high beneath an insulated ceiling that looked like it was thirty feet high. The walls were rock, and the floor was slate-tiled. Any large winery would have been proud to have a cellar like this.

He asked what type of wine I preferred. I responded with the names of some Italian wines like Chianti, Amarone, Della Valpolicella, and Barolo. Having friends that were wine connoisseurs came in handy at that moment. Sal seemed impressed. He called to Joseph, who appeared instantly—and just as instantly reminded me of Geppetto, the toy maker who created Pinocchio, with the hair style, mustache, and clothing of an Italian tradesman. I smiled as the thought arose, but Sal was already introducing us. "Joseph," he said, "This is my Irish friend who loves good Italian wine."

Sal explained that each season he selected grapes that were then flown over from Italy and that Joseph was his vintner. "What do you recommend?" he asked Joseph.

Joseph gave him a twinkling eye and a mustache-mouthed smile. I looked at the expanse of kegs and wondered which he would choose.

Then Sal said, "Let's sample some of the better ones, Joseph. Choose the best ones."

Joseph took us to several barrels and offered us a one-ounce sample from each. After I had tried four different wines, I was asked which I preferred. They were all excellent, but I picked barrel number three.

They congratulated me. I had chosen Sal's own special blend of grapes. Joseph filled a pitcher with the wine, and we all headed back to the elevator. Upstairs, we found a table set for us with two glasses for the wine, a plate of various cheeses, and a loaf of homemade Italian bread. Sal filled our glasses and offered me one of the cheeses which he described as his favorite. One taste confirmed that it was no ordinary cheese. And Sal told me that, indeed, relatives of his in Italy made it especially for him.

Although I felt that I was doing a good job of hiding my nervousness all this time, I had long since realized that there was a reason that Sal was going to such lengths to indulge me. He may have been the kind grandfather he appeared to be, but he was something else as well—which became apparent when he got down to business.

He started by saying that he had heard that I was able to supply gasoline components when they were scarce.

Okay. Now I knew where we were going. The Canadian government had put price controls on all oil products and would not allow for any increases, but the U.S. government, which did allow for the fluxes in the market, saw their prices escalate immediately and significantly.

I shared with Sal that when the shortage hit, George had reminded me that I was customs bonded on both sides of the border. Also, I had the right to buy from the refineries and had good credit with most of the refineries and chemical plants. Two large international trucking firms knew me well. I also had chemical distributors in the U.S.

In short, I told him, I was in the envious position of being a small, international import-export chemical marketing company. I explained also that while the refineries boycotted American plated trucks—for they wanted all the exports to themselves—with the help of a friend, I was able to use local trucks and storage tanks for pick up and could then transfer refinery products to U.S. plated trucks.

Also, I let him know that I made sure that my distributors did not undercut the high market price. I made them appreciate that if they did, the big oil and chemical companies would find a way to shut me off. The only way I could sell to them was if they cooperated. As long as I did not get greedy, they could always claim that they did not have a monopoly. I was an independent.

Finally, I joked to Sal that I had asked my kids to say at my eulogy, "My Dad was able to do many things. His greatest achievement was he could buy retail, sell wholesale, and make money."

Sal gave me an approving nod. He asked how many shipments a day I made.

I told him, but I got the feeling I was being solicited. Still, the wine, cheese, and bread were excellent.

Then Sal surprised me. "You were brave to name your son Michael," he said. "Tell me a little about him."

I explained, "Michael can appear stubborn. He has his own mind and is not very flexible. His mother handles him by giving him choices and not backing him into a corner. I handle him by firmly guiding him to new experiences like traveling and trying different foods. I love him. He is a good kid. Unfortunately, he has inherited some of my demons."

Sal's response was, "I thought so." To me, that seemed like such an unusual remark that my guard went up further, but Sal simply asked me if I knew the history of the name Michael.

I told him that it comes from Michael the Archangel and means, "He who is like God."

Sal nodded his head. "There is a wonderful story about this Archangel that I would like to tell you," he said. "Michael the Archangel, the only Archangel to do battle for God, was chosen to be God's 'right-hand man.' As God's Commander-in-Chief, Michael was responsible for defeating Lucifer during the war of the angels.

"Michael was well aware of what he considered his strong points, but God viewed these same attributes as flaws. For example, Michael was stubborn; he wanted to do things his way; he always questioned everything, including God's authority. For Michael's part, he felt God was holding him back. He felt bored and restricted and was constantly complaining to God.

"Finally, God had had it 'If you don't like it here you can always go to Hell,' God said.

"You do not offer Michael a challenge and not expect him to take it! True to his nature, Michael said, 'So be it. I am out of here.'

"A short eon passed and then God got a message from Lucifer. 'Hey, God,' the message read, 'I will return 100,000 souls to you if you will just take Michael back. No, make that a million!'

"God accepted the deal, and ever since then, God and Michael have been loyal to one another. Their relationship is set to last for an eternity."

Sal paused for me to take the story in. I think he could tell that my hearing it had helped me see how appropriate it was that my middle name is Michael and that my son's first name is Michael. Suddenly, I was able to understand both myself and my son better.

Across the hall, we could hear the sound of voices. The meeting was getting louder. Sal told me that he thought George would not be able to make a deal.

I said that I had suspected that was so.

Then, he made an offer. "You are an experienced man," Sal said. "I need men like you. I would like you to look after and mentor my son."

Oops. That was not what I had expected. In the privacy of my own mind, I thought, "Mentor your son and what else?" Then, in a flash, I knew: "This is why he had studied up on me and my business. He wants all of my connections."

My thoughts turned to my Uncle Roy and his refrigeration business. He had taught me that in business you have to work directly with those paying the bills. While you could help the family, never let them help you. Above all, never get too close, lest they turn you into one of them

Remembering Roy's guidance, I knew that this would not be a good situation for me. I tried to be diplomatic. "I live in Canada," I told Sal, "many hundreds of miles from here. It would be impossible for me to do as you ask."

Sal countered, "Not if you move here. You would never want for anything. Your family would be well looked after. Your children would have the best schooling money can buy."

I remained firm, but polite, thanking him and saying, "My kids are doing well in school. I have a small, successful business. All our family is there. I appreciate your intentions but it is impossible."

To my surprise, Sal let it go. "I really did not think I would be able to persuade you," he said. "I understand. But if you ever need anything, here is my private number. Now, Let us just finish the wine and talk about life, until they discover their futility," he ended, with a nod towards the banquet hall.

With Sal's acceptance, I felt the protective influence of Michael's mighty sword—again.

On the other hand, George, as predicted, did not get his deal. Looking back, I have to believe that George Lodick's spiritual mentor was St. George the Dragon Slayer. That is the only reason which would explain why he kept dragging me with him into the dens of dragons.

Goodbye

It was January, 1977. Joan, our three kids, and I were living in St. Catharines, Ontario, and I was working at my office in Niagara Falls, New York. We had gone to the Regent Street house with the kids for my father's birthday. He was not well, but we did not understand how ill he was. Even when the five of us—Joan, Kelly Jo, Michael,

Andrew, and myself—visited him in the hospital in St. Catharines, we still did not realize exactly what was wrong or how bad it really was.

Then, on January 25th, Andrew's fifth birthday, I left work early so I could stop by the hospital and visit my father. There, I spoke with my brother Len's friend Dale who was a lab technician at the hospital. Dale met me in the hallway, looked me in the eye, and said, "I am terribly sorry." But when he saw the look on my face, he realized I did not know: My father had been diagnosed with cancer.

I was confused and upset. My oldest brother, Jack, had spoken with the doctor, and there had been no mention of death. Up until that moment, I thought they were still trying to figure out what was wrong with Dad. Looking back on it now, I wonder if someone was in denial about the whole situation. I could understand that, as I did not want to accept the diagnosis and its inevitable outcome.

With a heavy heart, I walked into the ward which I had heard called the "Last Goodbye Ward." My father was one of four men, there, and looked a waste of his former self.

I wanted to scream, but my choking tears took away my voice. I managed to simply say, "Hi."

His meek response was, "Thank you for coming."

I stayed with my father for a little while, and before I left, I told him, "I love you." He told me he loved me too. Then I kissed him on the forehead. Since then, I have regretted giving him such a reserved show of affection. It seemed meager compared to the love I felt for him.

Just a short while before, Joan and I had returned from a Marriage Encounter, and, full of love, we went to check on Dad, who seemed to be feeling strangely tired all the time. When we entered the family room of the Regent Street house, my dad got up from the couch to greet us. I walked straight over to him, gave him a big hug and a kiss on the mouth, and told him, "I love you." Before that, I do not remember ever kissing my father, as it was not a thing that straight men did in the world that I came from.

As if he had been waiting for that moment for years, my father hugged me and kissed me back, saying he loved me, too. This was a red-letter day, a very special moment.

So I am not sure why I held back at the hospital, held back on the last kiss I would give my father while he was conscious. Was it that I was self-conscious before the other three men on the ward? Perhaps? But that kiss marked a last, lost opportunity between my father and me.

I drove home from the hospital that day, saddened both by the news and by the diminished presence of my dad. But I tried to put on a good face when I got there. It was Andrew's birthday, and I did not want to spoil that for him. But when I entered the house, I believe all the children could tell that something was wrong—especially Kelly Jo, who met me in the front hallway with a warm and loving hug.

For the next couple of nights, Joan and I visited my dad, but he was heavily sedated, so we just took turns holding his hand and softly hugging him—and also spent time in silent prayer.

It was midday on January 28, when the phone call came to my Niagara Falls office: My father was dying.

I called my mother and told her to get ready; I'd be by Niagara-on-the-Lake to pick her up shortly. Then I asked my business partner to cover for me, explaining that I had to go to the hospital.

He looked at me in disbelief and said, "Have you looked outside, Bill? There is a blizzard, and it's hitting us hard and fast. We should spend the night close by, as there is an emergency storm warning in effect. We are to stay off the road."

I was determined, though. No one was going to stop me on my way to my father's deathbed. I just knew that somehow I would be kept safe. Besides, one good thing about driving in a blizzard is that usually there is no one else crazy enough to be on the road.

On the way, the brilliant torrent of white snow charged at my windshield to be slowly swept aside by the wipers; the defroster blowing at full blast, kept the windshield reasonably clear.

I found the streetlights had been turned on, which allowed me to follow their haze to the border at Lewiston. Once I started the approach to the bridge, I could make out a dimly flashing light shining through the blowing snow. As I got closer, the light became more intense. Then I heard a police siren howling from the booth. A man decked out in Arctic gear approached my car, and I could see a barrier was blocking my way.

Officiously, the man demanded, "And where the hell do you think you are going? This bridge is closed."

I explained my predicament to him, and I guess my words tugged at his heart, because he lifted the barrier and said, "God help you! You will have to deal with Canadian Customs when you cross." But when I reached the other side, there was no one there; there was not even a barricade.

I was home free—or so I thought.

Actually, it wasn't until I hit the River Road that the real driving adventure began. Up until that point, the roads had been at least partially plowed. On the River Road, however, the snow was at least a half-foot deep. Even with winter tires it was rough going. Off and on, the tires lost their traction and just spun, but when I took it slowly, I was able to plow my way through. Then the only problem was trying to figure out, in all the blowing snow, where the road actually was.

Taking my best guess, I drove down what I figured was the center, and, somehow, with inner strength—and all the late-night drinking and driving miles I'd logged on this familiar road—I remembered where the trees lined the road and how it curved. It was like driving in a dream. My mind was on the road, but my heart was with my dad. I do remember feeling relieved when I passed the tree where the Elliot girl had been killed. That area was like the "Bermuda Triangle" for car accidents.

Eventually, I made it to the Regent St. House, but, as in a dream, when I arrived, I could not remember most of the places that I'd passed—and the drive that would normally have taken twenty minutes at most, took well over an hour-and-a-half.

The fun began once I entered the house to pick up my mother and take her to the hospital. She had not been drinking, at least not as far as I could tell. But she still simply refused to go with me. I got tough. "You have no choice. Your husband is dying, and you have to say goodbye," I told her. I put her into her boots and coat, found her gloves and scarf, made sure she had her rosary, and then I virtually shoved her into the car.

Highway 55 had been plowed a short while before, but the whiteouts were nerve-racking. Once again, I drove down the middle of the road, as I was the only driver stupid enough to be on the road. My mother, who was a very nervous passenger at the best of times, was petrified. Even with her rosary to keep her mind occupied, she kept insisting we turn back.

I convinced her that we should continue, as we were more than halfway there. Then she started asking how we were going to get home. I explained that she was not going home; she was staying at our place in St. Catharines. Finally, I pulled into the General Hospital following the ambulance tracks. I left the car in the fire lane. I did not give a damn if I was towed. I had made it. When I think back on that drive, I still don't know how I accomplished it.

Once in Dad's room, we found him highly sedated. Mom was denying that her husband was dying, but I forced her to recite her prayers and say goodbye to him, anyway. Then I said my own final goodbye, sobbing and sobbing. The adrenaline that had surged during the stormy drive from New York had drained away, and my stomach felt raw.

I took my Mother to our house, where Joan settled her, and I had a drink of Dad's favorite scotch, the special one that I kept for his visits. Then I went to bed and cried myself to sleep in Joan's arms.

The next day, the storm was over, the roads were plowed; I drove Mom back to Niagara-on-the-Lake. Unfortunately, I had to return to work in Niagara Falls N.Y., which made daytime visits to the hospital in Ontario difficult. Fortunately, Doug had arrived along with Jack. They stayed at our father's side. In the evening, Joan and I did faithfully visit what seemed to be just the shell of my Dad.

But none of us were there when he died.

At approximately three in the morning, I awoke with a start. I was flooded with a glowing, soft light that drifted off. I woke Joan and said, "I do not know if it was a dream or not, but Dad just died."

About an hour later, I received the phone call from Jack confirming this. Whether or not the "visit" I received that night was at the exact minute of my father's passing, I do not care. All I know is that I felt his spirit say, "Goodbye."

Dad had made a success of his vision for Niagara. In order to prosper, it had to go backwards, which meant back in time. His leadership in this and other endeavors earned him such great respect, that the day of his funeral, the storeowners closed their doors during the funeral and the flag at the clock tower was flown at half-mast, an honor usually reserved for dignitaries.

While I felt myself to be an escapee from Niagara at the time, on this occasion, I appreciated the tribute the town offered to the memory of my father. My heart swelled with pride for Dad, and my tears poured freely for both of us.

***

My Dad's famous Gene Autry cowboy jacket became a family heirloom. I had permanently "borrowed" it from him a few years earlier, and it became my trademark as it had been his. Years later Kelly Jo incorporated it into the latest style for young girls, for it was the fashion to wear hand-me-down clothes from a recent era. Then Michael claimed it until Andrew commandeered it. Together, we honored the legacy we had inherited, and Dad lived on, his essence enfolding his child and grandchildren through the jacket he had worn.

Encountering Marriage

There is a saying that I like: "Behind every good man is a good woman." In my case, the "good woman" is Joan. When we got married, the priest said, "Now the two of you are one." This might have been true, but the first fifteen to twenty years of married life were still not easy for us.

In fact, those years were difficult. Joan and I were complete opposites who were trying to appreciate each other. In the language of the Myers-Briggs Type Indicator (a psychological instrument that evaluates preferences in how individuals perceive the world and make choices),

Joan is an ISTJ, while I am an ENTP. These two "types" do not have a single preference in common. In short, Joan and I are fundamentally as different as it is possible to be.

Our differences, as identified by the Myers-Briggs instrument, suggested that the chances of our marriage surviving were extremely slim—less than two percent, in fact. And there were many instances where we simply did not understand how to communicate, and pushed against each other, rather than finding a way to cooperate. Still, we were able to go forward and believed in ourselves, and made our children and the church our glue.

In the meantime, I was charging ahead in my business, like a bumbling Don Quixote who somehow ends up on his feet. I met with what was best categorized as a disorganized success. The accountants were not happy with me.

Joan, who was very detail-oriented and had strong organizational skills, came to the rescue. She took over the billing and filing, learned the rudiments of accounting, and even the complexities of commercial border crossings. She shored me up so I could do what I did best: make new contacts and increase the business.

There was a catch 22, however. The more the business increased the more work Joan had on her hands. And, of course, she was raising three children! Add to this the fact that my long-suppressed dysfunction had begun to raise its complex, confused, ugly head, and I could no longer keep the anxieties from my past sealed into the cemetery of my mind, and you can imagine what a lot of pressure this placed on a marriage that was already strained.

We were so fortunate, though, that just at this juncture, friends of ours had completed a weekend-long, religion-based marriage renewal event called "Marriage Encounter." They had enjoyed it so much that they encouraged us to go on one too.

We agreed, and our weekend was a success, in my eyes, for during it, I revisited Don Quixote and learned about Dulcinea. I realized that if I did not change my ways, if Joan and I did not fight for our marriage, our relationship would end in divorce.

The Impossible Dream, the theme song from *Man of La Mancha*, called me to engage on my own quest, a quest "to right the unrightable wrong" in my life, a quest which I would have to undertake in my own way, bulldozing forward, blindly, quixotically, and with all the faith I could muster.

But not without Joan.

She and I committed to reviving the spirit of our vows and accepted an invitation to become a Marriage Encounter Team. This was a particular challenge to me, because the assignment entailed learning how to give talks. But thanks to one couple's relentless coaching, I finally got a reasonable talk formatted. Also, they told me about a great Spiritual Director at Mount Carmel. As I was struggling with my faith, I tucked this information into my memory bank for future use.

In our role as a Marriage Encounter Team, Joan and I were asked to help with weekends in Toronto, Waterloo, and other centers, as well as giving some of the "home weekends" in St. Catharines. In the course of our work with Marriage Encounter, we met many caring couples. Unfortunately, they seemed to look up to us as having it all together. If only they knew how fraudulent we felt when they held us up as this ideal couple.

Nonetheless, we enjoyed meeting these couples, and we felt redeemed by the fact that we were offering them hope through the miracle of the Marriage Encounter weekends. Eventually, we became county coordinators. At that point, we learned that Marriage Encounter was, sadly, similar to any organization run by volunteers in that at times, politics can create friction. Fortunately, in addition to the politics, there were also great, loving people who managed to maneuver around those individuals who were vying for influence and just got the job done.

Eventually, we decided to take a rest from our Marriage Encounter duties in order to concentrate on our family and business. But I learned much from participating in that program. In particular, I took away the healing idea that "Feelings are neither right nor wrong, they just are." From that concept I developed another: It is what I choose to do with my feelings that make them right or wrong for me.

Even though we had moved on from Marriage Encounter, my learning curve was not complete. Joan signed up for a Dale Carnegie course and convinced me to do likewise. She liked the course so well that she was asked to teach it. Instead, she wanted to sell it.

I was delighted! This was an idea that suited my salesman's personality perfectly. Together, we ended up helping the Carnegie program by assisting with classes, and both of us grew from the experience.

To this day, I find Dale Carnegie's principles sound. Two still resonate with me to this day, as my grandchildren, who know my quotes by heart, would attest. They are: "If it is to be, it is up to me," and "No stinkin' thinkin'." These two guidelines remind me that it is always possible for me to improve my lot in life.

And, certainly, from our Marriage Encounter and Carnegie experiences, Joan's and my unlikely marriage improved as well.

Search

Kelly Jo was a challenge for us, as she knew how to push her mom's buttons. We decided that I was best suited to handle her, so I instituted the tough love approach that I had learned. But I knew she was a good kid and that I had had a poor upbringing. Therefore, I was determined to do better for her than had been done for me.

Finally, Joan and I ended up exploring a program called *Search*, which offered weekends for teens, to see if this might be the answer for Kelly Jo. Finding nothing in our area, we went to Buffalo to investigate their program. There, we met Father Gary Bagley, and the next thing we knew we were enrolled, along with Father Peter Rowe, who acted as spiritual guide, training assistant, and musical inspiration, and a group of CORE kids, to learn about *Search*—and a loving fire was lit in us.

The *Search* program offered an opportunity for teenagers to ask important questions of themselves, like, "Who am I?" "Where am I going?" and "How am I going to get there?" Through the guided self-reflection process of *Search*, the kids discovered new answers and possibilities. Joan and I were to train a team of kids in such a way that they felt free to give their own input in talks and leadership.

The Myers-Briggs idea of psychological types was so helpful in this process. It was Buffalo *Search's* Father Gary who first introduced us to Myers-Briggs with the book *Please Understand Me*. This book helped me to understand myself, Joan, and our children. In fact, I have to say that it was a bridge between Kelly Jo and Joan and me.

With a bit of salesmanship, Kelly Jo was able to see this book as if it were describing different astrological signs. She realized it showed how she could be her own unique person and did not have to be a carbon copy of Joan; this was a huge breakthrough for our relationship.

As our association with *Search* developed, *Please Understand Me* became an immensely valuable tool for us to use to communicate with the teens who came to us.

In a truly uplifting coincidence, on a return business trip from Lake Forest, Illinois to Chicago, I casually introduced myself to the gentleman across from me, only to discover that he was David Keirsey, co-author, with Marilyn Bates, of *Please Understand Me* and also the sole author of *Please Understand Me II*. Somehow, I ended up having this greatly influential man all to myself for well over an hour. I do not accept that this was a coincidence. In the most bizarre circumstances and unrealistic places, people come out of nowhere to give me assistance and insight.

In addition to our training work, we offered ourselves to help *Search* in other ways. Joan came to the rescue as an organizer of details, while I looked after the marketing. We became temporary mentors—a surrogate Mom and Pop, known as Mr. and Mrs. B.—for the team. We also acted as chaperones, along with the terrific Father Peter, because, with up to 45 teenage girls and boys housed for a weekend separate dorms, one important job was keeping the kids where they belonged. The three of us formed a unique trio. The teen leaders completed the dynamic team.

Nonetheless, the teen leaders were very aware that Joan and I had very different gifts. They observed how our approaches to the same subject would sometimes conflict. While they seemed to take this in stride, we sensed them watching to see how we would resolve our divergent positions. For our part, we hoped we were demonstrating good problem-solving skills and not just airing our discord.

The teen leaders stayed until they went off to University, and then the next group of leaders built on what the previous group had created. In this way, *Search* became an evolutionary process that was guided by the caring hearts of the teenagers it served.

With the kids' help, Joan, Father Peter, and I took the program to a new level of successful retreat. *Search* got the blessing of the Bishop and more importantly, received high approval ratings from the participating teens and their parents.

Search was a place where secrets—and the fear of secrets—would have a "Search light" shone on them, exposing them for what they really were. The teens themselves resolved to banish the idea of labeling each other "weird" or creating situations in which some of the kids felt like outsiders: No secrets. No labels. No outsiders.

Within these parameters, the *Search* teens were able to build a place for healthy interpersonal interactions.

Our three children contributed to *Search*, each in their own unique way, and we found that the *Search* community allowed Joan, me, and our children to experience a new and lasting trust within our own family. We learned more about our kids through *Search* than we ever would have in our regular home environment. But, for our own kids and all the others in the program, despite the emphasis on truth and not keeping secrets, *Search* did have guidelines which protected the "Searchers" from revealing too much.

All in all, *Search* provided a balanced environment, a garden of sorts, in which these teens could grow. And some of the growth Joan and I witnessed was almost miraculous! For instance, one of the younger girls told the team that her best friends were ostracizing her, which not only ousted her from her own group, but made joining a different group difficult as well, because she was seen as an outcast. The young lady in question shared that she had begun to feel unworthy and unwanted.

On their own, some members of the senior team who hailed from distant schools decided to adopt this girl as their friend. They showed up at her school and made it apparent that they, a group of older, cooler kids, appreciated her. Thanks to their intelligent response to the problem, quite soon, the juniors who had rejected this young girl in the first place, once again sought her friendship.

The wisdom of this approach was passed along. After that incident, each new group of teen leaders introduced themselves to the various school chaplains. Then the leaders made themselves available to their schoolmates. Approachable and kind, these special angels offered comfort and open arms to their peers, not only helping them find the support they needed, but standing by them as that support was affected.

We adult members of the team felt such glad pride as we learned of the ways that these *Search* leaders circumvented suicides and abortions, found aid for those suffering from depression and anorexia, and just generally reached out their helping hands.

Joan and I are still reaping the rewards of our eight years of personal "Searching." The growth we experienced as we worked alongside the *Search* teenagers is tremendous. Like many survivors of alcoholic parents and childhood sexual abuse, I had developed a protective bravado that made it nearly impossible to experience humility. But the willingness of these youngsters to give—with no strings attached—worked a special change in my heart: As I saw what they were able to accomplish through their freedom of spirit, I found myself humbled. I am proud to have been associated with them.

Through our years' association with *Search*, we were witness to the outstanding accomplishments of so many of the teenaged participants that it would require an entire book to do them all justice. This does not lessen the treasures we hold in our heart of each and every one of those teens that took the risk to share beyond their normal limits.

This story, Dave's story, is just one example.

When Dave first attended *Search*, he looked like he was dressed for the rumble in *West Side Story*; he even had the motorcycle. His walk, his talk, was all bravado, and I knew the stage was set for trouble. As a new Searcher, on his weekend, he left the retreat property to buy cigarettes and snacks for the other Searchers. But once I took him aside and talked with him, Dave seemed to settle down and have a good weekend.

After each weekend, a meeting was held to see what we could be doing to improve our program. At these meetings, we also picked new teen leader candidates. Not surprisingly, Dave's name did not come up. Or, not until I suggested that instead of choosing only "good kids" who obviously had team potential, we should consider doing something a little different. Considering our goal was to help a wide variety of Searchers, why not one of the rougher-edged teens as team candidates?

My suggestion was met with dead silence. Everyone knew who I was talking about. That was one of the very few times I ever pulled rank, but I felt that Dave was worth the risk. Perhaps I recognized myself in him. For whatever reason, I felt strongly enough about giving this kid a chance that I volunteered to take responsibility for him. Dave's name was put on the list.

From then on, it was soul-enhancing to see his growth. From being a tough, street-wise kid, he softened and became the kind of person that adds to the goodness of the world. The last I heard, Dave was working with handicapped people.

Our Last *Search*

In 1985, the Pope declared it to be the Year of the Youth. The Bishop asked Joan and me to be youth ministers and assist in a Diocesan study. We gathered information from the individual parishes. The next step was a council was formed. We logically assumed because we had done all the legwork we would head up the council. Wrong!

The Bishop chose one of his priests to head up the newly formed Youth Ministry Council. We were suddenly considered to be only lay ministers, and were required to report to the new head.

Why? What did a priest really understand about the struggle of youth? Why does the Church always have to put one of their own in control.

The first meeting was one of everyone getting to know one another. Father "B" had a proud opinion of himself. What he lacked in experience, he tried to make up for with the power of the collar. He ended up disagreeing with the rest of the panel. Because he was challenged, at dinnertime he sulked off to eat by himself.

This situation was the first serious crack in our trust of church leadership. With the support of some good priests, *Search* continued. We repeatedly tried to recruit help, but the program was intimidating to those interested in helping us. After eight years of *Search*, other cracks surfaced.

The sad ending is the commission fell apart, we the people of the church, were expected follow blindly, and we, were not trusted. They claimed it was our church, but only to the limited extent they wished it to be. The resulting loss was the missed opportunity for the youth.

This situation made it clear that it was time for Joan and me to move on. But there was still one last *Search* weekend to lead.

The last *Search* was overbooked. And then I got a call from a desperate mother who wanted us to find room for her daughter. She was seeking a miracle—and hoped that a *Search* weekend would provide one. I explained that we only had a limited number of beds; we already had over forty -eight teens registered and a waiting list, besides.

In response, she told me that her daughter had been in a serious car accident; that while the daughter had survived, her best friend had died; that her daughter had been driving, and was now taking all the blame she felt and turning it inward.

Search was not a program for teens needing psychological help, I said. She still felt *Search* was the right place for her daughter, as the girl had refused to talk about the accident to anyone, and was becoming somewhat of a recluse. The mother hoped that at a *Search* weekend, her daughter might at least begin to talk to other teens.

I could see her logic, and agreed to fit the girl in somehow. We reworked the dormitory arrangements and squeezed her in.

The girl came on Friday night, but kept to herself. We had already explained to the team that she needed space, so they allowed her to observe, even though she did not participate. As for the adult members of the team, we were so busy with the other kids that we just let her be.

That was how it went all day Saturday. Then, late on the Saturday night, which had actually become Sunday morning, when we were gently encouraging the team to get to bed, the girl came up to me and said, "I am ready to talk."

In my exhaustion, it took me a moment to realize who she was and why she wanted to talk—but when I made the connection, I listened as she outlined her sorrows.

I told her that I knew a good counselor; that I would talk with her parents; that, together, we would do all we could to get her the help that she needed. I also told her how proud of her I was and kissed her on the forehead, thanking her for taking the monumental step of reaching out to speak to another person about what was in her heart. Then, assuring her that everything would work out, I sent her to sleep.

Somehow, the atmosphere of trust and safety at the *Search* weekend helped that troubled girl to move forward. I heard much later that she was able to drive to the spot where the accident occurred and, with her stuffed animal and prayers, she was able to free herself of the cycling thoughts that had haunted her: I wish I didn't . . . I could have . . . I should have . . .

I could not have dreamed up a better way to sign off *Search*.

***

I would like to conclude my thoughts about *Search* by remembering one of the earliest team members, Anne Marie Potton, who froze to death on Whistler Mountain, in British Columbia, in 1994. Anne Marie was a talented, feisty, bubbly, adventuresome young lady, who will never be forgotten. Joan and I took a special trip in 2000 to visit the place where she released the last of her energy; we said our own special prayers there.

DON QUIXOTE RIDES AGAIN

A New War

It came to our attention that something was not right with one of the priests, Father James Kneale. This was the second time I had had suspicions. However, when we confronted our Bishop with our concerns, he insisted that suspicions were not enough to instigate an investigation. For that, we would need a parent to confirm our concerns with concrete, factual evidence of wrong-doing.

The Bishop basically stonewalled us. He was not even willing to discuss implementing preventative measures to safeguard the kids. I shared my personal history of abuse at the hands of Father Weaver, hoping to elicit his understanding of the potentially serious consequences of ignoring the situation. Instead, he told me that the issues from my own past should be brought to the attention of the Diocese of Toronto; at the time of my abuse, Niagara-on-the-Lake was in the Toronto diocese. And that was the end of the conversation.

At that point, it was evident that Christian authoritarianism and Christian spirituality were in complete opposition. Children under his protection were being left vulnerable by the Bishop who was supposed to be their protector, the man who was seen as the holder of the keys to heaven.

It was at this moment that I remembered my brief discussion with the psychiatrist at the asylum: "How do you distinguish the sane from the insane?" I had asked. "It does not matter," he had replied. "Just find out who has the keys."

The Journey Towards Confrontation

The Call to Right the Unrightable Wrong

I was devastated by my Church. At every opportunity I got, I skipped Mass. The anger I was experiencing had been triggered by the Bishop's rejection of my concerns, but it went far beyond that. The two dogs inside me were fighting big time.

I did not like my spiritual life. I was living a lie, and I wanted no more of the pretense. I was frustrated. I thought I had put all of this garbage behind me after Marriage Encounter, yet there it was again.

I was in counseling at this time with a great counselor, whose name was Sam. In response to Sam's suggestion that I look for further spiritual guidance, I sought out one of our Marriage Encounter veterans. From him, I got the name and phone number of Father Gregory Battafrano of Mount Carmel in Niagara Falls.

Before Father Gregory would see me, he insisted I send him a letter which introduced my family and myself and explained why I wanted a meeting. With Joan's and my secretary's help, I wrote the letter on May 21, 1993, and Father Gregory agreed to see me.

And once again, just when I was ready to take another step in my personal growth, a caring, understanding mentor came to the rescue. In this situation, Father Gregory helped me learn that I was not alone. He lent me books so I could educate myself, and then we would discuss the spiritual ramifications of what I read and how to apply the ideas and principles to my own life.

SPEAKING MY TRUTH

I learned that courage was not the absence of fear, but the triumph over it. The brave man is not he who does not feel afraid, but he who conquers that fear.
—Nelson Mandela

Father Gregory guided me forward, inviting me to take my abuse story out into the open. In fact, as the Diocesan Retreat Director for the very diocese that was denying me, Gregory proposed his program as a fine "pulpit" for me to speak from. Before I did so, though, he encouraged me to rid myself of some of my anger and to focus on my good purpose, rather than on revenge.

I did as he suggested, and when I was finally ready, he and Joan proofread my talk many times until it—and I—was balanced and presentable.

I was scheduled to present my talk after the noon break. I was nervous and focused on staying calm enough that I would not blow my opportunity by getting angry. Then I received the news that the Bishop and a questionable cohort of his priests were not going to attend. As one priest told me, they were voting against what I was going to say. They were "voting with their feet."

Included among those who walked was James Kneale, the priest we had gone to talk with the Bishop about. Kneale would later be convicted of a sex crime. Joan and I attended his trial and found that the Diocese had hired the most notorious lawyer in Ontario. This lawyer had defended serial killer Karla Homolka and managed to get Kneale a reduced judgment, of which Kneale eventually served only house arrest. He is now labeled a felon. Even worse, Kneale's accuser and his accuser's family were badgered in the process. Watching these proceedings, it seemed to me that the Inquisition was alive and well, but Christian charity did not seem too healthy.

Fortunately, some of the more caring priests did attend my presentation. The brave souls who did not join the Bishop's boycott gave me hope.

With Joan at my side, on March 15, 1994, I stood up and read what I had written:

> *The only way I could come here today was by being assured that my being here and my sharing will be kept confidential. I respect you for this. What I have prepared has been worried over, prayed over, and cried over. Torn up and*

started over. This has not been easy. I could not have done this alone. A few close confidantes, one of them being my wife, have encouraged and nurtured me.

This is not meant to be eloquent or profound. It tends to be disjointed, but that is me and my life. I am using my notes in order to keep from rambling and to help me get through this.

I am so sad that I have to be here today. I am not here to share my anger. I am not here to get even, to threaten, or blame. I am not here for money or for notoriety. I am here because I have to tell the truth. A truth no one wants to hear. Most would rather that I just go away and not rock the boat. I love parts of my Church and I believe that with open wisdom and faith, it can be rebuilt.

Joan is here with me today, as she has been with me throughout our marriage. She married me knowing the outline of my history. We struggle to try not to have any secrets in our family. We make an effort to deal with issues in an open responsible manner. I appreciate her support.

I have spoken many times in public. I have given numerous spiritual sharings. This is the first time that I have ever spoken to a group about the breach of trust. My sexual abuse caused by my Church. You must understand that a young boy sees his priest as his Church. It is difficult for me to talk about this even on a one-to-one basis. It has been always difficult for me to talk about this with Joan.

You see, I do not want to be here. I did never want to meet the requirements to be here. The breach of trust is such that a survivor like me finds it extremely difficult to trust you—after all, my unwanted knowledge makes me very wary. I am emotional about this. However, I believe I have a right to be emotional, for I have been degraded. I am a survivor: that is, someone who is able to overcome the control that was held over me. I did this by making myself always to be in control. I am vigilant about this. I am not used to being out of control. Throughout this sharing, I may have to pause to gain my energy.

Please understand.

Sometimes I wonder if my child within will ever be happy, ever be free of the sadness given to me, in a premeditated, clandestine way, at a very tender age. This could have, would never have happened if the Church, the Mass, the confessional, and the power of the collar were not an integral part of this black entrapment. It was as though this person had the power to reach into the computer of my mind, placing a virus into my immature logic. Taking my very inherited graces, my own spirituality, and using these against me.

These "people of the lie" known as pedophiles, what a tangled web they weave. The devil himself could not make evil sound more righteous and holy. I do not wish to go into the depth of how this affected my life. However I will say that it has affected every area in my life. Not only am I reluctant to trust, I am also very vigilant. I am vigilant to the point that I will not let any of my children serve at Mass. In my dealings with priests, yes even some of you, I had to have the assurance of your integrity before I could I could even start to accept you.

The fear of being found out, the fear of being judged is very suffocating. Secrets are very terrifying things. They are living nightmares. When, as a teenager, I had to have some surgery, I must have been babbling under anaesthetic, for when I was recovering the nurses wanted to know the great traumatic secrets of Niagara.

Perhaps you can imagine all the cover-up masks I had to wear: the altar boy, the normal son, the average, prepubescent boy, mischievous, and the loner. I was always feeling sad, never knowing why. I had no one to turn to. My brothers and friends would have branded me a "faggot." My parents worshipped this spiritual leader who was guiding me. I attended a public school where the teachers openly ridiculed Catholics. No help there. No help anywhere.

When I reached out to other religious or people who might know and understand, I hoped they could help; however, they avoided me turning their heads, pretending not to comprehend. They rejected any overture of hope I might have had. It was as though I did not count. After all, bad things happen to bad people. Somehow I knew that I must be bad.

The breach of trust still exists to this very day. I cannot make any sense of it. Perhaps you can. When I learned in 1992 that the Canadian Catholic Bishops had published recommendations dealing with sexual abuse within the church, I read the books. I found the recommendations to be minimal. However they are a good start. It was my understanding that the recommendations were being put into action throughout our Niagara diocese.

I was told that a system and a committee had been put into place to deal with abuse. I could not find anyone who could direct me to said system. I believe in my heart that such a system does not formally exist. If it does, it is only in avoidance pretense, at best a secret. I judge once more I have reached out, taken a risk, and have been rejected.

In the report "Sexual Abuse by Priests" by Richard Sipe, on page 15, it states that "approximately six percent of Roman Catholic clergy have some sexual contact with minors."

Further on, Sipe says, and I quote,

"I realize that in many ways, we, too, were part of an atmosphere that confused confidentiality and secrecy. I can appreciate that many Bishops have still not solved this dilemma, although difficult. Secrecy must be distinguished from confidentiality. Confidentiality is a personal communication that must be protected at great sacrifice, not only out of professional duty, but because it is in the service of, and necessary for, transformation of growth. Secrecy is a stance that reserves access to knowledge in the service of power, control, or manipulation. Secrecy is often rationalized as the only way to avoid scandal. St. Paul knew that when it came to religion, truth is always a scandal." End of quote.

The way I relate to this is that your covenant, given to me today in confidentiality, is necessary for my transformation and growth. Secrecy is the living nightmare that surrounded my being sexually abused. I was told sexual abuse is out there, but not in our backyard. The truth is it happened in the past, it happened here, it happened in Toronto, and we know it recently happened in Buffalo. As well, I have knowledge of other victims, in particular one living here, who has similar circumstances to mine. Yet there are no safeguards to prevent it from continuing to happen here.

To me it is like knowing a fire has happened in the past, that a fire has happened in a nearby neighbourhood, but we do not need a fire prevention program. It appears that the avoidance approach, the denial approach, the study-it-to-death approach, the procrastination approach, the it-can't-happen-here approach, the hoping-it-will-go-away approach is dangerously looming here. I am real. I am telling the truth. What happened is a fact and cannot be denied. I have no assurance that this fact is accepted, or that anyone cares to put into place a system that will help avoid abuse in the future. All I have heard is vague verbiage.

I see myself standing here not as a protector of future youth. I see myself as an advocate. I am very comfortable to be an advocate of truth. That is, an advocate of quality, ethics, knowledge, integrity, and serenity. I believe that if a format that encompasses these values is put into place, there will be no need to protect our youth from the evil within.

I refuse to go away. I am prepared to keep on struggling, to keep risking rejection until some compassionate persons will hear the cry of my child within. This is my Church. It is my beacon of faith. I choose not to reject it as some people have rejected me. As I stated from the beginning, I am not here for money, not here for revenge, not here for notoriety. I need your help.

I cannot do this alone. I refuse to believe that you do not care.

I risked this sharing with you; my soul tells me there has to be hope. My hope depends on the Holy Spirit and you. There are enough programs in existence to borrow from. There are enough professionals available to assist us. I will not be comfortable until I have been assured that there are no more secrets, and that I am able to have the confidence level of trust that something concrete, not just lip service, has been put into place. Please do not deny this opportunity to correct the evilness of the past. We need to rebuild the confidence in our Church.

My hope and prayers go with you.

When I finished sharing, I realized I had made a breakthrough. In just a few short years I would understand how much I had changed. The priests that did attend thanked me; some took time to search me out. I received two letters saying how they were touched.

Another Candle Lit

It was in the summer of 1994 that Joan, our new friend Father Gregory, and I made a voyage to what seemed to me another world when we travelled to Linkup's Second National Conference for Victims of Abuse by Clergy.

The conference was held at St. John's Abbey, at St. John's University, in Collegeville, Minnesota—ironically, a place where much of the Catholic literature is printed. There, we found an entire community of humans struggling with and surviving the same sort of situations I had found myself trapped in when I was younger.

Before we even arrived at the conference proper though, we were made to feel particularly welcome. The driver who picked us up at the airport, Rick Springer, had a kind, worn face told me he had "been there and seen it all."

I offered to pay him for his gas as he drove us to the abbey. His response was that driving attendees to that conference was not, in his eyes, an expense, but rather, it was a reward. He was honoured to support victims of clergy abuse in this way. He wanted to be part of the process in which we learn we are not alone.

In his cab, Rick had pamphlets from an organization called *Bishop Accountability*, which compiled data concerning sexual abuse in the Catholic Church. Rick, who was abused by a priest, was one of the cause's greatest advocates—and his generosity to victims travelling to The Linkup was one way that he showed his caring.

On that summer day, as is always the case when a special person comes into my life, with his kindness and openness, Rick lit another candle in my soul.

Tom Economus

It would take more than one candle to light my way out of the darkness, however, and Rick Springer's friend Father Tom Economus had a whole candelabra-full to brighten the path. This path would eventually blaze a trail into the halls of the Vatican. A priest of the Independent Catholic Church, Father Tom's own past included sexual abuse at the hands of clergy. These facts made him the perfect person to speak out on behalf of himself and other victims of perpetrator-priests.

He was one of the first to blow the lid off of clergy abuse in a public arena, and I marvelled to hear how, with great determination, he got an opportunity to speak out on *The Oprah Show*.

He told of his years as a "front man" for Father Don Murray, Director of Sky Ranch Group for Boys in South Dakota. Tom shared graphic details about how he would be taken to fund-raising events and conventions with Father Murray to raise money for the school; how Father Murray would position him, Tom, next to him on a stage and say, "This is a troubled child. This is a bad boy. This is a kid who's been in trouble with the law, with drugs; he comes from the streets of Chicago," when, in fact, none of that was true.

It was usually after those events, after Murray had one too many drinks, that the priest would sexually abuse young Tom.

I have heard Tom bravely tell his story so often that I can almost see the expressions on his face, his gestures, even his aura, as I write this.

He was usually trapped with Father Murray somewhere isolated, in a hotel room, for instance, where there was no one around to tell. Although, Tom says he didn't think he would have told anyone, anyway. "Many times," Tom said, "when I had threatened to expose

[Father Murray], he would tell me, 'I have legal guardianship over you. Who are the people going to believe, you or me?' And so I was manipulated into silence for seventeen years."

Tom also described his assault by the psychotherapist priest who was supposed to be helping him deal with the years of abuse he'd suffered in Father Murray's care: During Tom's ninth or tenth session, the priest/rapist began telling Tom about his own sexual appetite, saying he thought he was homosexual, that he had been with other men. And then he showed Tom a picture of a young man he said was 15 or 16 years old, with whom he said he was sexually involved.

At that point Tom said, "I felt very uncomfortable and I got up and asked him if I could use the restroom. In order to get to the restroom, we were in his sitting room, which was connected to his bedroom, and the restroom was on the other side. I had to go through the bedroom to get to the restroom.

"When I came out of the restroom, he was standing there in a T-shirt, and just a pair of underwear. And lunged at me, and knocked me onto the bed. He started kissing me and, wanted to have sex with me. I continued to refuse that, he . . . you know, I'm not very big, and he was a pretty tall person, and he managed to hold me down . . . and he was trying to force himself on me. He pulled his penis out and tried to put his penis into my mouth, and then he finally ejaculated, and when he did I was able to get away from him, and I ran out of the rectory and never returned."

And when Tom tried to train to be a priest himself, as he shares, he had this experience:

"In the seminary program, I remember the first day we went to classes. I felt like I was at a meat market, because everybody checked you out. But it wasn't like, 'Hi, how are you?' It was like, (flirty) 'Hi, how are you?' People were checking you out, scanning you over. It was the most uncomfortable feeling. But I thought it was me, at the time.

"Then, as I got into the program, I realized people were both heterosexually and homosexually active. There were people who lived in our house who were accused of sexual abuse of children. There were people in the house that had very obvious, apparent alcohol problems. There were two people in our house who had very apparent eating disorders and were very much overweight.

"And all of a sudden I was in the middle of all of these people, and the expectation was that I was to hug these people in prayer every day, and I was to love them as my brothers, and continue with my studies. And not to be concerned with what they were doing. The whole thing was dysfunctional."

At that point, Tom Economus dropped out, drank, did drugs, went to rehab, and became ordained in the Independent Catholic Church. I knew him as a vibrant, energetic, caring person. He was on a mission, his own personal quest.

***

Rick Springer remembered when Tom was on *The Larry King Show* in the early 1990s. "We were in the

Tribune Tower in Chicago," Springer said. "The lawyers were in Dallas, others in Washington, D.C., King moderating. Tom just chewed them up. He tore them apart."

The first time the two men met was at the 1992 Chicago Conference. They staged a Victims' Panel during which perhaps ten people told their stories in front of the audience.

Springer said "It was quite daunting because there were TV crews from all over the world. This was the first conference ever on clergy sexual abuse, and it was when the story was just starting to break out all over the place.

"Chicago blew up; abuse cases all over Chicago and Massachusetts and New Mexico and Louisiana and Texas. It was just the beginning. After that, Tom was on the phone all the time. I can't tell you how many people had conversations with him—like, thousands."

***

Tom Economus and Rick Springer founded the quarterly newsletter for Linkup. Each issue featured an editorial written by Tom and information that Jay Nelson—who edited the newsletter and would go on to write the expose *Sons of Perdition*—assembled from his home in New Mexico.

Jay Nelson would highlight news of crimes of a sexual nature perpetrated within the auspices of the Catholic Church. These articles would appear in the Linkup newsletter under the column title, "Black Collar Crimes." In Rick Springer's words, the newsletter ." . . was like a

Bishop's accountability before Google." When Jay had finished compiling and editing all of the pieces for an issue, then Tom, Rick, and Rick's sponsor from Alcoholics Anonymous would put together the mailings, including labeling and stuffing envelopes.

"It was big ritual," Rick said.

When I first met Tom, he had enough energy for ten men, and he sure knew how to delegate. Before Joan, Father Greg, and I left that conference in Minnesota, Tom had enrolled me to start Linkup Canada and put me on the advisory board. With Tom's and Rick's great support behind me, I used that forum to try to rattle the Ontario Bishops into action.

Eventually, according to Rick, they "held, I think, a total of twelve national conferences. The one in Toronto in 2001 was the last one [Tom] went to. Everything seemed to be okay," said Rick. "[Tom] had just gotten a settlement from the archdiocese. He bought himself a condo in Evanston. He moved there, and it was about that time the cancer came back.

It is with deep regret that I write here that on March 23, 2003, Tom Economus died—just as the stories about pedophile priests were breaking in Boston.

Deliver Us From Evil

"The Lord's Prayer" says, "Forgive us our sins, as we forgive those that sin against us," but it also says, "Deliver us from evil."

What is "evil", though? Anyone can act in ways that could be called "evil", but does that make the person intrinsically evil? If a person shows remorse, if he or she makes amends, it seems to me that it was the actions, not the person that was evil.

In my experience, truly evil people do not believe they are evil. They neither show remorse nor try to make amends for their evil deeds. They see themselves and all that they do, no matter how hurtful to others, to be just fine. Their position is if you have a problem with them or their actions, you are the person with the problem!

M. Scott Peck wrote a classic book, *The People of the Lie*, which gives some clear guidelines to help identify what I would consider truly "evil." For instance, paraphrasing Peck, an evil person deceives him—or herself in an attempt to keep guilt at bay and appear "perfect"—at least in his or her own eyes.

As a natural outgrowth of this self-deception, an evil person is deceptive in relationships with others, as well. In another form of deception, the evil person may very well pretend to feel or offer love when he or she is actually feeling or offering hatred.

Further, it is typical for an evil person to focus his or her wrong-doing on particular people, while treating all others "normally." He or she quite often misuses the power that others have vested in him or her, whether that power is political or emotional, using that power to coerce or impose upon others, and is evidently not able to imagine situations from the perspective of those he or she victimizes.

Also, Peck points out, evil people make themselves seem highly respectable—and then will lie in whatever ways, necessary to maintain this illusion. They are also specific and "consistent in . . . [their] sins," rather than just generally badly behaved. And, of course, these people have a deep-seated aversion to any suggestion of a negative judgment of them or their actions.

Certainly, these attributes describe my abuser, Reverend Major Eugene Weaver. A decorated World War II hero, rescuer of struggling children, and savior of the St. Vincent de Paul parish, he appeared respectable beyond reproach, even though the nature of his evil was specific—and, with me, he directly demonstrated his inability to understand the perspective of his victim.

When we acknowledge and identify evil, I believe that the next discussions that must be undertaken are on the topics of guilt and forgiveness. I have observed that we survivors can, with lots of love and great effort, find our various ways of forgiving those who did us evil.

But while survivors can forgive others, forgiving ourselves, redeeming our self-worth from the guilts of victim-hood, is more of a challenge. The forgiveness of self may take years (even with love and support and guidance) beyond the forgiveness of the perpetrator. And even then, the wrongs done to us and those we have done to others may continue to haunt our psyches.

We may look like we have survived, but certainly, we have been changed in the process. I am not alone with this view; many, many abused persons have shared similar convictions. I now know I cannot change the past.

However, I do have the ability to forgive, thus changing the future.

As we attended many conferences, I observed many different types of victim survivors. First, there is the survivor who is in denial. These are victims who cannot move forward without help. Next, there is the survivor who has dealt with the truth, but who is still stuck in "survivor mode." Finally, there is the abuse survivor who is moving on. These are the individuals who a popular radio host and political commentator calls "victorious survivors." And once a wounded soul becomes a "victorious survivor", that person will, in turn, help other wounded souls on the journey towards recovery.

My Own Warrior

All along this journey, Joan had choices to make. Most Catholics would just have prayed. Some would have thrown up their hands and said, "What can you do?" Others would simply have denied the situation—it is difficult for devotees of Catholicism to believe that their Church would not do the Christian thing, would not address wrongs perpetrated by its own.

Not Joan. She chose to stand by me, her Don Quixote. My quest was her quest. As my life's partner, Joan was willing to fight against everything her Catholic upbringing had taught her. She had been such a good Catholic child. She was the little girl chosen to crown Mary with flowers. She grew up saying the rosary every night. She even let her family make me say the rosary with them before I took her out on a date.

This is a woman of the highest moral principles and greatest respect for her religion. And yet, she stood at my side at my darkest battles. She helped me confront bishops, even taking on one bishop on her own. She journeyed with me into many strange halls and monasteries. She spent days away from our children supporting me on my quest. She opened her mind and her heart to what was really happening within her own Church.

She has heard firsthand what the wolves in priests' clothing had done to thousands of children like me. She has been a witness to the sad and heavy truth of our stories, stories she will never forget. The majority of the stories she has heard have been from Catholics; however she has also heard from victims of clergy from a wide range of religions and denominations, including, but not limited to, Anglicans and Baptists, Mormons, Mennonites, and Jews.

Despite the stresses my past put on our marriage, Joan stood behind me, acknowledging what had been done to me and others, and the changes I was trying to effect. We, alongside many others, protested the Canadian Congress of Catholic Bishops, and Joan stood beside me as we defied and boycotted the Pope, who at that time had remained silent about sexual abuse, and his Church.

I do not recall any other wives who, not abuse victims themselves, braved being involved on behalf of their husbands. Only Joan, who helped make my impossible dream a reality.

Ray Brown

I met Ray Brown at the St. Cloud Retreat House, where the Bishop had asked us to hold our conference. The Bishop's hope was that the seminarians and other priests would attend and get some insight into the purpose of our organization.

The large campus had many buildings and, of course, a church at the center of everything. Respectful of our concerns, the Bishop had asked that the priests attire themselves in lay clothes so as not to upset any of the survivor participants—but he could do nothing to disguise the presence of the church, itself, nor to change the appearance of any priest within its walls.

Most of us are very sensitive. We tend to be guarded. The speakers were well qualified and were intelligent as they spoke about our shared predicament. Still, for our support, the conference offered trained counselors.

I had just met Ray. We clicked and quickly established mutual trust. We were walking toward the church, when a priest came through the doors fully flocked in old-fashioned black robes with a very visible Roman collar.

I glanced at Ray. He suddenly looked gray and shaken.

I asked, "Hey, are you okay?"

He turned and started walking in the opposite direction of the robed, fool of a priest. As he walked, Ray talked about his phobia of priests and churches. I understood. We shared experiences of having flashbacks triggered by the sights and smells we associated with the Church. Over the weekend, we discussed ways to handle our fears and memories in our daily lives.

When we met, Ray was the Deputy Chief of the New York Fire Department. He was in charge of all of New York's rescue service. But earlier in his career, he had been a fire captain, and was also in charge of New York's dedicated rescue squad, which was the squad that rescued trapped fire fighters. Ray was one of the founders of that specialized team.

In one of his last rescues, Ray was leading his men across a burning floor when it collapsed. They had to jump to safety with the floor literally disintegrating beneath their feet. After that incident, he told me, as Deputy Fire Chief, he started getting flashbacks. These flashbacks were about what had happened during his abuse with the priest and about all the narrow escapes he had as a fire fighter. He was experiencing post-traumatic shock. He just could not take the memories anymore and was transferred to another department.

Those bogeyman flashbacks left him defenseless, but he took on the emotional work he needed to do to survive. He worked through the baggage heaped on him by the Church. He worked through the reasons he thrived on the adrenalin of his rescue work. Then, having transferred to the Port Authority, he retired and went back to college to get his Master's Degree in Psychology.

Now he is a counselor for fire fighters. And he is a wise one.

He explained a Gestalt Therapy term to me called, "Person in Environment" or P.I.E., which explains that everything an individual is exposed to remains with the person. Therefore, to therapeutically serve a person, a counselor must take in not just his or her personality but the totality of environments which he or she has been exposed to, as well.

This is a man who took difficult life circumstances and translated them into opportunities to heal himself and then help others. I view Ray as a victorious survivor. He prefers the term "thriver." No matter which you call him, I am proud to call Ray Brown my friend.

Richard Sipe and Tom Doyle

Among the many, many people who truly impressed Joan and me were ex-priest and author Richard Sipe and well-known priest, Father Tom Doyle. While I only met each of these two men a couple of times, they both influenced me deeply.

Richard Sipe, author of more than ten books on celibacy, clergy abuse, and other topics of spiritual, religious, and political interest, spent twenty-eight years serving the Church as a Benedictine monk and Catholic priest. His credentials are long and impressive. He was trained to deal with priests' mental-health issues, and has done an excellent job of attacking the Church's on-going cover-up.

Married, now, and the father of one son, when Richard Sipe spoke, we listened. His authenticity reinforced my sense of purpose and re-fueled me for my sometimes difficult quest.

Father Tom Doyle was a canon lawyer on-staff at the Vatican embassy in Washington, D.C., but he could not tolerate Rome's position on sexual abuse. In order to avoid being ostracized while being vocal about his beliefs, he joined the U.S. Air Force as a chaplain. His rank was Major. In this position, Father Tom was officially employed by the U.S. government and could not be censured by the Church. (While I have heard that the Church has since been trying to breach this protection, Father Tom Doyle was able to prevail.) Awarded several times for his integrity, Father Tom is also a deeply intelligent man. He not only holds a degree in Canonical Law, but also five Master's degrees, as well.

For me, Father Tom Doyle, advocate and truth-teller, plays a particular and special role. As a decorated Major and Military Chaplain, he challenges the model of the first war-decorated Military Chaplain that I knew all too well: Reverend Major Weaver.

Nancy Mayer Helps Me Bear My Cross

When I met Nancy Mayer at a conference in Chicago, I had made plans to retire to Florida and was trying to recruit someone to lead the Canadian branch of Linkup. However, the wounded victims of our movement had their plates too full to take on much more. What we really needed was a very special person to take over.

What we got was a Canadian spirit who wore a name badge that said, "Nancy Mayer." An able professional, Nancy was blessed with the gift of being able to see all sides of the box that we survivors are in. She picked up the

Canadian leadership with grace, and I marvel at the progress she made.

Our first protest was at the meeting of the Canadian Council of Catholic Bishops, outside Belleville, Ontario. Nancy had booked us in the same hotel as the bishops. When the bishops discovered we had rooms there, they had the hotel cancel our reservations—"for security reasons."

Joan and I are fond of *Wedding Song*, by Peter, Paul and Mary. In it, we particularly appreciate the line, *For whenever two or more of you are gathered in his name/ There is love*. In Belleville, our group gathered, in love, to protest the abuse of children.

But the bishops? When two or more bishops gather, not in his name, not for love, but rather to contain secrets, then there is collusion afoot!

While we were there, we heard what can only be described as the "waking nightmares" which had been experienced by some of the Indian children of that area, who had then grown up and joined in the protest. They told us stories of themselves as six-, seven-, and eight-year olds who were taken from their homes by white strangers knocking on their doors and shipping them off to various religious boarding schools called "residential schools," where the government paid for their room and board.

Once at the schools, they could neither leave nor communicate with their parents. At the same time, their parents were being told they had no rights. Their children had to be sent to the residential schools to be Anglicized. "Anglicized" was only part of their education. They quickly learned that as children they did not count. They were beaten, abused and raped with no recourse, until they were dumped on the streets at eighteen, when the Government subsidies ran out.

This, it seemed to us, was just another example of how a supposedly loving Church "shepherded" and "protected" its children when no one was looking—or, at least, no one who had the power to make a difference. Our protest was a signal to the Church and government authorities that now, finally, many people were looking. And together, we did have the power to make a difference.

***

Nancy Mayer arranged for another a clergy-abuse protest, this one in Toronto, in July, 2002, when Pope John Paul II was scheduled to make his visit to that city. Our hope was that our presence would force the Pope and the Canadian Church out of their stance of denial.

The only church that would accept us was the Holy Trinity Anglican in downtown Toronto. Holy Trinity is a small, historical, Tudor-style church, and ideal for our protest. In it, Nancy set up a ceremony for the stations of the cross.

Nancy knew that the cross was a perfect symbol to represent the different "stations" of our lives, the different passages we had each traveled bearing our unique but secret pain. Since members of the local, national, and international press were already covering the Pope's visit, Nancy felt they would be interested in what we had to say, as well, and she arranged for them to cover our protest.

At our station, Joan and I held a black, six-foot tall, wooden cross. The crosses were decorated with teddy bears, hearts, and other symbols of childhood.

Then the press arrived.

I had no idea what I was going to say. I thought of some pompous-sounding statements, and then my mind went completely blank. As I began to speak, it was as if I was hearing a strange but familiar voice: "I was born in Niagara-on-the-Lake, Ontario." I said. "The more that I and other survivors tell our stories, the more likely the prospect of the Church listening to us."

With Joan standing beside me, in my squeaky voice I choked out my story of abuse. "I was the salt of the Earth; I was the light of the world. I was abused by an evil priest. He abused my body, but I own my soul."

I grasped my wooden cross and continued. "My prayer is for the youth of today, that they have the strength to challenge the Church, to get the truth and the strength to protect them."

My statement resounded across Canada and throughout many other countries. Siblings and friends who knew nothing of my involvement found out via their television screens.

Yes, I was granted a fleeting second of notoriety. Much more importantly, in the time it took to speak those sentences into a microphone, the mistakes and lies I had buried were released, and I got my unencumbered soul back. It was now mine and God's.

From that day forward, the cross had a new meaning for me. It no longer belonged to Christianity or to

Catholicism. I was no longer nailed to the Church, no longer had to carry her stigma. The cross Joan and I had held that day was the cross of my own personal liberty. Finally, my soul was free.

To Sleep Or Not To Sleep . . .

"Not all child abuse is obvious."

After I came forward and publicly revealed my secret, others, some of whom were old acquaintances, some of whom were strangers to me, shared their similar stories.

An old school friend phoned and asked if she and her husband could come to talk with Joan and me.

I had not seen her for some time and I was looking forward to catching up on old times.

I was delighted. That is, until she told us her story. It was so painful to hear. But in some ways, it was just the same—all of these stories, always the same, always about fear, always about the secret.

I knew her well-neither of us knew about the other. We buried our secrets deep.

This woman's story went deeper for me, though. For some reason, it reverberated in such a way that I had to express it in the form of a poem that I titled "To Sleep or Not to Sleep is Not an Option."

I feel the fear.
It is Daddy's voice.
His footsteps near,
I pretend,
but that does not fool him.
He rolls me over.
He does it again.
I scream. I cry. (I must be bad.)
"Mommy! Mommy! Stop him!"
All I hear is her laughter from the kitchen.
My little sister in the next bed
blocks out the scene.
I hurt.
I cry myself into a blackout sleep.
(I must be bad.)
Eventually, I grow into puberty.
I am left alone,
For a while.
You know who is next.
I try to stop him.
Now it is my turn to block out the screams.
No Mother. No Father. No love.
I am alone with just my fear
and the chilling dark secret.
I am entrapped by his decadent power over me
until he dies,
until I die.
Why me?
Why? Why?

Of course, I could not answer her question, the most important question, "Why?" But I understand that there is some solace in knowing you are not alone, so I am glad to have shared my story with this woman and to have listened openly to hers. She thanked me for allowing her to tell her dark secret with someone who had first-hand understanding of what she had gone through.

I am happy to report that, as horrifying as her years of abuse had been, this woman was a "victorious survivor." She eventually found love and happiness, and her marriage was blessed with children, for whom she was thankful. As she and I focused on the joys of our respective lives, we enjoyed a few good laughs. Before she left, I told her that she was a true survivor: that I loved her just because she was who she was, and that I acknowledged her for taking evil and, with love, turning it into good.

The powerful theme of "Not all child abuse is obvious" comes through loud and clear. Secrets destroy the soul. While my friend was to become a survivor, her sister survived by becoming an angry recluse.

The Fight Continues

The Church has claimed to be the rock of faith, to hold the keys to heaven. It has claimed that its servants—priests, bishops, and monks—are the shepherds of the souls entrusted to them. But my experiences have uncovered some of those would-be shepherds and revealed them as wolves in false-hope clothing. They have shattered my trust, which is the very anchor of my spiritual being.

***

While most survivors do not commit suicide, still, many get stuck. They want to start anew, but they can't. Their nightmares keep them connected to the past. I have empathy for these people. I know how difficult it is to be able to stay in the present, let alone to forge ahead to the future.

Tom Economus, Rick Springer, Richard Sipe, Tom Doyle, Ray Brown, Gregory Battafarano, Nancy Mayer, and most especially Joan—these people revived me when I became too tired to fight. They revived me, and I survived.

Why? Was I lucky? Special? Did I have a purpose to fulfill?

If so, did I fulfill it? Or did I just let it slip right by?

***

With sheer strength and force of will, I have pried open tombs of the cemetery of my mind: shame and fear. I have had to learn to deal with the dark spirits rising from those tombs, as I forced them into the bright light. And, over time, I have had to respond to the wisdom that guided me to forgive those spirits, even to embrace them. But as difficult as these parts of my process have been, they have been not nearly as difficult as my continuous struggle to forgive myself.

The hardest part of all is that the situations that have caused me and so many other victims of clerical sexual abuse are not contained safely in the past. No. Scenarios such as I have recorded or alluded to in these pages, are still occurring today.

So often, I still hear of bishops' involvement in sexual abuse or cover ups. Rome continues to deny knowledge of the crimes perpetrated by its ordained shepherds. Sexual crimes and their subsequent cover-ups at the Congregation of the Christian Brothers, the Belleville Diocese, in the Indian Residential Schools, in Ireland, Germany, Poland, the vast Irish cover up, the German, Polish, Penn State, Syracuse University, even the Boy Scouts did not surprise me. All the signs were there—all of these churn my guts. (Upon learning about pornographic pictures coming to light, I experience flashbacks of myself as a trusting kid being conned into having Polaroid pictures taken to record my prepubescent development. My heart palpitates and I have to swallow hard to rid myself of the shadow of fear that haunted me for so long that those sick pictures of me will somehow make an appearance.)

My personal victimization may have long been at an end, but, as the list above shows, the bad news just keeps coming—despite the many promises made to obliterate sexual abuse visited by those in power upon those who are in their thrall.

While steps are being taken, the fact that they have been made only after the Church, or the organization, has lost a huge amount of money to the battle, as well as many of its followers, makes me wonder if even those steps were examples of repentance. Or maybe all those dollars were spent as payoff, a way to make the Church and others look as if it cares without requiring a substantive change in policy or attitude.

After so many years of fighting, it is draining now to try to muster up the energy for the war against the perpetrators. I have to leave that to younger warriors. I have to accept that while I cannot change the past for myself or any others whose innocence was lost at the hands of trusted authorities, I am grateful to know that through the efforts of thousands (millions?) of us who are sharing our stories with the world, changes are being made to protect the innocence of the future.

2013 - 2014 UPDATE

Staunch Catholics still have a hard time accepting that the church failed millions of us. When some friends said that only a small number of priests are pedophiles, they ignored the fact that, as Richard Sipe has stated, "Well-established studies show that the average pedophile has 250 or more victims over his lifetime." They also ignore that this has been going on for decades, perhaps centuries.

Some say that they are old men now. Why can't they just be left alone to live out their life in peace?

Why? Because the survivors cannot live out their lives in peace. Instead, they experience nightmarish flashbacks, even when we become old men. No, peace does not come easily for us.

Understand this: The pedophiles abused us first—and far too many bishops and cardinals were among them. The second level of abuse occurred when were not believed. The third level of abuse occurred when those who had full knowledge of the first and second levels of abuse just shipped the offenders into the next unsuspecting parish, so they could abuse anew.

The fourth level of abuse occurred when the hierarchy lied, misled, and stonewalled investigation, so as to protect the perpetrators. We now know, because the Church was finally forced to release many secret documents that the sin, the crime of the cover-up extended even to the Popes.

The fifth level of abuse occurred when victims bravely came forward to press charges, and the Church used her monetary and legal might to discredit them, not caring if the victims were destroyed along the way.

The sixth level of abuse is the destruction of faith and spirituality, which the first five levels of abuse leave in their substantial wake. Mortally wounded souls do not heal easily.

Inquisition. Evil. Abuse. Defamation. Shady dealings. Mortal wounds. These, then, are what we protest against. Not harmless old men who deserve their peace.

Most survivors I know do not wish to destroy the Church. The Church seems to be doing that well enough all by itself, as its sins are being vomited forth for the world to see and judge.

Many priests are trying to resurrect the faith. I don't see how they can do this without openly dealing with the sicknesses of the past and preaching *Mea Maxima Culpa* from the pulpit.

The recent HBO special on *Mea Maxima Culpa* seems to have served justice when it revealed that Cardinal Ratzinger instructed all sexual abuse cases go to his desk. That would mean that Pope Benedict XVI would have the inside story. The question is, what did this "Keeper of the Keys" do with the information? Ah. He protected the pedophiles and turned his back on the victims, just like the popes before him.

Is he then not as guilty of sin as the pedophiles themselves?

My understanding is that according to the Vatican Council, three conditions must be met in order for a pronouncement by a Pope to be infallible:

The Pope must speak ex cathedra, from the chair of Peter, in his official capacity

The decision must be binding on the whole Church.

It must be on a matter of faith or morals

I, like many Catholics, accepted this for many years. This newly revealed breach of trust, however, shows explicitly how the working of the internal Church itself has destroyed our faith.

Pope Benedict is the first Pope to resign in six hundred years. Public statement reports that he is tired. Tired of what? Tired of the inescapable glare of hundreds of thousands of the people's candles? Tired of the long-secreted truth being illuminated? Tired of what has been hidden in the Vatican being so blazingly exposed that the lawyers and the press could no longer ignore the horrors the brilliant light revealed? Tired of the financial scandals.

"You are the light of the world." With the sparking of those candles, this Bible quotation has taken on a whole new meaning. "We," the collective "you," have taken our lights and lifted them up so the world can see. Our fiery candles have blazed a path to the sacred halls of the Vatican.

Yes, as I learned from Dale Carnegie, "If it is to be, it is up to me," or, in this case, it is up to us.

***

Friends and staunch Catholics, please understand we are against not the teachings of Christ, but the perversions and abuse of pedophiles that are hidden within His Church. We are against those who did not commit acts of abuse directly, but who are complicit in the evil that is the worldwide cover-up.

One of the greatest criticisms Joan and I have of the Church is its inability to grasp the problem, to understand the damage done by the breach of holy trust.

I have learned that so many priests turned their backs to what was happening because, having their own faults and fears of exposure—whether it was gambling, drinking, womanizing, theft, or being gay—it seems that to report someone else's derelictions of duty is to risk exposure of oneself. However, know that great harm has been done.

On the other hand, we are very appreciative of those brave religious who stood beside us. And, of course, special kudos are deserved for Tom Doyle and Richard Sipe for their relentless perseverance on behalf of an unpopular truth.

Joan and I can attest to the fact that their dedication has been a guiding light for individuals and organizations worldwide, including *Linkup* and *Snap* and many others.

Maybe, just maybe, there is hope: Cardinal Marc Ouellet of Montreal grasps the massive blow they've caused by the Church's moral authority. In Rome, he's seen to be among the reformers; during an international summit on the abuse crisis in February, 2012, he led a liturgy of repentance in a Roman Church in which victims of clergy abuse participated.

Ouellet called the crisis, "a source of great shame and enormous scandal," and said sexual abuse is not only a crime but also an "authentic experience of death for the innocent victims."

***

At the time of this writing, Pope Francis is the new Pope. He chose the name Francis after Francis of Assisi. It appears he is the Pope of peace. The Prayer of St. Francis is well known by many of all faiths. It offers hope. It is one of Joan and my favorite prayer-hymns. It is a prayer I use to diffuse my anger, to focus on forgiveness.

Lord, make me an instrument of Thy peace.
Where there is hatred, let me sow love.
Where there is injury, Thy pardon, Lord.
Where there is doubt, let there be faith.

Oh Lord, make me an instrument of Thy peace.
Where there is despair, let me bring hope.
Where there is darkness, let there be light.
Where there is sadness, let there be joy.

Oh Divine Master, grant that I may not so much seek
To be consoled as to console,
To be understood, as to understand,
To be loved, as to love.

Lord, make me an instrument of Thy peace.
Where there is hatred, let me sow love,
For it is in giving that we receive;

It is in pardoning, that we are pardoned.

And it's in dying that we are born
To eternal life, to eternal life.
Lord, make me an instrument of Thy peace.
An instrument of thy peace.

Christ is the Prince of Peace, St. Francis an instrument of peace. Both were not devoid of using anger first—the peace came later. Mahatma Gandhi was for peaceful resistance. I could not find where he acted in anger. However he did cleanse his country of the English rule. My present -day hero, Nelson Mandela, is an exemplary example of the power of peace and forgiveness.

My wish is the new pope will be able to overcome. In my opinion the Vatican needs to be swept clean. God utilized Michael to kick out the devil angels. Christ chased the moneychangers from the temple. It will be interesting to see how the new Pope accomplishes cleaning out the decay within.

***

I have been asked where I am regarding my religion. My Jewish friends tell me that if your mother was Jewish, you remain Jewish no matter what religion you might practice or convert to. Similarly for me, it is said that once you are baptized in the Catholic Church, some part of you remains Catholic forever.

Although I no longer attend Mass, I do miss some of the pomp and ceremony. The orations of a well-written sermon used to stimulate my soul and the holy music moved me—although, having been born in what was probably a filthy stable, the music that greeted Jesus' newborn ears was more likely the noises emitted by the animals that were his stable-mates, rather than the song of a choir of angels. And I truly doubt he had a halo over his head.

Yes, there are deep truths to Jesus' life that need to be remembered: He was criticized in his hometown. He spoke of being homeless, of sleeping on the ground in the open. He sweated and went long periods without bathing.

He hung out with a motley crew comprising twelve renegades, and a prostitute. He did not have much respect for religious teachers, calling them "snakes." He threw the moneychangers out of the temple. And I bet the only parade Jesus ever willingly marched in was the one we call Stations of the Cross.

Eventually, some of his critics threatened to throw him off a cliff because his teachings infuriated them. Ironically, they accused Jesus of being a heretic.

I can accept Jesus as my spiritual guide. He's the type of defiant hero I can respect. But I cannot get beyond the blatant cover up sanctioned by the very top leaders of the Church. I still have some growing to do before I can decide what to do with any religion.

A friend suggested that the church needs another reformation. Perhaps if the Church really wants to be the Church of Christ, it should go backwards to the beginning in order to go forwards.

REVELATION

The Keys

Despite all of its testing, my faith has a truly quixotic spirit.

Many decades ago, as a teenager, I found the courage to conclusively end my sick entanglement with Weaver. I destroyed all the photos in my possession that would remind me of the relationship and returned any gifts that he had given me that had not been stolen, broken, or lost. Among these were my coveted guns and knives.

However, I did keep one single object that Weaver had given me, a crucifix that was purported to have belonged to the French-Canadian Jesuit priests, martyred in the 1600s. Somehow, in the purge, I neglected to return this religious relic. My reasons for keeping it are a mystery to me—and as mysterious are the ways it has appeared, disappeared, and affected my life and thinking.

I thought I had lost the crucifix when I left Niagara for St. Jerome's. But then it reappeared. Not wanting anything to do with my sordid past experiences, I gave it to my religious girlfriend, Joan. When her brother dropped the crucifix, it broke. I took care to glue it back together properly and handed it back to Joan. When she and I married, the crucifix returned to my possession, but we moved five separate times and misplaced it with each move—and each time it reappeared.

Over the years, I thought seriously about giving it away or donating it to a museum, but I just never seemed to get around to following up on the impulse, and now that crucifix, an abandoned, broken, patched, relic of survival, occupies a special spot in our bedroom.

It was after we protested the Pope's visit in Toronto that I finally made peace with that cross. I accepted its presence in my life, although I still did not understand its significance.

Years later, I understood: I discovered that when I look at this rejected, abused crucifix, a symbol of martyrdom and survival, a relic dating from a time before my grandparents or even my great-grandparents were born into their Christian faiths, I am able to let go of my own past. This cross shouts at me "to love the unlovable; to forgive the unforgivable." With this revelation I am able to love and forgive myself.

Finally, in the presence of that crucifix, which has traveled through so many years and miles and hands to reach mine, I find my key—or, rather, my own pair of keys—given to me to turn any locks that I encounter.

My keys are named, *"To Love" and "To Forgive."* As the psychiatrist explained to me, be the holder sane or insane, just find out who has the keys. Now, I have my own sane keys.

Finding these keys was a major breakthrough. However this left me reflecting on my life. I now knew the keys to *Who am I?*, but I also knew I had to keep searching to find out what all the misaligned past pieces meant. My search journey needed to continue.

What Is This Journey All About?

September, 2000

We decided to take a vacation to see the west coast. One of the spots we put on our itinerary was Whistler Mountain in British Columbia, where one of our precious *Search* team leaders, Anne Marie Potton, froze to death while hiking.

We felt compelled to visit the spot where her body was discovered. We wanted to share our spirits and let her know that she made a difference in our lives.

After holding Anne Marie in our prayers and thoughts, we took time to experience what it felt like to be on top of the world. We were above the tree line, the place where the snow seldom melts. It was breezy and cold, but the sun, shining, seemed to be almost within our fingers' reach.

Huge, fluffy cumulus clouds were a backdrop behind and below us. A friendly tourist took a picture of us with our camera. When we developed it, we found an image of us floating in the clouds. This photo is certainly a reminder of that special day, and a reminder of what happened next.

Monks Santy Sismobath and
Jum Jujawro, with Bill

As I glanced down the steep mountain, I saw a pair of brown-robed Buddhist monks beside a man wearing a dark, summer suit. What a contrast they made! Robes versus suit; sandals versus loafers. I just had to get a picture of this.

Joan cautioned me to be respectful, and I approached as humbly as it was possible for me. I half-bowed, half-nodded my greetings, and offered a warm smile which was returned with warm, giggly smiles in return.

I asked if I could take the trio's picture, which led to happy chatting. With broken English and the help of the accompanying business man, Mr. Theeraisin Thaimsak, I learned that the three were from Thailand and were here to open a new temple in British Columbia.

The older monk's name was Santy Sismobath. He seemed to be the hierarch, if there is such a thing in Buddhism. His radiating warmth reminded me of some truly holy men I have met, including Father Pythian, and Father Gregory Battafrano, while the younger monk, Jum Jujawro, reminded me of a loving puppy.

I said I was impressed that they were here to open the temple. But Santy, as he insisted on being called, informed me that the reason he was here was not the reason that he came.

While that didn't make immediate sense in my Western mind, I had learned enough of Buddhist philosophy to understand that sometimes what was said was meant to stimulate a person to think differently.

Then Santy said, "The reasons that you think you are here are not the reasons you will ultimately learn as to why you are here."

For some reason, I wondered if what he meant was that I was there to meet him. But I doubted it.

It grew late, so we hugged goodbye and exchanged addresses and phone numbers so that, in the event it was meant to be, we would be able contact one another and perhaps meet again.

When Jum said his goodbyes, he added, "See you round."

I asked, "Like 'round' as the top of the world? Like where we are? Is this another Buddhist saying?" He just giggled and patted his well-endowed stomach.

We didn't see Santy and Jum again, but what Santy had said to me about why I was really at Whistler kept edging forward from deep inside me: When I visited a new place I could hear his voice. He even entered my dreams, challenging me to find a solution.

Then it happened. One day as I was meditating, it came to me like a sunburst: It was not about me! The "you" Santy had referred to was plural; it meant Joan and me—the two of us.

How could I have foreseen all of this, when, at seventeen years old, I took my compass and carved the outline of a heart into the wood of my desk, and then, inside the heart, inscribed this:

♥ BB & JT

The Bill and Joan who overcame Feeney's vendetta.

The Bill and Joan who survived our honeymoon challenges.

The Bill and Joan who raised our family.

The Bill and Joan who were business partners.

The Bill and Joan who were Ministers of Youth.

The Bill and Joan who were Ministers of Communion.

The Bill and Joan who were county coordinators for Marriage Encounter.

The Bill and Joan who assisted in the Dale Carnegie classes.

The Bill and Joan who, along with Father Peter, founded the teenage *Search* program.

The Bill and Joan and who took on the Diocese of St. Catharines, and the Bishops of Canada, for sexual abuse.

The Bill and Joan who defied the Pope, getting worldwide attention by demonstrating at Nancy Mayer's "Abuse Stations of the Cross."

The Bill and Joan who fought against sexual abuse on many fronts.

The Bill and Joan who, for ten years, fought off and settled favorably, a multi-million dollar lawsuit.

The Bill and Joan who went to share our spirit with Anne Marie on top of Mount Whistler.

The Bill and Joan, who for no logical reason, met Santy Sismobath, my challenging monk.

The Bill and Joan who, although according to Myers Briggs had a less than two percent chance of staying married—that is forty-nine-to-one odds against—made it, surviving together against all the odds, despite wavering and finding ourselves often scathed, sometimes scarred, but still remaining Bill and Joan.

How, when I was seventeen, could I have foreseen this life? How could I have understood the truth it has taken me so many years to learn? That when two people who seem to be complete opposites nonetheless find a way of creating of themselves a single one, the synergy that is created is love. I, we, could not have accomplished all that we have, could not have kept our marriage alive and well, without both the gift of determination and our full, mutual commitment.

Two giving as one—this is what overcame all odds.

Now my gift of determination made sense.

Now I know why **WE** really went to Whistler.

EPILOGUE

And Finally...

On a fine fall day, I park my car at Queens Royal Beach. I want to have a long look at the Niagara River spreading out into Lake Ontario, Fort Niagara completing the scene. I inhale the surroundings, along with the cool air and with nostalgia for my past, I am ready for my short journey.

First, I walk up Front Street to the Golf Club, still the oldest golf course in North America, which boasts old Fort Mississauga as a back drop. Memories flood my mind. I wonder where Neil, Pat, Jack, and Mike are. I wish they were here to assist me in recalling some of our laughter, our fears, and our ridiculous stunts.

I sip a beer on the renovated Golf Club patio, and allow the old scenery in my mind to blend with the new spread in front of me. It seems that even the shoreline has been updated. It is beautiful, but it is no longer my shoreline. The forts on both sides of the River look the same, but they are not. While Fort Mississauga has become even more decrepit, Fort Niagara has been kept polished and spit-shined for its visitors and tourists.

I finish my beer—and my dreaming—and head toward Victoria Street to Maw's house, which, of course, is not Maw's anymore. Once there, I see that they were building a new house where Tobe's barn burnt down.

I walk up Victoria to Queen Street, where I find that McClelland's has been sold and the store front renovated. As I continue up Queen Street, I realize that while the businesses along the street might change, according to the plan my father fought for—go backward to go forward—the buildings that house those business are not supposed to. And I am sad to see that the green English Ivy is still missing, stripped from both the Cenotaph and the Court House.

George Bernard Shaw's statue is on prominent display, standing right next to an ultra-modernized wine bar. The Brock Theater is now the Royal George. Greaves is still there, but their elixirs no long longer perfume the streets. Still, you can purchase their jams and chili sauce in the updated store.

Niagara Home Bakery has been sold, but still looks familiar. Bates Rexall Pharmacy is long gone. Now, the storefront is occupied by a clothing/souvenir shop, whose interior has been completely modernized—as are most of the other stores. The exception is Field's Drug Store. Now a museum, it has been made to look and feel as old as it is.

As I walk down Regent Street to our old house, I see that, while it has been renovated, its exterior has been kept. I feel satisfied that, in this case, anyway, the change is for the better. I turn right on Prideaux Street and pass many familiar, if updated, houses that bring equally familiar names to my mind. I meander past the former Masonic Lodge, which looks just the same, and the park, to find that St. Mark's Anglican Church has retained its Olde English splendor—and still provides a shortcut to the dock. (I think briefly of the new generation of urchins who must play hide and seek at night among those tombstones, and wonder if they have discovered that it is a great spot to steal kisses!)

I arrive at my destination, the St. Vincent de Paul cemetery. Just before the Polish cemetery altar, to its right, lie the remains of my genetic past—my mother, father, grandmother, aunt and uncles. I have stood here before, saying my goodbyes, meditating on my forgiveness, saying prayers for the dead.

Now I look around me and see the rectory of corruption and the Church that protects the power of the collar. Beyond the church, the Shaw Festival entertains throngs of tourists who are unaware that Shaw embraced the idea of euthanizing those he deemed useless to society.

Beyond the Festival is the Commons where the Boy Scout Jamboree was held. This vast acreage is vacant, and my father's concept of a re-enactment of Niagara-on-the-Lake's historic past has long since died. I have a bitter taste for the politics that killed it. I know, of course, that governments come and go, but I am sad that dreams and heroes do, as well.

I try to muster a spiritual prayer for my great mentors, Maw and Dad. What comes to mind, however, is the title of a Berenstain Bears book: *Inside Outside Upside Down*.

And that feels right, somehow, because, here I am, at long last, standing outside up, looking down at the upside green grass, knowing that downside, the upside boxes hold your remains inside up—and I am at peace knowing that your spirits are upside, way outside, up.

I bow my head and say,

"Even in death, your spirit is not forgotten. I love you."

As I stand at the graveside, I remember excerpts from W.H. Auden's poem "September 1st, 1939." They echo in my mind.

> . . . *I and the public know*
> *What all schoolchildren learn,*
> *Those to whom evil is done*
> *Do evil in return. . . .*
> *All I have is a voice*
> *To undo the folded lie,*
> *The romantic lie in the brain*
> *Of the sensual man-in-the-street*
> *And the lie of Authority*
> *Whose buildings grope the sky:*
> *There is no such thing as the State*
> *And no one exists alone;*
> *Hunger allows no choice*
> *To the citizen or the police;*
> *We must love one another or die.*

I look back at the graves of my family and wonder again why so much evil must exist. Suddenly, I know the answer: Evil cannot exist without good. As my father would say, "There would be no yin without yang." I reflect further, no hard without soft, no dark without light, no diamond without black carbon. And as Maw would say, "Glory be," from the prayer, "Glory be to the Father and to the Son and to the Holy Ghost. As it was in the beginning is now, and ever shall be, world without end. Amen."

> *We all have problems, imperfections, neurosis, sins, failures. Our imperfections are among the few things we human beings all have in common.*
> ~M. Scott Peck, *The Different Drum*, p230.

ACKNOWLEDGEMENTS

It is over eight years since I started to write *The Cemetery of My Mind*. The number of people who gave me a warm hand is legion. At the risk of senior mind moments I include those that made a pertinent contribution. However, I wish to thank all those who guided me, as well as those who gave me moral support.

My dear friend Fran Shaller of Boynton Beach, FL, took time to teach me the rudiments of Word 2003. Jim Smith, Niagara's historian was a shoulder to lean on. Big Brother Doug listened to my much rambling, adding some of his memories.

Jamie Morris, Jamie@WoodstreamWriters.com, took many hundreds of pages of those rambling notes, organizing them into a book. Judy Borich of Middle River Press, Fort Lauderdale, introduced me to Jamie. She gave me encouragement and understanding when I once again had to move on.

I appreciate Richard Budnick, Harvey Baron, and Ted Wolpe for their willingness to help as needed.

I thank Jon Fear, reporter for The Record, formerly, K-W Record, for assistance on accessing and referencing previously published material.

The Niagara-On-The-Lake Library taught me how to research my needed material. The *Niagara Advance*, with its records archived at the Library was invaluable. Many thanks to The Niagara Historical Society (contact@niagarahistorical.museum) for graciously making available much needed research data, in particular the files on Niagara District High School.

I sincerely appreciate all the handholding and encouragement from the Lewiston (NY) Writers Group, and The Lewiston Public Library for supporting us budding writers. Thanks to Bob Giannetti of Bob's Olde Books, Lewiston, for getting me started. Jennifer Hedges (Jennifer.hedges@sympatico.ca) guided me in the right direction.

A special thanks to my daughter-in law Wendy Butler, a graphic artist, whose insight, imagination, effort, and inspiration working with us created the cover befitting the book.

We used the photograph of the clock tower made by Jim Smith. Wendy Butler, Mike Miller, and I enhanced it into the final version. My friend Mike Miller, pubyourbook@gmail.com, from the Lewiston Writers Group, came to my final rescue. He encouraged me to find old photographs to include in the book. I had been told by many experts that old photos would not print, not so for Mike. Mike, thanks for all the organization and push to finally publish.

William Bates

SURVIVORS NETWORK OF THOSE ABUSED

The **Survivors Network of Those Abused** (formerly the Survivors Network of Those Abused by Priests, but now open to all victims of abuse) is a national support organization. Information on the organization is available at www.snapnetwork.org. The website contact page provides additional information. Quoting from their website:

"We are **SNAP**, the **Survivors Network of those Abused**. We are the largest, oldest and most active support group for women and men wounded by sexual abuse. We have broadened our original charter which focused on abuse by religious authority (priests, ministers, bishops, deacons, nuns and others). We are an independent and confidential organization, with no connections to any religious organization or religious officials. We are also a non-profit, certified 501 (c) (3) organization and we are here to help."

Windsor
Contact: Brenda Brunelle
Phone: 519-800-3492
Email: windsor@snapnetwork.org

Toronto
Contact: Marion Kelly
Phone: 416-274-5954
Email: Marion.Kelly12@hotmail.ca

Quebec Regional
(SNAP is partnered in Quebec with
   Mouvement-Action-Justice)
Contact: Yves Manseau
Phone: 514-525-5273
Email: mouvementactionjustice@hotmail.com

British Columbia
Contact: Leona Huggins
Phone: 604-240-3741
Email: SNAPVancouver@SNAPnetwork.org

For general SNAP information:
Phone: (312) 455-1499
Fax: (312) 455-1498
Phone: 1-877-SNAP-HEALS, (1-877-762-7432)
Survivors Network of those Abused
PO Box 6416
Chicago, IL 60680-6416

SNAP President:
Barbara Blaine
Phone: (312) 399-4747
E-mail: bblaine@snapnetwork.org
PO Box 6416
Chicago, IL 60680-6416

SNAP Outreach Director:
Barbara Dorris
Phone: (314) 862-7688
E-mail: SNAPdorris@gmail.com
6245 Westminster Place
Saint Louis, MO 63130-4849

SNAP Director:
David Clohessy
Phone: (314) 566-9790
Fax: (314) 645-2017
E-mail: SNAPClohessy@aol.com
7234 Arsenal Street
Saint Louis, MO 63143-3404